# NO PLACE FOR SAINTS

WITNESS TO HISTORY

Peter Charles Hoffer and Williamjames Hull Hoffer, Series Editors

*No*

# PLACE FOR SAINTS

## MOBS AND MORMONS
## IN JACKSONIAN AMERICA

ADAM JORTNER

Johns Hopkins University Press | *Baltimore*

© 2021 Johns Hopkins University Press
All rights reserved. Published 2021
Printed in the United States of America on acid-free paper
9 8 7 6 5 4 3 2 1

Johns Hopkins University Press
2715 North Charles Street
Baltimore, Maryland 21218-4363
www.press.jhu.edu

Library of Congress Cataloging-in-Publication Data

Names: Jortner, Adam Joseph, author.
Title: No place for saints : mobs and Mormons
    in Jacksonian America / Adam Jortner.
Description: Baltimore : Johns Hopkins University Press, [2021] |
    Series: Witness to history | Includes bibliographical references
    and index.
Identifiers: LCCN 2020047868 | ISBN 9781421441764 (paperback) |
    ISBN 9781421441771 (ebook)
Subjects: LCSH: Smith, Joseph, Jr., 1805–1844. | Church of Jesus
    Christ of Latter-day Saints—History—19th century. | Mormon
    Church—History—19th century.
Classification: LCC BX8611 .J67 2021 | DDC 289.309/034—dc23
LC record available at https://lccn.loc.gov/2020047868

A catalog record for this book is available from the British Library.

*Special discounts are available for bulk purchases of this book. For more
information, please contact Special Sales at specialsales@jh.edu.*

For David and Susan

Open your ears; for which of you will stop
The vent of hearing when loud Rumour speaks?

WILLIAM SHAKESPEARE, HENRY IV, PART II

# CONTENTS

# ACKNOWLEDGMENTS

THIS BOOK RELIES on archival research and assistance from a variety of extraordinary institutions, including the Church History Library of the Church of Jesus Christ of Latter-day Saints, Harold B. Lee Library at Brigham Young University, Ohio Historical Society, State Historical Society of Missouri, Library Company of Philadelphia, American Antiquarian Society, University of South Carolina Library, and others. Brent M. Rogers, Spencer McBride, Kristine Haglund, and Roger Launius all read drafts or pieces of chapters. Their advice has made this book better. The anonymous reviewers at Johns Hopkins University Press provided valuable assistance. Laura Davulis and the entire staff at Johns Hopkins University Press worked tirelessly over several years and a pandemic to bring this book to press. I am grateful too for the love and support of Emily, Charles, and Sam; this book would not exist without them.

*Note to the Reader*: I have sought to keep the spelling and grammar of nineteenth-century sources just as they were, but where it would impede comprehension, I have silently corrected it.

# NO PLACE FOR SAINTS

# Miracles and Mobs

A GROUP OF AMERICAN CITIZENS met in orderly fashion on July 20, 1833, and decided to attack their neighbors.

Between four and five hundred residents of Jackson County, Missouri, were led by an appointed group of "gentlemen." They convened a public meeting intended to deal with the twelve hundred Mormons who had also settled in the county and who needed to be "blasted in the germ." Mormons were "a set of fanatics," "pretended Christians," and "characterized by the profoundest ignorance, the grossest superstition, and the most abject poverty." Should Mormons win elected office, the other residents of Jackson County would be subject to "the vexation that would attend the civil rule of these fanatics."[1]

The real crime, though, was Mormon religion. Mormons believed in modern revelation and a restoration of New Testament miracles in the American nineteenth century, and the July 20 meeting declared that such a belief was dangerous. The assembled citizens did not trust Mormons as jurors, witnesses, or sheriffs, because Mormons "do not blush to declare and would not upon occasion hesitate to swear that they have wrought miracles, and have been the subjects of miracles and supernatural cures; have converse with God and his angels." They hated the Mormons for speaking in tongues. The Mormon faith could not be trusted, because its beliefs were "extravagant and unheard of." Five hundred Gentiles (non-Mormons) had decided that twelve hundred Mormons would have to go.[2]

So they voted—unanimously—to expel them. Hundreds of citizens (and several elected officials) signed a pledge demanding that the Mormons leave the county and never return. They insisted the Mormons must shut down the *Evening and Morning Star* (the local Mormon newspaper) as well. This action would occur "peaceably if we can, forcibly if we must." If the Mormons refused, then "their brethren who have the gifts of divination" would know what awaited them. The comment was at once mockery and threat. One member of the meeting insisted he would expel the Mormons from Jackson County even "if he had to wade up to his neck in blood."[3]

The assembled Missourians appointed a committee of twelve to march into the Mormon neighborhoods of Independence and demand to meet with Mormon leaders. The committee presented their demands and gave the Mormons fifteen minutes to comply. Flummoxed, the Mormon leadership declined. The twelve returned to the group, who (in their own words) "unanimously resolved" to destroy the Mormon printing office. The group became a mob, marched to the office, and tore down the two-story building, smashing the press's type and scattering it in the street. The Mormon bishop Edward Partridge was dragged to the town square, stripped, and covered in tar and feathers. The mob then gave the Mormons three days to think about it.

On July 23, the attacks resumed. The mob arrived in Mormon neighborhoods carrying "a red flag in token of blood." Several leading Mormons, including David Whitmer, were brought by bayonet to the town square, tarred and feathered, and held at gunpoint. "The commanding officer," wrote John Greene, then threatened them "with instant death, unless they denied the Book of Mormon and confessed it to be a fraud: at the same time adding, that if they did so, they might enjoy the privileges of citizens." Whitmer and the others did not deny their faith that day, but they did sign an agreement—under threat of further violence—that they would leave the county.[4]

The expulsion of the Mormons from Jackson County is one of the great acts of religious violence and repression in United States history. The July attacks were just the beginning. In September, the mobs returned, demanding Mormons leave immediately and declaring that any effort to defend themselves would be taken as an act of war: "The mob threatened, that if we petitioned or prosecuted, they would MASSACRE us *in toto*," wrote one Mormon. In October, the mobs struck with fury, leaving "houses in ruins, and furniture destroyed and strewed about the streets; women . . . weeping and mourning, while some of the men were covered with blood." Militias swarmed upon Mormon homes and gathering places. In response, the Mormon prophet Joseph Smith gathered several hundred faithful believers in Ohio and marched across the country to help his brethren fight back. A church raised a battalion to fight a militia spawned by riotous meetings intent on expelling a new faith.[5]

It had all seemed to begin so politely, with a popular meeting adopting the forms of self-government and Jacksonian democracy. Those who wrote the "Mob Manifesto"—as the document recording the demands that Mormons leave Jackson County has come to be known—repeatedly referred to themselves as "citizens." They met peacefully and voted on resolutions. They expressed concerns about their local government, and then they decided to destroy and assault Mormon properties and persons to make their point. By calling *themselves* citizens, they implied that somehow the Mormons were not. (Mormons of 1833 were virtually all Americans, with a few Canadians mixed in.) What the Gentiles meant, of course, was that Mormon citizenship was contingent on religion, not law or birth. The voting Gentiles defined citizenship as a kind of ideology—*their* kind of people counted as citizens, and others did not. Those who could not meet their standards had no rights. That was how five hundred "citizens" could take it upon themselves to make policy for twelve hundred of their neighbors—and how they justified the violence against them. In this, too, the riots against Mormons echoed themes of Jacksonian America—a great era of political and religious violence when repeated efforts were made to define some religions (Catholicism, Mormonism, Judaism, and others) as antithetical to America, the First Amendment be damned.[6]

Yet Mormonism differed from many religions because it was so new. The Church of Jesus Christ of Latter-day Saints—"Mormon" was a derisive nickname the church later embraced—had been founded just three years earlier, by a self-taught farm boy who claimed divine inspiration and miraculous proofs of his mission. Joseph Smith Jr. claimed to have unearthed golden plates inscribed with an ancient text called the Book of Mormon, which he translated supernaturally. The appearance of the new scripture, claimed the Saints, was an indication that God had restored the one, true Christian church, and Smith was its prophet. With virtually no money and little organization but great confidence, Smith and his fellow believers spread rapidly across the Northeast and the frontier in the 1830s. The Mormons reported a bevy of angelic visitations, healings, exorcisms, and other miracles as evidence of the truth of their claims and insisted that any church that could not show such signs could not be a true church.

At least at first, critics laughed rather than rioted. Smith's previous association with digging for magical treasure in particular made for comedic fodder. Detractors mocked the "huge magic spectacles" Smith used to translate the golden plates, and claimed Mormon newspapers were staffed by "magicians and soothsayers."[7] Someone wrote a parody called the "Book of Pukei" in which a magician with a "*magic* stone, and his *stuffed Toad*, and all his implements of witchcraft" passed his mantle to Joseph Smith, who then, according to Pukei, "obtained the Gold Bible."[8] The Book of Pukei parody was in circulation almost as soon as the Book of Mormon rolled off the presses.

Making fun of other people's religion is a long-standing tradition in human history. The Mormons were not different in this part of their fate. What *was* different was the way in which anti-Mormon animus quickly coalesced into violence. Ruffians broke up Mormon baptisms. Two years after the church was founded, Smith and other leaders were tarred and feathered. Violent mobs in Missouri attacked Mormon homes and neighborhoods for days in July and October 1833. Militia forces joined in the expulsion. Both Mormons and non-Mormons were killed, and by December 1833, more than one thousand Mormons had been forced from their homes by their fellow Americans.

Religious conflict in America was not new. Mormon expulsion was nearly simultaneous with the burning of a Catholic convent in Massachusetts. It was just two years after the Virginia uprising of Nat Turner, a revolt against slavery inspired by religious tenets. Repressing Turner's revolt resulted in major restrictions on African American churches.

But tensions between Catholics and Protestants and between enslaved and slaveholding Christianity were decades or centuries old. Anti-Mormonism grew and developed into a violent force in just three years. Sometimes Americans assume that anti-Mormonism in Missouri was a response to Mormon polygamy—but that unusual doctrine was not practiced in 1833, not mentioned before 1835, and not announced among the Latter-day Saints until 1852. Anti-Mormonism preceded polygamy.[9]

What happened? How did jokes and theological arguments turn into riots, mobs, and expulsions? The United States in the 1830s was experiencing a massive religious reorganization, as new forms of Christianity rose up and old forms restructured themselves. It was also undergoing a communications revolution: cheap print and an expanding press put novel ideas and news items into the hands of the public more quickly than ever before.

In such a situation, rumor took root and spread readily. Rumors abounded in the early republic, and they reshaped the way people thought about their politics, religion, and neighbors. Isaac McCoy, a Baptist minister involved in the Mormon expulsion, justified the action based on rumors that Mormons had formed a military alliance with nearby Native Americans. McCoy admitted he had no "legal evidence of that fact," but the rumor was enough, McCoy wrote, to justify efforts "to throw down houses, to whip their leaders, and to apply tar and feathers."[10] Another Missouri Baptist minister declared that Mormons believed to know the location of the Ark of the Covenant (they did not), and he personally went from house to house spreading such rumors. The story of the Ark then got reprinted across American newspapers.[11]

These rumors shaped how non-Mormons responded to the new religion. Indeed, since there were so few Mormons in North America in 1833, Americans were far more likely to have read about Mormons than to have met one. And as rumors began to insinuate that Mormons were bad for the country, advocates emerged who applied notions of ethnic cleansing to American religions. Those who believed falsely should be removed or destroyed in the name of democracy.

This is a book about rumor and religion. These subjects sometimes make it hard to distinguish facts from beliefs from opinions. And since rumor and religion can and did lead to violence in early America, it's important to take the topic seriously despite the difficulties.

So two quick points before we go any further.

First, I have tried to write about early Mormonism from the perspective of the ordinary people who embraced it and the ordinary people who rioted against it. In the case of the former, I have included many accounts of supernatural experiences. I have tried to record these as much as possible in the words of the original sources. Therefore I have dispensed with the cumbersome apparatus of writing "Smith *believed* an angel appeared to him," and simply written that "an angel appeared." In terms of the latter, I have included many hard words about the Mormons, and I have likewise mostly avoided qualifying terms. Readers should understand that I write this way to recapture the anger and fear of anti-Mormonism and the chaotic, high-stakes world of early-national religion. I am not writing an epistemological affirmation of Mormon beliefs or of the anti-Mormon criticisms of those beliefs.

My second note follows from the first. I have sought here to recapture these beliefs, because it is from their beliefs and reactions to what they heard that we can draw conclusions about what they believed and how it came to violence. The process of conversion and the recourse to violence, as another historian has written, "took place in people's minds on the basis of what they knew, or thought they knew. It is useless in the process to consider all the things that we know."[12]

The rapid expansion of Mormonism and anti-Mormonism provides a remarkable case study of religious conflict in America. Many of the issues at stake in the rise of Mormonism and its almost immediate expulsion from Missouri will also be familiar to Americans in the twenty-first century: Religious tensions. Claims of divine right. An anxious public. A changing democracy. Advancements in communication creating an unmatched new rumor mill. Of course, the 1830s are not today; the religious context and social world in which Mormonism emerged were quite different. But the stories of magic, miracle, hucksterism, democracy, and rumor that came together in the expulsion of 1833 are still valid today—as is religious violence. If we are seeking to understand how competing faiths can coexist in one town or city or country, and to find the difficult line between theological and moral criticism on one hand and the propaganda of prejudice on the other, the Mormon example is of profound importance.

# 1

## Lo Here! Lo There!
*The Sectarian Dilemma*

IN 1805, VERMONT HAD NOT yet earned its reputation for New England quaintness. It was a severe frontier landscape, more H. P. Lovecraft than Robert Frost. In this land of stark realities, religion assumed intense and jagged forms. Renegade Baptist sects—once banned by New England's Puritans—sprouted across the state. Methodists sent circuit riders trudging through rain, snow, and summer heat to preach outdoors to an absent or impertinent public. Revolutionary War hero Ethan Allen, leader of the irregular patriot Green Mountain Boys, published a theological screed denying the physical existence of the devil and the Christian doctrine of miracles. Elizabeth Babcock and her husband founded a church predicated on angelic communication. A collection of religious seekers in the town of Whittingham recorded their dreams of buried treasure and practiced occult rituals to obtain the lost gold.

This was the world into which Joseph Smith Jr. was born, and he found it a burden. To him, religious variation meant religious anarchy, "stir and division among the people, Some crying Lo here and some Lo there. Some were contending for the Methodist faith, Some for the Presbyterian, and some for the Baptist." All that competition, Smith wrote, led to "great confusion, and bad feeling." American religious liberty had bred a wealth of choices, and to choose wrong meant damnation. Worse, it raised the specter of atheism, for "how could God be the author of so much confusion?" For Smith, sectarianism was a religious challenge that challenged religion itself.[1]

Smith found a way out of this maze by building an unconventional church, one he believed would put all the others to rest. It was not exactly a *new* church, Smith taught, but a *restored* church, the true faith of Jesus Christ, which all others had forgotten. Along the way, Smith found thousands of like-minded men and women who also believed the true church had to be restored. They helped Smith organize it and start it on a remarkable and unlikely journey in US history. Building that church was no simple matter, for the restored church of Christ possessed a score of seemingly unusual practices: translation by seer stones, direct revelations from God, intense missionary work, pooling of resources, legends of hidden gold, and the construction and dedication of a new temple of God to replace the one lost in Jerusalem in AD 70.

This was the Church of Jesus Christ of Latter-day Saints, or as they were more colloquially known, the Mormons. For adherents, then and now, the Mormon faith is the living word of God on earth. For nineteenth century critics, Mormons were "fraudulent exorcists," "a gang of impostors," "engines of death and hell."[2] Even today, observers sometimes reduce Mormonism to its most uncanny and outré elements. Yet much of what stands out about Mormonism today could be found in many sects and denominations in 1830. Mormonism resembled much in the United States from 1776 to 1840—a period historians call the early republic—a period filled with itinerant prophets, religious experimentation, new cities on the frontier, magical gambits, and endemic violence.

Consider the story of yet another new church, one whose faith was also daubed with magic implements, gold buried in the earth, sacred temples, condemnation of the Gentiles, and violence that came for the believers. A Vermont prophet standing apart from other churches launched his own missionary endeavor. His followers claimed "*it was revelation*" and possessed the ability "to cure diseases, in many cases . . . thought almost miraculous." The prophet "regarded himself and his followers as modern Israelites or Jews" and taught that God would "visit their enemies, the Gentiles (all outsiders), with his wrath and vengeance." His followers "professed to believe in supernatural agencies" and began building a temple in their hometown. The prophet was even condemned for lascivious behavior, as when two young female followers were informed "that the devil was in their clothing" and were subsequently ordered to strip naked.[3]

This prophet was Nathaniel Wood, not Joseph Smith Jr. Wood's New Israelite movement flared briefly in Middletown, Vermont, from 1789 to 1802, then vanished into the antiquarian twilight. Excommunicated by the Congregationalists, Wood founded his own, New Israelite church, which soon became as large as any other Middletown denomination. Wood received revelations through divining rods, used the Bible to dig for treasure, built a Hebrew temple, and became convinced that God would send a destroying angel against his enemies on January 14, 1802. Faithful New Israelites inscribed "Christ our Passover was sacrificed for us" above their doorposts the night of January 13 to ward off destruction. Destruction came anyway: the local militia was called out to disrupt any Israelite activities for fear of civil insurrection. The failure of the January 14 prediction apparently crippled the Israelite movement, and the town council of Middletown drummed Wood and the remaining believers out of town—no small feat, since several of Wood's sons held elective office there.[4]

The "Wood Scrape," as it is known, comes to us through Barnes Frisbie, who wrote a history of his New England hometown in 1867. Frisbie did not hide his disgust at the "disgraceful conduct" of the Wood Scrape, which he cited as the "main source from which came this monster—Mormonism."[5] An association between one of the treasure diggers and the father of a later Mormon apostle (Oliver Cowdery) cemented the case for Frisbie. Some modern historians have agreed, but others have searched for a different origin for Mormonism. One award-winning book posited that Mormonism was built on the ancient art of alchemy, which had some avid practitioners in the early republic. Others have pointed to the presence of folk magic—charms, countercurses, and divination techniques—that flourished in the nineteenth-century age of cheap print and the free press. Still others have claimed that Smith borrowed inspiration from similar prophets like Jacob Cochran in Maine or Ann Lee in New York, or that Smith copied utopian ideas from the Seneca prophet Handsome Lake or the Jewish reformer Mordecai Noah.[6] At times, it can seem as if the entire history of early Mormonism is a search for the exact group that preceded Mormonism—and many such potential groups have been identified. But the significance is perhaps not in one group or another but in the fact that *many* such groups have been identified. There were many new religions in early

America, shearing and buckling the religious landscape like tectonic plates: "stir and division among the people, Some crying Lo here and some Lo there."

Mormonism did not emerge as a clear-cut alternative to all other forms of Christianity in America; there was not one form of American Christianity and a Mormon alternative. Rather, Mormonism developed in the world of sectarian conflict. Its initial appeal—and the subsequent alarm that followed—was part of a larger cultural and religious contest where old and new faiths pressed in on one another. The English wit Frances Trollope wrote that in America, the "whole people appear to be divided into an almost endless variety of religious factions. . . . Besides the broad and well-known distinctions of Episcopalian, Catholic, Presbyterian, Calvinist, Baptist, Quaker, Swedenborgian, Universalist, Dunker, &c. &c. &c.; there are innumerable others springing out of these" of which "the most intriguing and factious individual is invariably the head." Trollope never met Smith, but she agreed with him that the presence of such a "fury of division and sub-division" had the "melancholy effect of exposing *all* religious ceremonies to contempt."[7]

Literally and figuratively, Smith set himself in this lost world of sectarian competition, frequently comparing his restored faith to that of the Presbyterians, Methodists, Disciples of Christ, and others. He sent missionaries to the Shakers, Catholics, and Campbellites, and he set up his Ohio church next door to a utopian Christian experiment and not far from where the Shawnee prophet Tenskwatawa had proclaimed a new divine dispensation in 1806.

Other Americans also worried about having too many churches to choose from. Methodist preacher Peter Cartwright grumbled about Baptists, Universalists, classical Calvinists, infidels, and several kinds of Presbyterians in his Kentucky neighborhood—and that was before the arrival of the "self-deceived Millerites," the "blasphemous Shakers," the "diabolical Mormons," and the "modern spirit-rappers [Spiritualists]."[8] Revivalist leader Barton Warren Stone recalled that "our preachers, and our pupils, alarmed, fled from us, and joined the different sects around us. The sects triumphed at our distress, and watched for our fall."[9] The Universalist minister Caleb Rich had a visionary experience in which a glowing angel brought him to a mountaintop; at its base were dozens of sets of footprints, each representing a different sect, but no steps reached the summit.[10]

This sectarian dilemma is almost invisible today, but it was commonplace in the nineteenth century. Modern American Christianity usually coalesces in the popular mind into an evangelical subculture arrayed against a secular state, or sometimes as evangelical Christianity set against the so-called main-line churches. In either case, the choices are (at least rhetorically) reduced to two. Earlier generations of Americans had a much wider array of choices, the product of an unprecedented flood of new church buildings and institutions borne on a wave of new religious ideas. Established denominations often split, compounding the choices. Methodists had broken into four organizations by 1830. Presbyterian schisms gave way to new branches of Christianity—the Disciples of Christ and Churches of Christ. By the time Smith published the Book of Mormon, the famously fractious Baptists had Regular Baptists, Primitive Baptists, Separate Baptists, Freewill Baptists, Seventh-Day Baptists, and others—all of which had significant organizational and theological differences. In 1827, even the Quakers split.

Some believers even rejected the divinity of Jesus, becoming Unitarians—believers in one Christian God, who inspired a human Jesus. As one closet Unitarian wrote, "I am a Christian, in the only sense he [Christ] wished any one to be; sincerely attached to his doctrines, in preference to all others; ascribing to himself every *human* excellence & believing he never claimed any other." That closet Unitarian was also president of the United States. Thomas Jefferson had an uncommon view of Christian theology, but there was a lot of that going around in the early republic.[11] The array of choices was astonishing. Smith's cry of "Lo here" and "Lo there" has become unfamiliar to modern experience. The dominance of evangelicals today means that modern American Christianity is only "Lo here." Frenetic interchurch competition, backed by supernatural proofs, was common to nineteenth-century America but has become largely absent two hundred years later.

This spiritual upwelling was not limited to churches. Esoteric practices boomed in the early United States. Magical-treasure digging, for example, became something of a cottage industry in the early republic, practiced by Smith, Wood, and a bevy of other votaries. "Settlers in New England," wrote one observer in 1808, "indulge an unconquerable expectation of finding money buried in the earth."[12] In the 1780s in New Jersey, there was a "prevailing opinion that vast sums of money had, at some earlier period of time, been deposited in the earth at Schooley's mountains, with an enchantment upon it; which could not be obtained without a peculiar art in legerdemain to dispel the apparitions and hobgoblins."[13]

Treasure hunting had Christian antecedents. Medieval Europe's treasure hunters understood that money was the root of all evil and, when buried in the ground (home of the devil, demons, and spirits), was evil twice over. Yet purification was possible and profitable; Christians could dismiss the demons and pray to put ghostly spirits to rest. Treasure hunts came to involve a mix of Christian prayers for the dead, magical symbols to contain devils, and a rigorous personal morality—an adventure more *Pilgrim's Progress* than *Indiana Jones*.[14] Indeed, one Massachusetts treasure hunt was undertaken by "pious and godly Christians, with the Bible, Prayer-book, and Pilgrim's Progress lying near them."[15]

The early republic and its freewheeling faith rediscovered these Christian themes and made treasure digging a Christian activity. Universalist preacher Miles Wooley used a magical stone "to discover hidden treasures."[16] In New Jersey, Ransford Rogers led a host of citizens to find treasure guarded by "*the spirit of a just man, sent from Heaven.*" A constant refrain heard from the apparition was "LOOK TO GOD!"[17] Congregationalist William Bentley—a famous defender of orthodoxy—provided a Bible and psalmbook to the treasure-hunting efforts of a conjuror in 1808.[18] And if the relationship between strict biblical Christianity and magical-treasure hunts seemed a little slippery to Americans, proponents could point to the diabolical origins of the treasure *guardians* as a good reason to search and pray. The seeker known as "the Commodore" made preparations to counter "the malevolence of the devil, or evil spirit, who was put in charge of the money."[19] Other guardians included demonic dogs, apparitions, an "evil spirit" who "would rise up and blast them with his vaporous breath," and, in one case, an entire deceased crew, "rowing the spirit of their mouldered boat."[20]

Then there were the witches. In South Carolina, Joshua Gordon handwrote an entire book of spells that promised everything from luck in court to efforts to cure bewitched firearms. The fortune teller Moll Pitcher headed a going concern in Lynn, Massachusetts; she envisioned how to find lost loves and predicted whether ships would survive their passage. In at least one case, an impending voyage had to be canceled when Pitcher foresaw that the ship would sink. A printed book of spells, *The Long-Lost Friend*, appeared in 1819 and taught numerous magical techniques, including how to reverse a witch's cattle curse by feeding cows paper inscribed with a version of a first-century AD spell. And where there were rumors of witchcraft, there were witch hunts. Mobs lynched suspected witches in North Carolina in 1792, Maine in 1796, South Carolina in 1814, and elsewhere. In 1822, Joseph Lewis of Virginia shot and killed a free African American named Bass on suspicion of witchcraft. Lewis had consulted a fortune-teller who had named Bass as a witch.[21]

These are lesser-known entries in the American history of religious violence. The topic receives scant attention in history textbooks, but violence was there. The religious outpouring of early America was pockmarked by small-scale thuggery and widespread riots in an effort to impose religious order on communities by force. An old woman was lynched in Philadelphia for witchcraft in 1787; the angry mob beat her and paraded her down the streets past the Constitutional Convention. She died from her injuries. Mobs sacked villages of Cartwright's "blasphemous Shakers," sometimes burning crops and killing cattle and other times beating or kidnapping the believers. When Renegade Baptists in Pepperell, Massachusetts, tried to perform their namesake rite in 1778, a mob came upon them, broke up the ritual, beat the penitents, and baptized a dog instead. In the summer of 1834, a series of riots broke out around the Catholic convent at Charlestown, Massachusetts. Whipped up by the anti-Catholic sermons of Lyman Beecher, a mob eventually burned the place to the ground. When Andrew Jackson attacked the Creek armies in Alabama in 1814, he encouraged his troops to destroy the Native American forces for religious reasons. Creeks had to learn not to listen to the new "Red Stick" religious message: "They must be made to know that their prophets are impostors."[22]

Both the sectarian explosion and the stoking of religious violence derived in part from the emergence of religious freedom in America. The colonial British world had been a religiously diverse place, too, but its legal regime was predicated on established churches and a tradition of deference to clergy. Religious practice that did not conform to the official church faced some level of scrutiny, ranging from official disapproval to mild suppression. In New England, Baptists faced harassment and discrimination from the state-supported Congregational (Puritan) church. In Virginia, the Anglican church was the state church. Presbyterians and other non-Anglican Protestants had to pay taxes to support churches they did not attend; when ministers refused to pay, they were thrown in jail. Maryland had been founded as a Catholic colony, but by 1689, Protestants had taken over and had banned the public practice of Catholicism in the colony. Catholic priests and parishioners could practice their religion only in private homes, out of sight of good Protestants. Odd little Rhode Island had no state church—which perhaps explains why it was an early adopter of many magical practices. (By the 1740s Rhode Island had earned a reputation as the best place to consult astrologers and alchemists.)[23] But even Rhode Island had its limits; in the 1680s, the government attempted to forcibly seize all Jewish property in the colony.[24]

When the colonies broke from Great Britain, nearly all of the newly independent states retained some kind of religious establishment at first. States' constitutional provisions ranged widely. Delaware's 1776 constitution required officeholders to take a test oath confirming faith in "God the Father and his Son Jesus Christ." Massachusetts went into the American union with a state church intact. Massachusetts's 1780 constitution promised free exercise of religion while also authorizing the government to require attendance in church and public exercise of religion. The state legalized government-supported "maintenance of public Protestant teachers of piety, religion, and morality."[25]

Yet, as Americans settled into independence, these rules crumbled. Virginia led the way in 1786 when James Madison, Thomas Jefferson, and Virginia's hard-pressed Baptists successfully pushed for a disestablishment of the state's Anglican church. In a free nation, Madison wrote, "the Religion then of every man must be left to the conscience and conviction of every man . . . in matters of Religion, no man's right is abridged by the institution of Civil Society."[26] A free society could not allow compulsion in matters of conscience or worship, and religious taxes, preferment for office, and state-supported pastors were all forms of compulsion. The battle to disestablish Virginia's church was difficult; opponents argued that a government that did not officially recognize Christianity would invoke divine displeasure and would be "swarming with Fools, Sots and Gamblers."[27] Madison in turn dismissed the notion that religious oaths guaranteed moral politicians. "The inefficacy of this restraint on individuals is well known," he wrote, pointing to the corruption and crimes committed by oath-bearing Christians.[28]

In 1786, despite objections, the Virginia Statute of Religious Freedom became law; henceforth, neither Anglicanism nor any other faith would receive state support. The statute invoked "Almighty God [who] hath made the mind free," declared that "civil rights have no dependence on our religious opinions," and pointed out that Jesus Christ never himself made any effort at religious coercion while on earth. Virginia law now held that no one could be "compelled to frequent or support any religious worship" or "suffer on account of his religious opinions or beliefs." Matters of religion "shall in no wise diminish, enlarge, or affect their civil capacities." In Virginia, all religions were now legally equal.[29]

Other states soon followed suit. Georgia removed religious requirements for office in 1789, Pennsylvania and South Carolina in 1790, and Delaware in 1792. The Bill of Rights was adopted in 1791, the First Amendment ensuring that the federal government would not legislate a national church or prayer. The sectarian results were easy to predict; if conscience alone could dictate religious choice, then the power of "tradition" would be lessened. The venerability of a denomination no longer necessarily spoke to its authenticity, and sects would inevitably multiply. Madison himself understood this; indeed, he wrote to Jefferson that the "mutual hatred of these sects" was actually a reason why more Virginians would support religious freedom.[30]

Religious liberty was not the only freedom bringing forth new sects and inspiring revived magical and spiritual techniques. Freedom of the press played a key role as well. An explosion of print rocked the early American republic. While the old Protestant classics by Luther and Calvin hung around, a wealth of new information free of censorship found its way into the hands of religious seekers. Methodist tracts, Unitarian exegeses, attacks on Calvinism, Campbellite newspapers, Jewish sermons, chiliastic predictions, and theories about the descent of Native Americans from biblical Hebrews all rolled off the presses. Abel Sargent founded an obscure organization known as the Halcyon Church. Little is known about his religious practice—apparently he had twelve apostles, some of them women, and went around Ohio seeking to raise the dead—but his theology is readily available to modern historians because he published a hymnal in 1811.[31] It is not clear whether the Halcyon Church really intended to resurrect the dead, but that was what Peter Cartwright had heard about them, and it was the story Cartwright published in his *Autobiography*.

Stories of supernatural events also stirred the world of print. Sometimes they appeared in side comments—as when an 1850 publication obliquely referred to a mystic turnip supernaturally tossed through a Rochester, New York, window—but at other times they formed the centerpiece of conversion narratives or religious apologetics that could be purchased, shared, loaned, and read aloud. Baptists, Methodists, Catholics, and other groups published narratives of divine healing; one such report even brought in a US Supreme Court justice to verify the remarkable accounts. The Shakers published a host of miracle stories about their founder, Ann Lee, in 1816 in an effort to instruct existing converts and gain new ones. John Thayer wrote a pamphlet explaining how belief in miracles had brought about his conversion to Catholicism in 1783. In addition to explicitly religious works, there were also books of magic and associated phenomena. In 1807, the Library Company of Philadelphia owned two books it filed under "Occult Philosophy"; by 1835 it owned seventy such titles, including Ebenezer Sibly's *New and Complete Illustration of the Celestial Science of Astrology* (1784), John Heydon's *New Astrology* (1823), and Francis Barrett's *Magus* (1801). For those who could buy rather than borrow books on magic, the only question was which edition. *The Complete Fortune Teller* went through five printings in 1799 alone. Erra Pater's *Book of Knowledge*, a guide to dream interpretation, went through eighteen printings from 1767 to 1809.[32] A flood of books and other printed matter allowed religious ideas new and old to be thrown into an American religious milieu already swarming with new sects.

These postrevolutionary changes created an American landscape stocked with abundant new religious movements, sectarian carping, esoterica, magic, and violence. The new nation had a host of new ideas and new supernatural claims in an environment of reduced ecclesiastical authority. In the mid-eighteenth century, it had been difficult to start a new church, even if one had a founding miracle to base it on. The ability to preach, organize, and recruit new members was regulated by the state and higher social orders backed by the state. After the revolution, those restrictions went away. And the sects came.

The Smith family of Vermont was well prepared for this development. Joseph Jr. came from a long line of sectarians. His grandfather Asael left the Congregationalists to join the Universalists, a new sect that held that *all* human beings, even the worst among us, would be saved—even if they did not want to be. "Christ died for all," wrote Universalist Elhanan Winchester in 1791, "and died not in vain."[33] Reflecting this belief, Asael Smith instructed his grandchildren that "sinners must be saved by the righteousness of Christ alone . . . he can as well Save all, as any."[34] Asael's son Joseph Smith Sr. collected occult warding symbols—which he copied from the print edition of Ebenezer Sibly's book on astrology.[35] His mother, Lucy Mack Smith, shared her son Joseph Jr.'s reticence regarding the growth of sects, recalling in 1845 her anxiety that if she joined one church, "all the rest will say I am in error. No church will admit that I am right, except the one with which I am associated. That makes them witnesses against each other." Eventually she was baptized by a minister willing to perform the rite without having her join his congregation. The Smith family's eclectic religious interests did not necessarily make Joseph Jr. different from other Americans of his day. Born in Sharon, Vermont, in 1805,

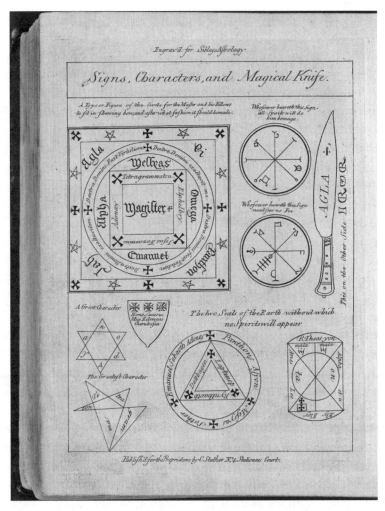

Sibly warding symbols. Illustrations for magical wards against evil spirits, offered to Americans in Ebenezer Sibly's *New and Complete Illustration of the Celestial Science of Astrology* (1784). L. Tom Perry Special Collections, Harold B. Lee Library, Brigham Young University, Provo, Utah (133.5 Sill 1788)

Smith inherited the kind of patchwork religion common to numerous families in an age of free preaching and free print

It is important to point out these commonalities because of a distressing tendency to explain religious change by pointing to a religious founder's upbringing. Mormon and non-Mormon historians have engaged in this tendency with

Smith, describing his visions and religious theologies as biographical development, from his beginnings in "the cabalistic ritual of rural wizardry" to his taking on the "satisfying role of prophet of God."[36] Early Mormons, meanwhile,
have been described as a "prepared people"—as though they were the only
Americans who dabbled in magical arts or questioned denominational alle-
giances. Many Americans did both and never became Mormons. Andrew Sheffield owned an entire library of magical books, which he consulted every day. He
came from old Connecticut Congregationalist stock and considered himself a
Christian astrologer—and made three hundred dollars a year at it.[37] Enthusiastic
revivalist Robert McAfee visited a "water witch" to stop a Kentucky drought in
between camp meetings. And plenty of Mormon converts came from standard-
issue Protestant households that had never dallied with any unorthodox beliefs;
for example, Mary Fielding Smith, an English immigrant to Canada, had spent
her whole life as a Methodist before she joined the Mormons in 1836.[38]

In other words, both general context and specific teachings are crucial to
writing religious history. The sectarian dilemma provided a general context
for Smith's crisis of faith, but the religion that he transmitted to the world—
Mormonism—was a particular series of doctrines, behaviors, and scriptures.
Mormon converts chose Smith's message from a number of options—the Disciples of Christ, Shakerism, Universalism, and other denominations trying to
"solve" the problem of sects. Caleb Rich echoed Smith in his fears over the
"hundred different denominations of christians" and "but one right way among
them all," but Rich chose to become a Universalist.[39]

Still, some of those confused by the sectarian crisis were perhaps more receptive to Mormonism. Smith remembered his childhood search for answers, in which one church "referred me to one plan, and another to another,
each one pointing to his own particular creed as the *summum bonum* of perfect." Smith elucidated a problem other Americans at the time would have understood. When John and Julia Murdock of Ohio moved from a Lutheran to a
Presbyterian to a Campbellite church and found them all "not according to
the scriptures," they probably had a similar feeling. They likely would have
agreed with Smith's 1842 assessment of his childhood thoughts: "If God had
a church, it would not be split up into factions, and . . . if He taught one society to worship one way, and to administer one set of ordinances, He would
not teach another, principles which were diametrically opposed."[40]

Much the same problem had struck at the heart of Kentucky and the Ohio
Valley in 1800, when a series of exuberant revivals were held at the Cane Ridge

meetinghouse. Buoyed by interest in an open communion service, thousands began showing up to the tiny church in Paris, Kentucky. Reports spoke of people coming in the thousands.

But there was a problem: officially, Presbyterians did not allow open communion. Before partaking of the body and blood of Christ, Presbyterian communicants had to pass a rigorous examination to be sure they understood exactly what they were doing. The Cane Ridge Presbyterians—led by Richard McNemar and Barton Warren Stone—decided they did not care whether someone understood the Westminster Confession before taking communion. It only mattered that they wished to give themselves to God.

It was a sectarian debacle. McNemar faced ecclesiastical trials in 1801, 1802, and 1803, a process he dubbed "the *Presbyterian Inquisition*."[41] Stone later recalled that "we saw the arm of ecclesiastical authority raised to crush us, and we must either sink, or step aside to avoid the blow."[42] They stepped aside. McNemar, Stone, and others broke away from their church and formed a new organization based on the Presbyterian model and centered on Springfield, Ohio. Thus began a long string of schisms over the following decade in which the Springfield Presbytery was declared dead and a new Cumberland Presbytery, a new Church of Christ (also called the Stoneites), and new Shaker families developed out of the shards of the revival. One preacher recalled a host of sects arising in the wake of the revival—the Halcyon Church, Hicksite Quakers, Universalists, and an obscure group motivated by immediate inspiration of heaven known as the Screaming Children.[43] Revivalists moved into northern Ohio where they made common cause with the preachers of Alexander Campbell's "Christian" movement—not to be confused with another movement, led by John Leland of Virginia, *also* called the Christian movement and also aimed at replacing all sects. A fair number of Ohio Campbellites later joined the Mormons, which so infuriated Campbell that he wrote *Delusions*, one of the first published attacks on the Saints. The spiritual ruckus across Ohio and Kentucky matched the uproar in Vermont. The denominational problem from which Mormonism emerged was national in scope, not the product of one family or one region. Indeed, Kentucky's schisms prove that upstate New York did not produce more schisms or religious fervor than anywhere else, as historians once argued, the so-called "Burned-Over District" of upstate New York was not so distinctive after all.[44]

The plethora of prophets makes the specifics of Smith's message all the more important. While context enables historians to situate and interpret the rise of and response to Mormonism, we cannot let context displace the particulars of Smith's message. Like all historical figures, Smith was a product of his time and place, but to say he succeeded *because of* his time and place slights contemporary Mormon belief—making the Latter-day Saint (LDS) message merely a cipher for nineteenth-century fears—and reduces historical investigation to mere social theory. It is not that Smith was simply one prophet among many, or even that he offered claims that no one else could match. It was that people found his claims and the claims of his followers convincing. Many Americans were looking for a prophet, and many were tired of sectarian quibbling. But they did not follow Smith because they wanted a prophet; they followed Smith because they found *his* claims convincing, as opposed to the claims of Shakers, Stoneites, Methodists, Catholics, or Screaming Children. They believed that Smith had recovered a golden bible containing the history of ancient Jews in America, and that he had been led to this discovery by an angel. Whether or not we find it convincing is beside the point. If we want to understand Mormonism and the crisis it provoked in American life, we must understand those claims.

The claims begin with a vision Smith experienced at age fourteen. Retiring to the woods outside his father's house in Palmyra, New York, Smith attempted to pray. When he later described his experience, he noted that he had been troubled for some time about his salvation. The division of Christendom into sects was on his mind, the "extreme difficulties caused by the contests of these parties of religionists."[45] Recent local revivals had exacerbated the problem for Smith. Historians have not been able to identify the exact revivals Smith was talking about, but his description, eighteen years after the fact, is pretty vague. What he described might have simply been the general status of American sects: "Some were contending for the Methodist faith, some for the Presbyterian, and some for the Baptist," a competition whose participants meant well but that ended with "priest contending against priest, and convert against convert so that all their good feelings . . . were entirely lost in a strife of words and a contest about opinions."[46] In 1817 or 1818, his mother had found a religious home in the Presbyterian church, while Joseph seemed "inclined to the Methodists," as Oliver Cowdery reported. Smith had also joined a debating society in which he encountered the arguments of the deists. He was being pulled into the sectarian divide.[47]

Alone in the woods, Smith prayed. He found himself bound by "the power of some actual being from the unseen world," and then the sky was filled with

Joseph Smith. This portrait was made after the prophet's death in 1844. Virtually no images exist of the young Smith as he organized his church and published the Book of Mormon. The Library Company of Philadelphia

a "pillar of light exactly over my head above the brightness of the sun." Then he saw "two personages"—God the Father and Jesus Christ. (Although Smith did not know it at the time, the presence of two divine beings underscored Mormonism's later anti-Trinitarian doctrine; Saints believe that the Father and the Son are distinct entities.) Smith had the presence of mind to call out and ask "which of all the sects was right." The personages answered that they were all wrong together and, indeed, "their Creeds were an abomination."[48]

Smith wrote several accounts of this experience, which has become known among Saints as the First Vision—including a short version, begun in 1832 and later abandoned, and an official version, written in several drafts from 1838 to 1841. Smith also gave oral accounts of the vision to close associates and sometimes to complete strangers; he told Oliver Cowdery, who later wrote about it in letters and newspaper articles, but he also explained it in detail to a man known as Matthias, another itinerating prophet whose credentials Smith did not accept.

The First Vision plays a significant role in twenty-first-century Mormonism: the church has canonized Smith's account, and the vision is often prominent in church promotional materials. It is harder to assess its impact on Americans in the 1820s and 1830s. No printed account of the vision was available until after the Missouri crisis had passed. The story of the two personages does not occur in any early Mormon sources outside Smith's close circle of confidants—which means that early Mormon preachers did not use the First Vision to encourage conversion, and Mormon critics did not use it to lampoon the faith.

What Mormons in the 1830s would have read about was the sectarian dimensions of early Mormon visions. Cowdery wrote a series of newspaper articles in 1834 about Smith's early visions. He did not include a description of the First Vision, but he echoed Smith's refrain about the difficulty in choosing right when salvation was at stake: "If he went to one [church] he was told they were right and all others were wrong—if to another, the same was heard."[49] And, when Smith did produce the story of the First Vision for publication, he emphasized the sectarian response. Indeed, Smith spent more time on the "hot persecution" that followed the vision than he did on the vision itself. "My telling the story," he wrote, "excited a great deal of prejudice against me among professors of religion." Smith apparently told a Methodist minister that he had seen a vision of the father and the son. The Methodist responded "with great contempt, saying it was all of the Devil, that there was no such thing as visions or revelations in these days." Smith remembered other Christians "heaped upon me bitter persecutions and revilings." In retrospect, he admitted that the stress induced by these "revilings" led to a period of bad behavior on his part. It was a rough start, but "I had now got my mind satisfied, so far as the sectarian world was concerned." He would join no churches.[50]

No other contemporary evidence links young Smith to any kind of religious hubbub in 1820, but the description he left of the Methodist minister was common enough in Jeffersonian America. While First Amendment freedoms permitted stories of miracles, prophecies, and visions to spread far and wide, these claims did not go unchallenged. A counterreaction denied the very existence of modern supernatural events and even suggested that to countenance such things was dangerous. What John Greenleaf Whittier called *supernaturalism*—"matters beyond and above the conception of [the] sharpened five senses"—threatened true Christianity, went this line of thinking, because supernaturalism elevated contemporary events and rumor above scriptural evidence. Critics blamed revivalist excesses known as "enthusiasm"—fainting, physical spasms, claims of divine healing, and crying out—for damaging true religion. Revivals were, in Trollope's words, "a terrific saturnalia." A careful contemporary of the Cane Ridge revivals, David Rice, worried that "under the influence of these enthusiastic mistakes men may positively conclude this or that doctrine to be true or false, not because they find or do not find it in the holy scriptures; but because they felt so and so, when praying."[51] A significant percentage of American Protestants thought, as did Smith's Methodist antagonist, that visions were "all of the devil."

Opposition to visionary experiences and even to revivals themselves may sound strange. Part of the reason that revivals seem so prominent in American religious history is that they have largely captured the interests of historians who study things other than religion. Given that antebellum revivals contributed to the rise of antislavery, temperance, and other social reform movements, and given that frontier revivalism helped build American national identity, revivals have been a favorite topic among history writers. Some have even gone so far as to classify all of American history as a series of "awakenings" that produced social change. Meanwhile, anti-revivalist critics of the period often made purely religious arguments—harder to situate in broader American history.[52]

To re-create American religion as the battlefield it was (and in the case of the Mormons, it could be a literal battlefield), it is necessary to understand how anti-revivalism also functioned as a powerful, active religious force. Anti-revivalists shared the Mormon anxiety about sects, authority, and false teaching. As Rice wrote, the problem with revivals was that the feelings and emotions of the revival might seem more real to converts than established biblical truth. If enthusiastic "exercises" became a proof of doctrine, Christianity was at risk. If "previous to their falling, their ideas are wrong . . . they imagine that these discoveries and impressions are made by the spirit of God, and are therefore certainly true, and out of this belief it is exceedingly difficult to reason them."[53] In such cases, wrote another set of critics, "one overflowing of a violent, ungoverned revival would snatch victory from truth." For more stri-dent critics, *all* revivals had this problem, for revivalism proceeded on "the mis-taken principle that the imaginations and passions of large bodies of men are to be excited without taking care, at the same time, to enlighten their under-standings."[54] This approach to visions and supernaturalism—that they killed true Christianity and were the product of "men of coarse and vulgar minds"—would also became part of the anti-Mormon literature. When Ezra Booth cri-tiqued the Latter-day Saints, he defined the visions of Joseph Smith as the product of "violent passions, bordering on madness, rather than the meek and gentle spirit which the Gospel inculcates."[55]

The reproach of Smith's vision by the unnamed Methodist therefore had deep roots in an American religious culture anxious about supernaturalism welling up from below. Yet, as Smith later recalled, he stuck to his story, main-taining that he had had a vision, like Saul on the road to Damascus. Years passed this way. Then, on a night when his family was once again discussing "the diversity of churches," he had a second vision. And this time, Smith would not be able to keep quiet about it.[56]

The vision came at midnight, and the darkness became as bright as mid-day. An entity came into Smith's bedroom with clothes of "exquisite white-ness" and a "countenance truly like lightning." This was Moroni, son of Mor-mon, father and son prophets of Christ who had once lived in ancient America. Both men had been Nephites, the descendants of Jewish escapees from the Babylonian conquest of Jerusalem. Moroni had written a record of the Nephites hundreds of years before. Three times the prophet explained to Smith the na-ture of those records—inscribed on gold plates and buried not far from the Smith farm in Palmyra, New York. He told Smith to "go and get them."

The records of the Nephites were, of course, the inscriptions that Joseph Smith translated and published as the Book of Mormon; curious inquirers wondered just where and how Smith had gotten word of such a treasure. Died-rich Willers thought very little of the Book of Mormon, but even before he had finished reading it, he knew that Smith claimed that "the angel of the Lord appeared to him and made known to him, that in the neighborhood of Pal-myra gold plates were buried in the earth on which the destiny of a Jewish prophet's family was written." Willers had little patience for the "plump fraud" of the "so-called golden book," but both converts and critics often heard the story of the Book of Mormon before reading its contents.[57]

It is also possible that the story of Moroni spread quickly for other reasons. This was not the first time Smith had been associated with supernatural beings in search of buried gold. Throughout the time he struggled with sectarians, angelic visions, and the lost unity of Christianity, Smith also sought answers to his Christian and mystical questions through the art of treasure digging. This, too, would form a recurring piece of anti-Mormon polemics, a constant accusation that in employing magical means to search for treasure, Smith had somehow violated Christian norms. But, as noted, Americans who engaged in magical practices did not necessarily believe they were abandoning their Christian roots. The astrologer Sheffield remained a lifelong Calvinist, stressing that divination by the stars was simpatico with predestination. Printed and handwritten grimoires laced spells with prayer and relied on the power of God to make the magic effective. Joshua Gordon wrote the phrase "Your Saviour sweating blood" multiple times on the flyleaves of his handwritten grimoire. The "Commodore," while hunting for treasure in Ohio, included as part of the search a reading from the Christian apocryphal Book of Tobit—a Hebrew scripture that also involved a search for hidden treasure.[58]

The Smith family earned a reputation as treasure diggers long before Joseph encountered the divine; they were known as jugglers—a nineteenth-century shorthand for magical con men. An 1830 critic pointed to Joseph Sr.'s reputation as "a kind of juggler, who has pretended, through a glass, to see money under ground."[59] Joseph Jr., meanwhile, had a reputation for "pretending, by means of a certain stone, or glass, which he put in a hat, to be able to discover lost goods, hidden treasures, mines of gold and silver, &c."[60] As the summer of 1825 turned to the fall, the Smith family finances went south; they had long been tenant farmers, and the bills came due. Even as Smith began to converse with divine personages, father and son turned to their treasure seeking as a means of financial support.

As discussed earlier, the Smith clan was not alone in leading treasure hunts. To find treasure, seekers needed a person rather than a map; X did not mark the spot. Treasure hunters with charisma and magical expertise were indispensable in these enterprises, and they hired themselves out like the specialists they were. Occasionally, these leaders were clergymen. A Methodist minister who preached in America and England came to New Jersey to divine treasure; an 1820s hunt for a "golden treasure or carbuncle" in the White Mountains of New Hampshire included a minister "well-qualified to lay the evil spirit" to rest. But official clerical titles were not necessary; indeed, one of the most remarkable aspects of treasure seeking was that it was a highly egalitarian activity, based as it was on hidden knowledge and faith. Although almost all treasure hunters were white men, the *leaders* of such enterprises could be all sorts of people. A "clairvoyant girl from Albany" led a treasure hunt in Oswego, New York, in 1851; an African American known as Mike saw buried treasure through a magical stone in Maine around 1812. An 1848 Staten Island treasure hunt was led by a "Guinea negro"—that is, a man born in Africa—who was considered a "great adept." Smith's status as an indigent teenager on the frontier was therefore no barrier to entry into the world of magic.[61]

What happened on a treasure hunt? What did the diggers actually do? Details are hard to come by, because the process of treasure hunting was at least nominally secret, and because no two hunts were the same. Some of the secondhand accounts were likely rumors—which told people what they expected to hear about treasure hunts, even if the listeners never went on one. Taken together, these accounts reveal some common aspects of American treasure hunting. An element of supernatural ability was required because treasure was something more than gold and rubies. It "was not some inanimate object," as historian Johannes Dillinger writes; it had "a life of its own."[62] Treasure was not bound to one patch of land; it could move or escape if it did not want to be found. It might sink deeper into the earth or simply fail to be in the same location from day to day. The treasure itself had magical properties and could be attuned to the moral qualities of the diggers—hence the need for prayer and clergymen. Treasure might not exist in sunlight; therefore, searches were usually conducted at night. Dreams could provide supernatural clues to locations. That was the case with a group of citizens in Whittingham, Vermont, who listed over forty mystical clues to buried treasure, such as the one that "a Pyrot hid" near Northampton, Massachusetts, or the money hidden "on fishers Island on mount Prospect near a Rock not the bigness of a haycock."[63] Chloe Russel, author of an 1824 treatise on dream interpretation, informed readers that she had been freed from enslavement when she dreamed of a pot of money and told the rightful owner where to dig for it.[64]

Treasure could move in other ways. As the 1850 account of the Commodore put it, "the human voice irritates the evil spirit who has charge of hidden treasures, and they vanish away." For this reason, silence was also a prerequisite. The unnamed African American who led the Staten Island search insisted on silence; he drew three concentric circles with mustard seeds, made magical symbols with a sword, and then, via a hand signal, instructed his silent followers to begin digging. Their silence extended to their breaks for alcohol, until at one horrible moment, a thirsty digger cried out, "The whiskey is all gone!" and this "unhappy exclamation destroyed the spells wherewith the spirit sentinels had been bound." The diggers abandoned the quest.[65] A Vermont treasure-quest in 1799 came to an end when the conjuror leading the quest, Ezekiel Perry, warned that a lack of faith, or any noise whatsoever, would cause the chest to move. The men worked in silence for two hours, until one of them stepped on another's toes. There was a cry of pain and exasperation, and the treasure moved.[66]

Edward Kendall wrote home to England about treasure digging. Quests usually began with dreams, he noted, but if dreams failed, "then mineral-rods are resorted to" and, after that, "charms and various observances, to defeat the watchfulness of the spirits that have the treasure in charge."[67] Kendall also noted that treasure digging opened a wide door for fraud. He reported the case of a Maine lumberjack named Lambert who began spreading rumors he had dug up a chest of gold using mystical mineral rods. Lambert's lavish spending on food and drink and the purchase of new horses seemed to confirm the stories, and "every day gave birth to new histories of the chest that had been found." Many others tried their hands at the task, believing "there were more pirates than one." Meanwhile, Lambert used his presumed wealth as collateral to take out massive loans from other settlers, then absconded with the money.[68]

Then there were seer stones—smooth, round stones that allowed those with magical powers to see at a distance. Seer stones appeared less frequently than divining rods in American treasure hunts, but they too had a long history in Christian magic. English traditions linked seer stones back to the Hebrew patriarchs. The court magician of Elizabeth I, John Dee, was a devotee of their use. Seer stones were not the stuff of forbidden, esoteric knowledge, however; readers could find a description in the US edition of the *Encyclopedia Britannica*, which described the process: "The seer looks into a crystal of beryl, wherein he will see the answer, represented either by types or figures, and sometimes, though very rarely, will hear the angels or spirits speak articulately."[69] Or, as the account of Universalist Miles Wooley's treasure hunt had it, seer stones were "mysterious" objects by which seekers "pretended to be able to discover treasure."[70]

Seer stones usually had to fit in a hat so the observer could cover his face with it, according to one account, and find "subterraneous wealth, which he could plainly see by looking into his dark hat, having this stone in the crown." Other than this size restriction, the stones had diverse properties. The treasure digger Zimri Allen used a small transparent stone, referred to as a "diamond." Joseph Stafford had a "peepstone which looked like a white marble and had a hole in the center." The family of apostate Mormon David Whitmer saved what they believed to have been his seer stone—a "trapezoidal gorget," a stone with two holes bored in it originally used by Native Americans.[71]

Seer stones chose their seer, not vice versa, and seers had to calibrate the stone to their abilities. Smith himself first borrowed a seer stone from "a neighboring girl," Sally Chase, apparently in order to find his own. One witness to the recounting of the tale recalled Smith taking Chase's "glass . . . placed in a hat to exclude the light" and immediately perceiving another stone, buried under the roots of a tree near the New York–Pennsylvania line. The stone began to glow "and after a short time became as intense as the mid-day sun." Now knowing where to dig, Smith unearthed the stone, "carried it to the creek, washed and wiped it dry, sat down on the bank, [and] placed it in his hat." Its supernatural powers were immediately apparent: "Time, place, and distance were immediately annihilated . . . all intervening obstacles were removed." Smith had his peepstone.[72]

Over the course of the 1820s, Smith apparently possessed several seer stones. A few are still kept in the Church History Library of the Church of Jesus Christ of Latter-day Saints in Salt Lake City. One is a smooth, egg-shaped stone, about five centimeters on its long axis, and mottled in brown and black. Other stones possessed by Smith were described as "composed of layers of different colors" or "white and transparent," and one as "a small stone, not exactly black, but was rather a dark color."[73]

It is unknown which of these Smith used in his divination by "Stone and Hat," as one witness recalled, but Smith attended several treasure hunts, though few of these are documented beyond hearsay.[74] William Stafford, in 1833, remembered the Smith family "tell[ing] marvelous tales, respecting the discoveries they had made in their peculiar occupation of money digging," including visions of "keys, barrels and hogsheads of minted silver and gold . . . large gold bars and silver plates."[75] Stafford joined the Smiths on one treasure hunt, during which Smith Sr. drew concentric circles on the ground and staked dowsing rods along them, while his son watched the activities of spirits in his stone. The spirits moved the treasure. A similar fate awaited Smith when he saw money buried with a tailfeather five feet underground; he and his compatriots dug for the money but found only the tailfeather, for "the money moved down."[76] Another time, Stafford heard the Smiths claiming they would need to cut the throat of a black sheep to make spirits release the treasure. Stafford gave them the sheep but suspected the Smiths ate it for supper rather than performing any ritual.[77]

Most of Smith's treasure hunts generated only oral or folkloric evidence, but at least one left legal evidence. In 1825, Josiah Stowell hired Smith to help him dig for hidden gold in Harmony, Pennsylvania. Apparently, "a woman named Odle, who claimed to possess the power of seeing under ground" located "great treasure concealed in a hill."[78] Oliver Cowdery insisted in 1835 that the cache had been gold unearthed by "a company of Spaniards . . . when the country was uninhabited by white settlers." The Spaniards mined it, minted it, and then reburied it.[79] Stowell tried to dig up the "valuable mine of either Gold or Silver" that he believed to be hidden on his Harmony property, but without success. Eventually, he sought professional help; he hired Smith for farm work and for his ability to "discern things invisible to the naked eye." Smith remembered being paid fourteen dollars a month to work the farm and search for the mine, above the going rate for canal workers and farm labor. It was both a magical and a capitalist venture.[80]

Things went wrong in multiple ways. The earth gave up no treasure, and one of Stowell's relatives hauled Smith into court on the charge of being a "disorderly person," producing the first (but not the last) legal imbroglio in Mormon history. New York state law banned "all jugglers, and all persons pretending . . . to tell fortunes, or to discover where lost goods may be found." Divining the future or the hiding place of lost gold was a crime in New York, and those who performed such rites were "disorderly persons." (Similar laws existed in Massachusetts, Connecticut, New Jersey, Maine, and Maryland.) Smith got swept up in an anti-magical sting.[81]

Such laws seem patently absurd today. They certainly violated the First Amendment's free-exercise clause—though modern interpreters should remember that the Bill of Rights did not apply to state governments until after the Fourteenth Amendment (ratified in 1868) mandated equal protection under the law. Perhaps that explains Smith's trial, or an 1818 arrest of a treasure hunter in New Hampshire, or the case against Alcut Stover of Maine, who called Eleanor Estes a witch in 1787.[82]

Or maybe it doesn't. *Why* exactly would New York State care if someone read another person's fortune or pretended to know magical spells? If Josiah

Stowell wanted to pay Smith money to dig for gold in a free and capitalist system, what was the problem? The answer lay partly in the colonial origins of the law and partly in the fears of a republican government.

Legislating against magic had not worked out well for European states. In the fifteenth through seventeenth centuries, European legal frameworks had generally permitted vigorous prosecutions of witches, including the use of previously banned practices such as anonymous accusations and torture to exact confessions. Tens of thousands of victims died in this "Great Witch Craze." Eighteenth-century jurists tried to make sense of it all; following emerging Enlightenment views of the supernatural, they argued that since witchcraft did not seem to leave any physical evidence behind, it either did not exist or could not be proved in court. These legal reforms slowly brought the trials to an end.[83]

That left a puzzling question for nineteenth-century historians and thinkers. If witchcraft was not real, then how had so many people been executed for practicing it? The answer for many jurists was that Reformation-era judges and lawyers had simply been duped. They were too "credulous"—too trusting of supernatural claims. Fears of demons, magicians, and witches were "images of straw" that nevertheless caused real fear—and encouraged Christians to overcorrect in response, according to the English thinker John Spencer. Believing in stories about witchcraft and the supernatural could thus disturb the "tranquility of the state"; therefore, the state ought to take no notice of such things. A host of European thinkers agreed with Spencer that the problem was not witches, but *stories* about witches. The threat to civilization was not witches making demonic pacts for which there was no evidence, but the fearmongering of witch hunters.[84] Several European nations began revoking their laws about witchcraft *and* making it a crime to claim anyone else was performing witchcraft. To secure the state against witch trials, it was not enough merely to end the penalty; if witchcraft did not exist, the state had to punish those who claimed it did. The Spanish Inquisition in 1614 adopted such high standards of evidence as to make witch accusations impossible. In 1624, France banned the practice of accusing witches. And in 1736, the British Parliament revoked its witchcraft laws and replaced them with a general ban on claiming that anyone could or did practice magic. As one historian wrote, "By 1750 it was not the witch but the witch-hunter who suffered the law's penalty."[85]

These laws were the ancestors of American codes against juggling and conjuring. Listening to wonder workers or magical claims, one Congregationalist minister wrote, tended "not only to destroy religion, but to dissolve our mutual confidence and subvert our social security. . . . On social, therefore, as well as religious grounds, these diviners ought to be prosecuted rather than encouraged."[86] Magic was bad behavior; it ruined morals, encouraged mobs, and promoted panic. States took the threat seriously. Maryland classified juggling and fortune-telling with prostitution, vagrancy, and public begging.[87] New Jersey forbade any prosecutions for "witchcraft, sorcery or inchantment" and also banned "pretences to such arts or powers . . . whereby ignorant persons are frequently deluded or defrauded," including claims to "skill or knowledge in any occult or crafty science." Those convicted of making such claims could be sentenced to up to three months of hard labor. These laws were listed in the statute books next to laws on adultery, fornication, and "open lewdness."[88]

But many Americans continued to practice magic—just as they continued to practice adultery and fornication. It was a difficult crime to prosecute, even when evidence of fraud was overwhelming. The grifter Ransford Rogers twice convinced Americans to pay him money to summon gold-seeking spirits—once in rural New Jersey and again in Vermont. When his powers of necromancy were revealed as gobbledygook and his customers demanded justice, Rogers fled to Quebec.[89] An anonymous exposé of New York City's dozens of fortune-tellers moaned that these "Witches of New York" had been "treated with such light regard . . . by the community they have swindled." They were "dangerous criminals," and the author could not believe they were not treated as such.[90]

Smith's trial was thus unusual: an actual prosecution for magic. It was such a rare event that one participant recalled "a large collection of persons in attendance" and that "the proceedings attracted much attention."[91] The original court records have not survived, save for a note by the judge, Albert Neely, referring to "Joseph Smith the Glass Looker."[92] Handwritten copies of the original records, however, along with some later recollections, form a reasonable picture of the trial itself.[93] Smith Jr. and Smith Sr. freely admitted their use of seer stones and divination, though the son claimed he "of late had pretty much given it up" and the father admitted regret that they had used this power "only in search of filthy lucre."[94] Stowell himself and another of his laborers both testified to their belief in Smith's abilities.[95] The Smith family defense was that they had not *pretended* to their abilities but had real powers with at least some Christian attributes, and therefore they had not broken the law.

Stowell's relatives testified that they, too, had seen Joseph Smith work his magic, and "the deception appeared so palpable" that they could not stomach

*Revolution of America*

America's horoscope. Practicing magic and divination could be patriotic. Astrology was a going concern in the early republic. Ebenezer Sibly wrote a horoscope for the United States of America, taking July 4, 1776, as its birthday. He placed his calculations of the positions of the stars on that day in the hands of an angel, with American symbols beneath. Sibly foretold good things for the new nation. L. Tom Perry Special Collections, Harold B. Lee Library, Brigham Young University, Provo, Utah (133.5 Sill 1788)

the matter. Indeed, the case itself was initiated by Stowell's relatives, who likely thought that the time had come for Stowell to stop throwing his money away.[96] Judge Neely therefore had an epistemological as well as a legal question to answer: Did Joseph Smith Jr. actually possess divine magical powers—and was he therefore innocent? Or had he faked it and thereby broken the law?

It is unclear what happened next. Cowdery wrote in 1835 that Smith had been "honorably acquitted." The extant copies of the court record claim the verdict was guilty, though this may have been a later addition. Joel Noble, a judge whom Smith had dealings with later, thought the teenager had taken "leg bail"—that is, run off to escape punishment. Whatever the case, it seems New York never imposed a fine, and one historian has suggested that Neely really believed that Smith had given up treasure digging and therefore let the matter drop.[97]

Smith was forever hounded by the "very prevalent story of my having been a money digger." Later writers and critics never let him forget it. The Book of Mormon was lampooned as merely "the counterpart of his money-digging plan," brought to light by "the same magic power by which he pretended to tell fortunes, discover hidden treasures, &c." A letter writer taking the name "Green Mountain Boys," in 1844, remembered Smith "digging for the money your Father pretended old Bob Kidd buried" in Vermont, then threatened to lynch him just as the British had hung Captain Kidd.[98] Smith Sr.'s treasure-hunting reputation allowed anti-Mormons to dub him "a great babbler, credulous, not especially industrious, a money digger."[99]

At the same time, treasure seeking paid. Sometimes it was reported that the finds really had appeared. Stephen Grindle stumbled across "some four or five hundred pieces of the currency of France, Spain, Spanish America, Portugal, Holland, England, and Massachusetts" on his farm in coastal Maine in the winter of 1840–41. Caleb Atwater reported finding Roman coins in Tennessee before 1820. Atwater—a noted scholar—passed on some rumor and speculation about their origins; they might have been lost by French explorers or soldiers in the decades of French contact, or "some persons [may] have *purposely* lost coins, medals, &c. &c. in caves which they knew were about to explored, or deposited them in tumuli, which they knew were about to be opened." That much, to Atwater, was "a fact."[100] And of course, there were fees to be charged for leading treasure hunts, even if the treasure never felt like showing itself. Smith was in business to collect those fees and those buried coins, whether they had been put there a thousand, a hundred, or ten years before. He needed to provide for his growing family, as he had courted and married his wife, Emma, over the course of the Harmony adventure.

Whether treasure seeking was real was a religious question, but whether people could practice it was a legal and political question. Freedom of religion had been established, but what counted as religion? John Adams mused that "authority in magistrates and obedience in citizens" derived from "reason, morality, and the Christian religion," but who precisely was going to define those terms in a world of expanding free print and rambunctious free speech? Adams specifically denied the role of miracle or mystery in defining how reason and Christianity worked, but did freedom mean the responsibility to carefully weigh each new piece of information as it came in—to evaluate it and cross-check it? Or was that too much to ask of free citizens, who might accept something in a newspaper as easily as their twenty-first-century counterparts click on a social media link to take them to fake websites that infect their computers with viruses and their minds with conspiracy theory claptrap? The same problems roiled the early republic. Not every conspiracy theory took root—John Symmes's theory that the earth was hollow inside and open at the poles never got much traction—but others did. Thousands of Americans believed novels and tracts that suggested that Catholic nuns were killing babies in nunneries and destroying the bodies with lime.[101]

And who got to say what counted as "Christian religion"? Could prayer for magical purposes count as Christian? What about those who accepted Christ but denied the Trinity? What about the hidden forms of Christian worship in the slave quarters—a Christianity that focused on Jesus *and* Moses and that emphasized personal freedom as God's will, ignoring Paul's tacit acceptance of slavery? What about White Protestants who began—very slowly—to argue that owning humans as property could not be Christian? John Adams had surely meant his own highly institutional Congregationalism of Massachusetts when he referred to a "Christian religion" keeping order in the state; at least, he wrote of a republic created "without a pretence of miracle or mystery." But that kind of Christianity was fading in the wake of the Revolution.

By 1820, ecclesiastical institutions were weak and ideas were strong. Christianity was now open to interpretation, and advocates on all sides were at one another's throats. This was the sectarian dilemma. No less a light than George Washington had more or less given up trying to solve it by 1785, when he made a radical suggestion that *all* religions could have state sanction; people should pay the state, which in turn would support the religion that "they profess, if of the denomination of Christians; or declare themselves Jews, Mahomitans, or otherwise."[102]

This was the world in which Joseph Smith began a spiritual quest to unearth and translate what Mormons consider sacred scripture, ancient plates of gold stored up in the earth. His quest—and the Mormon experience in Jacksonian America—is therefore not really a case of reason versus faith, religion versus folk magic, or even the people versus the pulpit. The genesis of Mormonism and the response to it pose a stack of questions and unsettled affairs about freedom, faith, Christian unity, virtue, morality, law, money, and authority, haphazardly balanced across the chasm of the early republic's penchant for violence. "There is no denying," historian Johannes Dillinger wrote, that the quest for the golden plates "is a treasure narrative."[103] Yet it is also true, as another historian countered, that "an early American could be deeply religious at the same time he was eagerly involved in the treasure-quest."[104] As Cowdery recounted the story, even as Smith dug for treasure and defended himself in court, he "continued to receive instructions concerning the coming forth of the fulness of the gospel." Looking back on her family's experiences in 1845, Lucy Mack Smith wrote that even though they had spent time "drawing magic circles or sooth saying," they "never during our lives suffered one important interest to swallow up every other obligation but whilst we worked with our hands we endeavor to remember the service of & the welfare of our souls."[105]

Mormonism was an outgrowth of, not an exception to, the American Christian world of the 1800s, part of an extensive concatenation of religious claimants set in motion by the Bill of Rights, the collapse of established churches, and a panoply of resurrected notions and practices from across Christian history. Early American religion did not feature a staid group of well-meaning Protestants who agreed with one another and constituted a mythical "Christian America" where faith was singular and unquestioned, nor was Mormonism a rebellion against such a mythical American consensus. Indeed, questions and conflicts defined the era. Americans of the 1830s had their own culture wars, and among Baptists, Methodists, Universalists, Churches of Christ, Presbyterians, Catholics, Unitarians, Swedenborgians, deists, Disciples of Christ, Quakers, Shakers, Jews, Wilkinsonians, Screaming Children, Nothingarians, and others, the Mormons arrived hoping to "solve" this crisis of division. Religion in the Age of Revolution was not a peaceful antidote to our own times. Indeed, it was so fractious, angry, supernatural, and cynical that we might almost recognize it as our own.

# 2

## The Bible Quarry

JOSEPH SMITH WAS NOT THE ONLY treasure hunter with a claim on the Book of Mormon. A seer named Samuel Lawrence showed up on Smith's doorstep in 1827. Lawrence and Smith had collaborated on treasure-digging exploits before, including an initial foray to find the golden plates. Now Lawrence had heard Smith had found the plates, and Lawrence wanted to "go shares" on the find. Just in case Smith was hesitant to show him the goods, Lawrence brought along a supernatural contingency plan—"one Beeman a grate Rodsman." If Smith would not share his treasure, Lawrence intended to match Beeman's magic against the young prophet's so as to find and seize the plates by force.[1]

Lawrence's claim had merit. He and Smith had worked together as diviners several times in the past as part of a group including one "Beman" or "Beaman" (almost certainly the same individual) and Hyrum Smith. It appears that Lawrence assumed that this prior arrangement entitled him to a piece of the treasure; they were, after all, *gold* plates, and times were hard in Jacksonian America. Smith demurred, perhaps explaining that the book was not *that* sort of treasure. When negotiation failed, Beeman "took out his rods"—enchanted sticks that knew where gold and water lay hidden—and began divining for the treasure; the rod pointed at the brick hearth beneath which the Smiths had secreted the plates.[2]

Like all evidence involving the coming forth of the Book of Mormon, the provenance of this story is convoluted and contested. Much of what we have comes from later recollections and hearsay collected from a bevy of sources. None of those involved in the recovery and translation of the Book of Mormon—and it involved a surprising number of people—kept detailed, day-to-day records; one of the most complete accounts of the Book of Mormon's emergence comes from Smith's mother, Lucy, who wrote her memoir in the wake of her son's 1844 murder. It is an invaluable source, but it was composed decades after some of the events it describes. More contemporary reports can be distressingly brief. A Gentile neighbor recorded in his 1830 diary that he heard of a "*new Bible, or Book of Mormon*," then never mentioned it again.[3] In other words, the stories circulating in upstate New York *about* the Book of Mormon were rumors about gold, treasure hunts, angels, and new scriptures. These were what most people of Palmyra heard the first time they heard of Mormonism.

They may well have heard the story of Lawrence and Beeman, who sought the book's gold (if not its message) with their divining rods at the ready. It is not clear how Smith got out of this scrape; Joseph Knight, who related the story in 1835, did not elaborate. One intriguing suggestion, however, is that Beman converted to Mormonism—perhaps right then and there. Several sources mention Alvin Beman as the person who helped hide the plates rather than reveal them; Beman and Beeman were certainly the same man, and dramatic conversions were not unknown in early Mormonism. Yet Knight never suggested Beman converted at that moment; Knight simply said that the Smiths "had to guard the house" in response. Possibly Smith had to throw the men out by force—a suggestion that violence between Mormons and their opponents predated the formal founding of the church in 1830.[4]

Tales of how Joseph and Emma Smith protected the golden plates have become an enduring part of Mormon folklore. The plates themselves consisted of a sheaf of thin pages, six by eight inches and fitted into something like a three-ring binder. For two years, the Smiths secreted these metallic records in a log, or under floorboards, or in a cherrywood box beneath a pile of flax. It is not entirely clear how many of the gambits made to steal the plates actually occurred, but the Book of Mormon had become something of an open secret by 1829, and interested parties made natural and supernatural efforts to secure the bible. Smith's 1838 assertion that "multitudes were on the alert continually to get them from me" is a point of pride if not an article of faith in modern Mormonism.[5] Smith described the desire for the plates as a sign of Gentile greed and as an indication of the hostility that Mormonism purportedly engendered in bystanders. The fight for the plates thus could even be considered the earliest form of anti-Mormonism—a belief that Smith and his relatives were either hoarding gold or plotting some form of religious radicalism. Indeed, one future Mormon became interested in the book precisely because locals were muttering that Smith "ought to be tarred and feathered for telling such a damn lie!"[6]

Such views even occurred within the Smith family itself. Jesse Smith (uncle to Joseph Smith Sr.) wrote to Hyrum that "the whole pretended discovery" was a "foolish deception, a very great wickedness, unpardonable." He chastised Smith Jr. in an 1829 letter for making "a gold book discovered by the necromancy of infidelity" and called the volume "a golden calf."[7] Charges of magic use and infidelity were prominent in these early critiques of the Book of Mormon, even though its contents were virtually unknown to anyone outside Smith's circle.

Smith himself told several versions of the story of the unearthing of the Book of Mormon. It seems likely that he included various details to various audiences at different points in his career, as is typical for oral communication. The stories likely circulated along with other rumors about the book. Smith's written versions assert that he, following Moroni's instructions, arrived at the Hill Cumorah on September 22, 1823. He discovered a "stone of considerable size" under which was a "box . . . formed by laying stones together in some kind of cement." At the bottom of the box lay the plates.[8] Joseph moved to take them—and discovered he could not. In his 1832 *History of the Church of Jesus Christ of Latter-day Saints*, he wrote that he "cried unto the Lord in the agony of my soul why can I not obtain them," to which he received the answer that his desire to obtain the gold for pecuniary reasons had sullied his soul; Smith felt greed like the Gentiles, and God could not allow that.[9]

In his 1838 *History*, Smith passed over this confession; Moroni simply appeared and said that "the time for bringing them forth had not yet arrived."[10] In 1835 Smith told a visitor that, when he first visited the plates, "the powers of darkness strove hard against me," and Willard Chase's 1833 recollection of the story that Smith told him (a convoluted provenance at best) specified that

Smith encountered a being shaped like a toad as well as Moroni, and that Smith received a physical shock that kept him from the plates. Truman Coe heard from Smith that the plates "eluded his grasp and vanished" until Smith learned to "cast away his selfishness."[11]

It took four years for God to forgive Smith, with annual pilgrimages made each year on September 22 to visit the stone box. In the meantime, Smith's family life turned upside down. His beloved older brother, Alvin, died in 1823. According to numerous recollections, Alvin had been the person Smith intended to take with him to unearth the golden plates.[12] But instead, in 1827, it was Emma Hale Smith who made the journey. She had met and married Joseph in a whirlwind romance when he traveled to Harmony, Pennsylvania, to dig for Josiah Stowell's missing mine. Emma and Joseph had to sneak out of her father's house to get married, and she was soon integrated into the Smith family quest for the Book of Mormon. Joseph and Emma traveled to Cumorah in September 1827; Emma waited on the road and prayed while Joseph went forth. Although in one account "a host of devils began to screech and to scream," Moroni at last gave the plates to Joseph.[13]

Smith was not the only person to see or interact with the plates. He appears to have worked from some object, though whether that object was actual

The Hill Cumorah in the twentieth century. Today, the site is home to several Latter-day Saint historical and missionary sites. Church History Library, Salt Lake City

ancient plates, a fabricated hoax, or something in between has been a matter of prodigious speculation. Emma Smith felt the pages underneath a cloth; Lucy Mack Smith admitted she saw and handled them. William Smith felt the plates and reckoned they were made of gold and copper. John Whitmer testified that "I handled those plates, there was fine engravings on both sides."[14]

Then there were the Book of Mormon witnesses. A collection of men—and they were all men—signed statements swearing they had seen the gold plates, and those documents were affixed at the end of every 1830 copy of the Book of Mormon. The testimonies combined a profound sense of religious awe with the framework of a legal document. The Three Witnesses—Cowdery, Martin Harris, and David Whitmer—wrote that "we, through the grace of God the Father, and our Lord Jesus Christ, have seen the plates which contain this record," and that the voice of God "hath declared it unto us; wherefore we know of a surety, that the work is true." Another collection of Whitmers, Smiths, and Hiram Page provided a more prosaic encounter with the plates: "Joseph Smith Jr. . . . has shewn unto us the plates of which hath been spoken, which have the appearance of gold." The plates, they affirmed, "we did handle with our hands; and . . . saw the engravings thereon, all of which has the appearance of ancient work, and of curious workmanship."[15] The testimonies now precede the text in all church printings of the Book of Mormon, and while not all readers (then or now) have found the statements convincing, these affidavits suggest the ways in which Mormonism based its claims on both the supernatural character of the Book (the Three Witnesses) and the physical existence of the plates themselves (the Eight Witnesses).[16]

The plates were not written in English, however, and the ordeal of translation made obtaining the plates look like a cakewalk. Since the original language and alphabet of the Book of Mormon had been lost, the process by which it was turned into English would be more mystical than linguistic. Smith rarely discussed the process of translation; most commonly, he simply noted that the book was "translated into our own language by the gift and power of God."[17]

It is a remarkable understatement for an ordeal that lasted nearly two years, involved multiple translators, and featured a number of unforced errors. For the most part, Smith dictated the translation to a scribe—Emma at first, then Martin Harris, one of the Three Witnesses. Harris, a Palmyra local, had become interested in the stories that were swirling around town. Upon visiting the prophet, Harris learned that God intended Smith to translate and Harris to scribe. Smith at first read the text via stones he found with the plates—

"smooth three-cornered diamonds," Lucy Mack Smith recalled.[18] These were the Urim and Thummim, first recorded in the Hebrew Bible and used in the Book of Samuel as a tool for divination. (This biblical precedent reaffirmed the long symbiosis of Judeo-Christian and magical practice.) The Urim and Thummim were secured in bows, forming a "a pair of spectacles."[19] Smith read the words through the stones, and Harris took the dictation.

At other times, Smith used his own seer stones, which were described by one Mormon as objects "made by the Lord" rather than naturally occurring geological forms. Smith also combined approaches. Joseph Knight watched Smith translate by putting "the urim and thummim into his hat and Darken[ing] his eyes," at which point the translation supernaturally appeared one sentence at a time, "in Brite Roman Letters. . . . Then that would go away the next sentence would Come and so on. But if it was not Spelt rite it would not go away till it was rite."[20] David Whitmer instead remembered a word-by-word interpretation, explaining that Smith informed him that the stones produced a vision of "an oblong piece of parchment . . . on that appeared the writing. One character at a time would appear, and under it was the interpretation in English."[21] At still other times, Smith copied the characters from the plates onto scratch paper. Lucy Smith remembered the process involving a transcription of "the Egyptian alphabet."[22] Sometimes Smith placed a veil between himself and his scribe, other times not.[23]

Smith and Harris did not make rapid progress as a translation team. It took them five months to produce 116 pages of material. Their slow pace was not the only problem; Harris had recurrent doubts about the validity of the plates. Harris asked Smith to copy down the characters of the Book of Mormon so Harris could take them to various authorities to validate their ancient origin. Although the Book of Mormon itself claims to be have been written in "Reformed Egyptian"—a language currently unknown to scholars—Harris nevertheless believed experts could confirm the characters as genuine. Perhaps he believed, as claimed in 1859, that the Book was in fact written in "Arabic, Chaldaic, Syriac, and Egyptian."[24] This kind of slight but significant deviation from Smith's teachings would become a staple of Harris's style—and a hallmark of the faith of many early Saints.

Other early Saints wanted to see the engravings. Both John Whitmer and Oliver Cowdery wrote down the "caractors" from the Book of Mormon; these symbols were probably transcriptions from the pen of Smith himself. Harris took three or four lines of characters and showed them to John Clark, a local

Episcopal priest, who pronounced them "as unlike letters or hieroglyphics as well could be produced were one to shut up his eyes and play off the most antic movements with his pen."[25] Undaunted, Harris took the characters to Charles Anthon, a man whom Edgar Allan Poe later referred to as "the best classicist in America."[26] Anthon and Harris produced different accounts of their meeting. Harris claimed Anthon told him the letters were Syriac, Chaldean, and so forth; Harris also reported that Anthon confirmed "the translation was correct."[27] Anthon insisted he told Harris the whole thing was a hoax and derided the "hieroglyphics" as "Greek and Hebrew letters, crosses and flourishes, Roman letters inverted," with Mesoamerican symbols tossed in for good measure.[28] Harris's version of events, however, became a public piece of Mormon proselytization efforts.

Oliver Cowdery also received a copy of the Book of Mormon letters, but he kept his copy of the engravings private, "for profit & learning." Another set of "caractors" was published in 1844 by a Mormon press in New York. The origin of these 1844 symbols is unclear, but they are consistent with the characters Cowdery and Harris collected.[29]

Despite his encounters with Anthon, Harris could not shake whatever was needling him about the book. He prevailed upon Smith to let him take the translated pages and show them to friends and family. Smith sought divine approbation, which came grudgingly and with a spate of provisos that Harris must not lose the pages. Harris promised and took the pages. Then he lost them.

Lucy Mack Smith provided dramatic testimony of this episode, complete with direct quotations for almost everyone involved; these recollections and quotations, however, were not recorded for almost twenty years. The prophet's mother recalled high drama, personal loss, and a host of tenuous excuses on Harris's part. In his 1838 *History*, Smith said almost nothing about Harris's blunder and instead focused on a direct divine manifestation: the Lord's chastisement of him and the removal and subsequent restoration of the Urim and Thummim by an angel. The missing 116 pages were the source of Smith's first divine revelation canonized by the later church, which insisted that, though the pages were gone, "the designs, and the purposes of God cannot be frustrated."[30]

When Smith realized the pages were gone, he received a revelation from heaven. God told Joseph not to retranslate the missing pages; the content of those pages, Smith learned, would be summarized and edited in another section (what today comprises the first six books of the Book of Mormon). One of the seminal anti-Mormon books, Eber D. Howe's *Mormonism Unvailed*, mocked this divine response, marveling that a "record made by a miracle, kept for ages by a miracle, dug from the ground by a miracle," could somehow be "*stolen* by someone, so that even a miracle could not restore it." Other critics of Mormonism have had similar responses in the past two hundred years. Yet, for the nascent Latter-day Saints, this divine arrangement *was* a miracle. For Smith, the loss was another in a series of supernatural events—a chapter in a series of chapters that involved angels, seer stones, and sacred history. The loss of the 116 pages was a site of divine communication and a providence. God preserved the Book of Mormon, and God knew the pages would be lost. Anti-Mormons interrogated each step of this process, but believers seemed to understand the coming forth and translation of the book as one seamless experience.[31]

Indeed, the loss of the pages and the restoration of the Urim and Thummim led Smith to one of the most prolific spiritual relationships in the history of Mormonism. After an extended break from the translation process, Smith met Oliver Cowdery in April 1829. Cowdery had heard the rumors and legends about the gold bible swirling in western New York, and he wanted to see for himself. Smith received a revelation for Cowdery, one that satisfied the visitor that the work was true. Cowdery began to serve as scribe. The two men finished the six hundred–page opus in less than three months.

Finding a publisher proved difficult. Smith and Cowdery approached several throughout western New York, including Thurlow Weed, a future confidante of Abraham Lincoln. Weed rejected the manuscript, even though he himself had once participated in a treasure hunt in which "the throat of a black cat was cut, and the precise spot was indicated by the direction the blood spurted."[32] Eventually, a Palmyra publisher named Egbert Grandin agreed to print it, even though he assumed it was "a gross imposition, and a grosser superstition." This time, Smith made a copy of the text before handing it off to Grandin. The first copies of the Book of Mormon rolled off the presses in March 1830.[33]

It was to be one of the most remarkable books in human history—not merely for its content but for the effects it had on readers. Indeed, the Book of Mormon itself seemed to work wonders on future converts. "I felt a strange interest in the book," wrote Parley Pratt. It awoke something in Pratt—something primal, beyond human need: "I read all day; eating was a burden, I had no desire for food; sleep was a burden . . . for I preferred reading to sleep."

Reading one of those first printed copies of the Book, Pratt absorbed more than names, places, and events. As he read, he realized that "the spirit of the Lord was upon me, and I knew and comprehended that the book was true, so plainly and manifestly as a man comprehends and knows he exists." The process of reading this "book of books" transmitted knowledge, truth, and a kind of transcendent gratification: "My joy was now full . . . and I rejoiced sufficiently to more than pay me for all the sorrows, sacrifices, and toils of my life."[34]

Pratt was not alone. As the Book of Mormon made its way across the nation, hundreds and then thousands of Americans picked it up, read it, and found themselves transported into religious awe. When Ezra Thayer opened the Book in 1830, he "received a shock with such exquisite joy that no pen can write and no tongue can express," and immediately testified that the Book was true.[35] David Patten became filled with fear and faith after reading only the preface and the accounts of the witnesses.[36] Abigail Leonard heard of the book in 1831; she prayed about it and felt "the gift and power of the Holy Ghost." When she finally found a copy, reading was a mere formality, and there followed "such days of rejoicing and thanksgiving I never saw before or since."[37] Benjamin Brown read the Book of Mormon and meditated on it before deciding to test it; if, as the Book claimed, "the Three Nephites had the power to show themselves to anyone they might wish . . . I asked the Lord to allow me to see them for a witness and a testimony of the truth of the Book of Mormon." The Nephites arrived five days later, and Brown subsequently became a Saint.[38] Sarah Pea of Illinois read the Book of Mormon one evening, yet "the book appeared to open before my eyes for weeks." She too joined the church.[39]

The Book of Mormon was not merely a book; it was a religious experience in itself. That fact may explain why Saints often preached about the "coming forth" of the Book of Mormon, as much or more than about the narrative within its pages. The Book was not merely text; it was an event. Such a book, written on gold, protected by angelic visitation, and attested to by witnesses, represented a miracle—or at least a potential miracle—in and of itself. Some of those who heard of the Book of Mormon went on to find and read a copy. Some of those who read it had the reality of the miraculous reports supernaturally confirmed in their mind. Noah Packard, for example, held the book to his forehead and asked God to manifest whether it was true. He then read it aloud to his wife, and the "Lord poured out His spirit upon me and the scriptures were opened to our understanding, and we were convinced that the Book of Mormon was a true record of the Aborigines of America."[40] The supernatural coming forth of the Book of Mormon combined with supernatural experiences of reading the Book of Mormon to produce thousands of converts in the first ten years after its publication.

These converts did not agree on everything—a fair number of them would turn against Smith at one point or another—but while they remained Mormon, they usually retained their faith in the Book itself. Indeed, one Gentile skeptic explained that Mormon missionaries had "full faith in the virtue of their Books, that whoever would read them, would feel so thoroughly convinced of the truth of what they contained, that they . . . would be obliged to unite with them."[41] Missionaries' *belief* that the Book would yield converts (even when it did not) seems to have kept them going, perhaps more so than the content of the Book itself.

This unusual situation may explain why scholars—even Mormon scholars—have paid relatively little attention to the content of the Book of Mormon itself. Indeed, the LDS church did not include a formal study of the Book of Mormon in its Sunday School curriculum until the 1970s. Scholars have tended to mine the book for evidence about Joseph Smith or the nature of Mormonism itself, while faithful Saints tend to do the same thing to make the case for the book's historicity or holiness. Yet, as the textual scholar Grant Hardy has pointed out, such efforts amount to beginning with something else—Smith, Mormon theology, ancient American archaeology—and using that as the lens through which to view the Book of Mormon. Indeed, modern-day Saints often follow the admonition of Moroni 10:4 to pray *about* the Book of Mormon "with a sincere heart, with real intent"—not to perform deep textual analysis of the work itself.[42]

Those who do investigate the Book of Mormon in its own right will discover an enormously complicated document; it contains summations and abridgments of over a dozen sets of records. Some books are presented in their entirety; others have been edited, re-edited, or condensed, but occasionally these emendations contain verbatim documents inserted into the text, to say nothing of recounting of earlier events and prophecies of the future. Mark Twain referred to the book as "chloroform in print," but it is not merely the endless repetition of "And it came to pass" that makes the text hard to read. It is a difficult book because its very structure is a series of layers of commentary on top of abridgment on top of summary. The scholar Terryl Givens has suggested the Book of Mormon reads more like Midrash than Bible.

# Book of Mormon Plates and Records

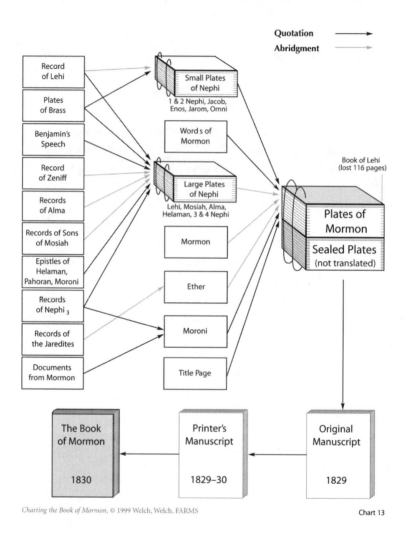

Quotation ⟶
Abridgment ⟶

| | |
|---|---|
| Record of Lehi | Small Plates of Nephi |
| Plates of Brass | 1 & 2 Nephi, Jacob, Enos, Jarom, Omni |
| Benjamin's Speech | Words of Mormon |
| Record of Zeniff | Large Plates of Nephi |
| Records of Alma | Lehi, Mosiah, Alma, Helaman, 3 & 4 Nephi |
| Records of Sons of Mosiah | Mormon |
| Epistles of Helaman, Pahoran, Moroni | Ether |
| Records of Nephi $_3$ | Moroni |
| Records of the Jaredites | Title Page |
| Documents from Mormon | |

Book of Lehi (lost 116 pages)

Plates of Mormon

Sealed Plates (not translated)

| The Book of Mormon | Printer's Manuscript | Original Manuscript |
|---|---|---|
| 1830 | 1829–30 | 1829 |

*Charting the Book of Mormon,* © 1999 Welch, Welch, FARMS

Chart 13

The Book of Mormon's structure. The Book of Mormon describes itself as a collection, emendation, and compilation of a host of Nephite sacred scriptures. Diagram by Jack Welch

Indeed, the Book of Mormon has often suffered in its comparison to the standard Christian Bible. As Fawn Brodie observed, Book of Mormon prophets tend to be uniformly good; nowhere in the Book's six hundred pages does a harlot speak in the name of the Lord. The chapter numbers in the original (since revised) could seem haphazard and occasional when compared to biblical arrangement. The Book of Mormon possessed a distinctive Christology; its Jewish prophets give much more specific forecasts regarding Christ as the messiah than anything found in the Old Testament. At the same time, this Christological specificity was interlaced with specifically Old Testament language. The Nephite prophets quoted long passages of Isaiah, and textual references and quips from other biblical books abound. Jesse J. Smith believed in the Book of Mormon because of its biblicism; his assessment of the book was based "wholly upon the bible," he wrote, and anything "that does not conform with the law or the testimony I place it entirely aside." He became a Saint. Scholar Paul Gutjahr writes that the Book of Mormon "echoed the Bible."[43]

But the Book of Mormon claims not to be another Bible but another *scripture*. The difference is important. The Old Testament represents a collection of diverse volumes written by different authors at different times and edited together by anonymous redactors; it contains creation narratives, family stories, political accounts, erotic poetry, theophanies, and poems. The New Testament contains four versions of one story, followed by a collective biography of the early Christian church, a series of letters by different authors, and an apocalyptic postscript seemingly so out of keeping with the rest of the volume that Martin Luther wanted to jettison it. The Hebrew Bible and the New Testament are really collections of sacred documents, not uniform wholes.

The Book of Mormon, on the other hand, *is* a uniform whole, self-described as the work of three men, "many hundred years after the coming of Christ." The prophet Nephi wrote much of the first two books, and the father-son prophet duo of Mormon and Moroni included Nephi's work in their abridgment of previous records, then added their own thoughts and experiences. The text is almost exclusively a political and military history of a religious movement, and is much more akin to the historical books of the Old Testament than to the Bible as a whole. If the Song of Songs is hot-blooded poetry, and if Ecclesiastes captures the uncertain fidelity of an anxious penitent, then the Book of Mormon possesses the straightforward sledgehammer appeal of Deuteronomy—if, indeed, it resembles the Bible at all.

The content of the Book of Mormon is—to put it mildly—dense. The opening book, 1 Nephi, begins amid the Israelite crisis of the sixth century BCE. God calls Lehi, a righteous Jew, to preach warning to Jerusalem alongside the biblical Jeremiah. This assignment does not go well, and Lehi and his family flee into the wilderness. Soon Lehi's son Nephi receives a divine warrant as prophet; he comes into possession of brass plates containing the records of Isaiah, and indeed, he incorporates vast swaths of Isaiah into his book. God further commands Nephi to keep two separate sets of records on a different set of sacred plates. This can get confusing, as in 1 Nephi 9: "[A]s I have spoken concerning these plates, behold they are not the plates upon which I make a full account of the history of my people; for the plates upon which I make a full account of my people I have given the name of Nephi; wherefore, they are called the plates of Nephi, after mine own name; and these plates also are called the plates of Nephi." The book of 1 Nephi *also* includes a fraternal rebellion, visions of a risen Christ, the construction of oceangoing vessels, and the promise "that the Lord God will raise up a mighty nation among the Gentiles, yea, even upon the face of this land [the Americas]. . . . And after our seed is scattered the Lord God will proceed to do a marvelous work among the Gentiles, which shall be of great worth unto our seed." And all of these activities occupy only one of the fifteen books of the Book of Mormon; most of the others rival 1 Nephi in complexity (and length).[44]

The basic plot outline of the Book of Mormon is not much different from that of much of the Old Testament: a bunch of Jews make a covenant with God, wander to different places over hundreds of years, establish a kingdom, and try to defend it. Lehi and Nephi become the protagonists of the first books, with Nephi's brothers Laman and Lemuel chafing under Lehi's righteous rule. The brothers have a falling out; Laman and Lemuel even tie Nephi up at one point and threaten him with death. The family sticks together for the long flight from the Old World, building ships wrought from "timbers of curious workmanship . . . not after the manner of men." These vessels take them to the promised land, somewhere in the Americas.

Identifying where exactly this land of promise was in the Americas has become something of a cottage industry among Mormons. Smith himself never definitively tied specific geographic sites to places in the Book of Mormon, though later in life he speculated that unearthed Maya cities in central America could be some of the locations of the Nephite exodus. Such a view restricted the events of the Book to the isthmus between southern Mexico and northern Panama; later Mormons suggested the drama unfolded across the entire Western Hemisphere, with the great cities of Zarahemla and Bountiful situated in South America, and military theaters extending northward to modern-day Hill Cumorah, near Rochester. By and large, however, these geographies are modern efforts. Only one such theory was published in Smith's own lifetime, and these theories have emerged despite the absence of archaeological or archaeo-biological evidence linking pre-Columbian American sites to ancient Israel.[45]

The Book of Mormon does possess an internal geography, one that expands as the Israelites grow, divide, and send out colonies. The brothers Nephi and Laman stay together until their father dies, but after that, the brothers part, each taking his followers with him. These two groups become the Nephites and Lamanites, and their descendants retain the fratricidal urges of their namesakes; within forty years, they "already had wars and contentions with our brethren."[46]

The long histories of the Book of Mormon are mostly stories of conflicts between Nephite and Lamanite civilizations. Their wars were furious and bloody. Whereas the Old Testament has Samson, who kills "heaps upon heaps, with the jawbone of an ass," the Book of Mormon has Shiz, whose rapid style of warfare leaves "the whole face of the land . . . covered with the bodies of the dead," which in turn become infested with worms and make a stink over the land. There are occasionally reversals and betrayals; Coriantumr the Nephite joins the Lamanites at one point, and a group of Lamanites converts to the Nephite faith and dubs themselves "Anti-Lehi-Nephi."

The climax of the redacted narratives is the arrival of Christ in the New World, fulfilling the promises and prophecies of Nephite holy men. Christ brings Nephite and Lamanite civilizations together and instructs them as he instructed his Israelite disciples. He heals the sick and cures the blind, appoints twelve New World apostles, and ascends to heaven. For two hundred years, the descendants of Laman and Nephi live in peace.

Then it all comes undone.

Nephite civilization collapses quickly; the decline and fall occupies less than twenty-five of six hundred pages in the original volume. New churches spring up that persecute true Christianity, and soon the conflict spreads and reignites the Lamanite-Nephite conflict. This time, the Lamanites triumph completely and the Nephites perish. Moroni concludes the narrative by stressing the spiritual gifts that accompany the true church of Christ: healing, miracles, speaking in tongues, "and all these gifts of which I have spoken, which are spiritual, will never be done away with." The Lamanites alone remain in the Americas, and nineteenth-century readers had little trouble identifying them as "the forefathers of our western Tribes of Indians," as Smith later explained.[47]

Smith's references to Native Americans were often the only connection he drew between the early American republic and the ancient world of the Nephites. Most early Saints followed his example, rarely discussing the book's inner complexities. More commonly, Saints who read the Book of Mormon and believed it spoke of the strange, preternatural experiences that clung to it. It was a sign as much as it was a story. As Joseph Smith explained to the Saints, the Book of Mormon "has sprouted and come forth out of the earth, and righteousness begins to look down from heaven, and God is sending his powers, gifts, and angels to lodge in the branches thereof."[48] The Book of Mormon itself was a miracle; the act of reading it, miraculous or nearly so. The preternatural experiences of those first Saints cannot be separated from the Book itself when explaining the rise of this first generation of Mormon faithful.

Such experiences were not limited to the Mormons—or rather, the Book of Mormon was not the only text to produce such experiences in the early United States. Both Protestants and Catholics had experiences with objects and wonders that brought them to conversion, if not with the Book of Mormon, then with some other text. Wonder stories had long been associated with the Bible, and the early republic had its share of bibliocentric wonders. Benjamin Randel had a vision during the Revolution that a bible was "presented before the eyes of my mind, and I heard a still small voice, saying look therein" to find "perfect connection to the universal love of God."[49] Randel went on to found his own denomination, the Freewill Baptists. John Jea, an enslaved person in New York, learned to read in one night by means of a mystical Bible. An angel, "in shining raiment, and his countenance shining as the sun, with a large bible in his hands," appeared to Jea and said, "'Thou hast desired to read and understand this book, and to speak the language of it both in English and in Dutch; I will therefore teach thee, and now read'; and then he taught me to read the first chapter of the gospel according to St. John; and when I had read the whole chapter, the angel and the book were both gone in the twinkling of an eye."[50] The African American preacher Rebecca Cox Jackson had almost the same experience through contact with a physical Bible;

she was illiterate when she prayed to God while holding the Bible, then opened it and began to read.[51]

There were other new scriptures in America, too. Several nineteenth-century Americans believed in "a bible with the back cover torn off," as historian David F. Holland puts it.[52] Several religious groups denied the closing of the Christian canon and offered additions. Shakers produced several collections of sacred works detailing the miracles and teachings of their leader, the Ever-Blessed Ann Lee. The *Testimonies* of 1816—a series of affidavits written in the King James style—eventually assumed canonical status among Shakers, but it followed two earlier volumes of sacred writing, the 1808 and 1810 versions of the *Testimony of Christ's Second Appearing*. These were also sacred scriptural histories of the church and Ann Lee. The *Testimony* declared Lee's life to be "a *marvelous work and a wonder*"—the exact phrase Mormons used to describe their new scripture.[53] In 1827 (the very year Smith unearthed the plates) the Shaker William Byrd defended the group's new revelation, writing that the "bible itself authorizes us to believe" that "an infinity of inspirations and miracles have existed not contained in the bible."[54] Later in the nineteenth century, Spiritualists and Christian Scientists introduced their own new texts that assumed canonical status.

New scriptures arose outside the Christian tradition as well. The Seneca leader Handsome Lake produced the Code of Handsome Lake, a series of visionary journeys that became the basis of his new religion for Native Americans. The *gaiwiio*, or Good Message, included both the story of Handsome Lake's own conversion and visit to the afterlife in 1799, and religious teachings from the Master of Life—a monotheistic god whose chosen people were the Native Americans. It was not an extension of the Bible but an alternative to it, one recited then and now by followers of Handsome Lake's teachings.[55]

The intense supernaturalism associated with the Book of Mormon had yet further analogues across the United States. John Wigger notes that "the quest for the supernatural in everyday life was the most distinctive characteristic of early American Methodism," and the Methodists were not alone.[56] Americans of all sorts became more open to "a variety of signs and wonders" and "an admission of increased supernatural involvement in everyday life."[57] Those who did not feel the touch of an angel or glimpse eternity could hear of such wonderful events related in sermons, stories, and printed pages, all of which burst forth with tales of wonder and miracle.

It is hard to separate the wonder stories surrounding the Book of Mormon from the content of its pages, but anti-Mormons did just that. Summations and abbreviations of the golden bible's plotlines were easily more common among anti-Mormon publications than in the Saints' own tracts. Eber Howe dedicated an enormous chunk of his vitriolic *Mormonism Unvailed* to a long recap of the Book of Mormon's plot; Alexander Campbell's *Delusions* (1832) did the same. When Diedrich Willers sought to discredit the book, he provided other ministers with a detailed summary of its contents, even though he admitted "I still have only read a little therefrom and would wish to be relieved from this trouble."[58] Howe provided running commentary on all the books of the Book of Mormon, occasionally tossing out zingers. Of Nephite prophets calling upon Jesus Christ, Howe wrote, "Wonderful preaching, considering the period in which it took place [was] at least 300 years before the nativity of Christ." Where the Book of Mormon explained that Nephite leaders were inspired by prophecy so that they could not be duped by mountain robbers, Howe wondered why God, having done so for the Nephites, could not prevent Smith from being duped by *Missouri* robbers? Howe spent sixty pages of his volume discussing each and every book in the Book of Mormon—a far more complete recitation than could be found in any Mormon publication.[59]

Howe had other, snarkier comments—referring to upstate New York as a "*bible quarry*," for example—but he hit upon the reason that anti-Mormons rather than Mormons provided extensive textual summaries. Howe cited the passage in Moroni that directed potential converts (then and now) to ask God "with a sincere heart, with real intent," as to the truth of the Book of Mormon. "Here we are directed as to how we can all become Mormons," Howe wrote, "believe all the fooleries, and forgeries and lies of Jo Smith's translation of the brass plates; and then pray to be convinced of its divine authenticity."[60] To confirm the Book of Mormon as true, one needed only to possess the text and await a spiritual experience. To prove the book a forgery or a lie required an enumeration of all the purported errors, misstatements, and painful phraseology in its pages. Thus, miracles from the Mormons and summations from the critics.

The first printed critiques of the Book of Mormon predated its publication. Abner Cole—writing under the pseudonym Obadiah Dogberry—published his *Palmyra Reflector* in 1829 from the same print shop that was typesetting the Book of Mormon. Dogberry printed whole tracts of the volume (despite complaints from Smith that he was usurping the copyright).[61] Most damning, how-

P. 275—276.

. . . " *Let the sots combine,*
" *With pious care a Monkey to enshrine.*"—DRYDEN.

Critiques of the story of the golden plates are as old as Mormonism itself. This 1834 cartoon, from Eber D. Howe's *Mormonism Unvailed*, features Smith holding the plates and getting a kick from the Devil. L. Tom Perry Special Collections, Harold B. Lee Library, Brigham Young University, Provo, Utah (M2209 .H83m 1834) ever, was Dogberry's comment in the *Reflector* that, having seen a scrap of the first chapter of the Book of Mormon, "we cannot discover anything treasonable, or which will have a tendency to subvert our liberties." Thus, upon hearing of a wondrous new bible and a restored religion, the editor *expected* that it would be treasonous or subversive of liberty.

The *Reflector* published not only extracts of 1 Nephi but also a Book of Mormon parody titled the "Book of Pukei." The satire, written in the style of the King James Version, referred to "Joseph, thou who has been surnamed the *Ignoramus*," led by "the spirit of the money-diggers." The *Rochester Gem* similarly listed the "books of Nephi, Nimshi, Pukei, and Buckeye" as "the mysticisms of an unrevealed Bible!"[62] Other parodies referring to contemporary politicians and treasure digging followed. There were spoofs named the Book of Daniel, the Book of Chronicles, and the First Book of John (which claimed Joseph came from "veracity corner"), and others.[63] Numerous articles that quoted the Book of Mormon accompanied their coverage with assertions that no one should believe the text, because it lacked proof. "I sought for evidences," wrote a correspondent to the *New York Telescope's* excerpt of the Book in February 1830, "such as could not be disputed, of the existence of this bible of golden plates. But the answer was—the world must take their words for its existence."[64] When the LDS church arrived in Ohio, the local paper reported that, "after having an opportunity to canvass some of its claims to [be] a true revelation from God, we have not been able to discover testimony which ought to elicit faith in any prudent or intelligent mind."[65] The plates themselves, early Mormons explained, had returned to heaven with Moroni, who, Smith wrote, "has them in his charge until this day."[66]

Early newspapers that did not quote from the Book of Mormon often gave long synopses of its coming forth and usually concluded in the negative. The "progress of the Mormon religion," averred the *New York Morning Courier*, was "one of the strangest pieces of fanaticism. . . . What a lesson it ought to teach us!"[67] Religious publications had understandably more direct theological responses. The *Evangelical Magazine & Gospel Advocate* condemned belief in the golden plates as a "blasphemous design" and worried about Mormons' purported "entire devotedness to the will of their leader."[68] The Book itself was dismissed as "a most bungling attempt to imitate the ancient English and Bible phraseology."[69]

The most famous early critique of the Book of Mormon came from rival reformer Alexander Campbell, who led his own restored church (what would become the Disciples of Christ). Campbell's tract *Delusions* mercilessly lampooned every miracle recorded in the Book of Mormon and savaged every inconsistency in the text. For example, responding to the Witnesses' claim that they had "handled as many of the brazen or golden leaves as the said Smith translated," Campbell wrote, "So did I." Like "credulous Jews," Campbell continued, the Mormons were following a false prophet—and then insinuated that all prophets eventually take up arms.[70]

From its very inception, therefore, responses to Mormonism contained multiple threads—exasperation merged with theological outrage at the very idea of modern miracles and new scripture. Critics took offense and made fun of the Book of the Mormon, occasionally making more serious hints about the treasonous and dangerous nature of Mormonism. Critics simultaneously dismissed Mormons and promised to watch Mormons, likely in part to "unmask the turpitude and villainy of those who knowingly abetted" Smith.[71]

Perhaps not surprisingly, the Saints encountered their first mobs around the same time. While conducting their services, Mormons heard cannons and pistols fired off outside. Smith recalled a mob "determined to commit violence on us" that descended upon them after their first public baptism. It may have been the same group of local toughs, "instigated . . . by certain sectarian priests of the neighborhood," who destroyed a temporary Mormon dam that had been constructed to permit river baptisms.[72] In Colesville, New York, public meetings of Mormons were met by people who "threatened to kill them."[73]

Reports of these mobs rarely name individuals, and certainly some later recollections by the Saints about 1830 are colored by their memories of the violence that occurred in Missouri and Ohio in later years. Nevertheless, hints of anti-Mormon violence emerged with the Book of Mormon itself; even as critics laughed off Mormonism and confidently predicted it would not survive, groups of Gentile observers took pernicious steps to watch the Mormons— and sometimes, to let the Mormons know they were armed. No critic openly called for violence against the Saints, but like the rumors that preceded the publication of the Book of Mormon, threats were already in the air.

# 3

## Kirtland

THE TERM *MORMONISM* WAS ORIGINALLY a critic's epithet, first used in print in 1831.[1] On April 6, 1830—the day of the church's official founding—the believers in the Book of Mormon incorporated themselves as "The Church of Christ." Other new sects had already snapped up the title "Church of Christ," so believers later adopted the name "Latter-day Saints." At that first church meeting, six of the Book of Mormon witnesses became members; Joseph Smith and Oliver Cowdery were ordained as elders. Samuel H. Smith departed soon after as the first in a long line of Mormon missionaries. Like most missionaries, he had a rough first day. Finding no takers at five houses, he slept outside under an apple tree.[2]

The church was already having problems with popular animosity against its members. In the summer of 1830, Smith was arrested for being a "disorderly person"—an event likely connected, once again, with New York laws that equated divination and treasure digging with vagrancy and disturbing the peace. Smith again faced jail time for "pretending to see under ground." The judge acquitted Smith, and the defendant was immediately served another warrant to stand trial for the same crime in a second county. Smith went off to another prison, withstood another trial, and received another acquittal.[3]

Court decisions did little to stem the rising tide of anti-Mormonism. Joseph Knight was a leader of the Mormon branch in Colesville, New York, where "People Began to Be angry and to persecute." The trouble only grew worse after Smith's acquittal: "The mob began to collect and gather and threaten and abuse us in a most Shameful and disgusting manner," Knight later recalled. Knight let word slip for the mob to expect him at the river, then he took his family and hid. Meanwhile, "the Mob watched all night at the bridge" and so "lost all their trouble."[4] Smith's followers were facing open threats. In December, he had a revelation ordering the Colesville Saints to Ohio, where the church was growing fast.

Mormonism is sometimes connected to a spiritual flowering from 1825 to the 1850s near the Erie Canal, along a corridor known as the "Burned-Over District." As one venerable American historian wrote, "Upon this broad belt of land congregated a people extraordinarily given to unusual beliefs."[5] Mormonism certainly qualified, but although it had origins in the canal zone, most of the growth in the early church came from Ohio converts. It was Lake Erie and not the Erie Canal that gave rise to the church.

The church had added more than a hundred converts in the Ohio township of Kirtland—twice as many as it then had in New York. By the end of 1831, there would be fifteen hundred Mormons, most of them living in Ohio.[6] These Ohio Mormons had not converted because of Smith's personal charisma or their engagement with him—he arrived only after the initial swell of conversions. They converted based on the word of missionaries and the text of the Book of Mormon, and they brought their own agendas and spiritual interpretations to the growing movement. Entire congregations moved into the Mormon church. Smith was suddenly faced with a lopsided geography of Mormonism, and a host of converts who seemed to have their own ideas about what the restored gospel—and the Book of Mormon—meant.

It was not the first time disagreements emerged about how the restoration operated. In the summer of 1830, Hiram Page (one of the Eight Witnesses) began experiencing revelations through his own seer stone. Ezra Booth—who had not joined the church at the time of the controversy—described Page as staring into "a smooth stone, upon which there appeared to be a writing, which when transcribed upon paper, disappeared from the stone, and another impression appeared in its place."[7] Page believed these writings to be divine. He wrote down at least sixteen pages of revelations from the stone, messages that caused "some dissention of feeling" among the Saints.[8]

That same summer, Cowdery challenged Smith on the wording of a revelation, raising an objection "in the name of the Lord" to alter the requirements for baptism as laid out in the church's Articles and Covenants. The Whitmer family sided with Cowdery, which meant that many of the Book of Mormon witnesses were now arrayed against the Book of Mormon translator. After a long discussion, Smith managed to prevail over Cowdery.

Then came Page's new revelations, which "most of the Mormonites" accepted "as an authentic document," as Booth told it. One of the Mormons who accepted the new revelations was Oliver Cowdery.[9] Although Page's revelations do not survive, they apparently concerned "the order of the church," as Smith recalled.[10] The church, only months old, already had recurrent problems concerning revelation and organization.

Historians often tell the story of Page's stone as a bump on the road of Smith's rising position in the church, for in the end, Smith's revelations became holy writ and Page's stony communiqués did not. But to view this crisis from the perspective of Smith obscures the world of early Mormonism for the converts themselves. It was a world brimming with possibility—a world in which God would end schismatic division and silence debate *directly*.[11] Nor was there any way of knowing, in the summer of 1830, how the fledging church would develop. Page and Cowdery certainly believed that God could speak to them. A shared system of prophethood was repeatedly suggested by early Saints; Smith's position as a sole prophet was not universally accepted by new Mormons. Page's seer stones were not a moment of peril for Smith's leadership but rather a moment of possibility for the Mormon movement.

Indeed, Smith himself appeared to take Page's revelations seriously, though he believed them demonic and not divine. He, too, found "many of the brethren . . . believing much in the things that were set forth by this stone." Smith did not immediately condemn the messages; instead, he wrote, "a few of us got together" and prayed for a revelation. The revelation confirmed that Smith alone was to receive divine messages, but that Cowdery was to participate in the process as Aaron to Smith's Moses. Yet Smith did not rely on the power of the revealed word to end debate, and he did not silence Page by fiat. Instead, he referred the matter to a church conference and with "considerable discussion, reason and investigation, Hyrum [Page] agreed to renounce the stone and its author [Satan], and the brethren unanimously agreed to renounce them also."[12] Page condemned his own work and destroyed the revelations.

Smith acted in 1830 not as an unquestioned authority but as an influential leader of a community—working to resolve conflicts rather than consolidate power.[13] He argued and acted more like a factional leader than a sectarian leader, even in a church he himself had founded. By claiming that the messages were demonic, the Smith faction actually validated the supernatural experiences of Page and incorporated them into church life.

Variant interpretations of Mormon supernaturalism would recur frequently in Mormon history. There was rarely a moment when Smith did not face some kind of challenge to his leadership. Often, those challenges (and the responses to them) were backed by supernatural events. Such events were to be expected, of course, in a movement that put a high priority on supernatural events as a way out of a sectarian morass. When the church members unanimously agreed with Smith and his allies about the nature of the 1830 revelations, they affirmed both Page's experience and Smith's leadership. Indeed, Smith's early willingness to discuss the stone's revelations with Page may well have been accepted by Saints as a template—something to expect whenever leadership questions arose. If we read Mormon history as merely a history of Smith, the result was a "victory" for Smith. If on the other hand we read Mormon history as the story of a church, we see a serious divergence of opinion on leadership and revelation brought back together in a kind of compromise: Page's experiences were real. They were not deliberate trickery or delusion. Other supernatural experiences that happened to Mormons were also, then, likely to be affirmed as real—and that interpretation, in turn, left the door open to further leadership challenges. The power of the supernatural would be a testing ground for Mormon leadership over the following decade.

The revelation about Page also commanded Smith to establish a presence "on the border with the Lamanites." That "border" was the Missouri River, which in 1830 marked the edge of legal white settlement—beyond its banks was land reserved for the forced relocation of Native American nations. The revelation about the Missouri was tucked in among other revelations, which condemned the visions wrought through Page's stone. Oliver Cowdery was simultaneously ordered to support only Smith's revelations and to travel west; the unsettled geography of early Mormonism was linked to its unsettled dynamic of leadership and spiritual gifts. Four Mormon missionaries dutifully set off for the Missouri River, beyond which the United States was aggressively resettling Native American nations. Mormon expansion west occurred as a response to leadership conflicts and competing interpretations of the supernatural.

One of the missionaries was Parley P. Pratt. He was used to an unsettled lifestyle; he had been an itinerating Baptist, then a Campbellite, and then a preacher without a church. When he discovered the Book of Mormon in up-state New York, Pratt and his wife, Thankful, joined the Saints. When he be-came a missionary to the Lamanites, Pratt suggested making a stop on the way to tell his former Campbellite friends about the golden bible. It would break up the thousand-mile walk to Missouri.

Pratt's time with the Campbellites in the 1820s brought him into contact with Sidney Rigdon, a rising star in the Disciples of Christ movement. Like Pratt, Rigdon had bounced around the religious world of Jacksonian Amer-ica. While serving as a Baptist minister in 1819, Rigdon encountered the Res-torationist teachings of Alexander Campbell in Pittsburgh and believed them, but he could not square those writings with his own Baptist creeds. Rigdon had a crisis of faith and quit preaching to work as a tanner. By 1827, however, he had returned to the Baptist fold, though people kept trying to kick him out for preaching what sounded like Campbellite views. Some considered Rigdon superior to Campbell in preaching. He was certainly one of the most promi-nent preachers and church leaders in the Western Reserve; his brother served in the state legislature.[14] Among Baptists and Campbellites, Rigdon earned a reputation for eloquence. After hearing one of his sermons, Mary Fielding Smith exclaimed, "He is a Masterpiece."[15] Not everyone agreed. One newspa-per smeared him as a man of "pride, ambition, and vainglory."[16]

Rigdon began to move beyond Campbell. Interested specifically in Chris-tian communalism, Rigdon thought the miracles of the New Testament should accompany the true church. Campbell disagreed and abandoned Rigdon, so some began referring to the Ohio preacher's followers as "Rigdonites."[17] Now out of Campbell's orbit, Rigdon became a supporter of Isaac Morley's attempt to share Christian goods in common, following the example of the Book of Acts. Morley gathered believers together to live communally on his farm. One of Morley's associates explained that after Christ ascended to heaven, "Peter . . . made an equal distribution by humbling the rich and exalting the poor" and, in so doing, was able to perform "signs and wonders." This was Rig-don's kind of place, and he supported Morley's establishment of what became known as the "Big Family"—a community of fifty or sixty people living on his farm, as well as in a few associated clusters across northeastern Ohio. They had a mile-long orchard, one hundred acres of wheat, corn, and vegetables, a herd of cows, and a cooper shop to engage in trade. Morley created all of this "to restore the ancient order of things," as a Gentile neighbor wrote at the time.[18]

Baptists, Campbellites, Rigdonites, and the Big Family: Ohio had opened itself to the same kind of sectarian division and efforts at restoration that haunted Joseph Smith in the 1820s. Indeed, Ohio pulled in many more new sects. A much larger communal experiment by Robert Dale Owen opened near Kirtland, offering a secularized version of New Testament communalism. (Owen and Campbell held a public debate against each other the year before the Mormons showed up.)[19] Shaker families, too, preached communalism and community in the name of Christ, and they had four villages in Ohio by 1827. The radical preacher Samuel Underhill thundered across Ohio, preaching Quakerism before embracing deism. Universalists, Unitarians, Separate Baptists, Zoar Separatists, and others were also jockeying for position in and around Kirtland.

Mormonism was in good company, therefore, when Pratt and the missionaries arrived in Ohio. Pratt likely believed that he had found in the Latter-day Saints a solution to the sectarian problem, and wanted to share the news with old friends. Rigdon dismissed the missionaries but promised to look at their book. Undaunted, the missionaries tried the local Shakers; the Shakers gave them hats and sent them away.[20]

Rigdon's heart softened. The Book had done something to him; he tried to preach and found "that all he had to say . . . was repent and humble ourselves before God."[21] Rigdon joined the new church. The missionaries preached to the Big Family, and Isaac Morley joined. A fair number of Rigdon's followers in the Disciples-Baptist-Rigdonite mold followed him, and most of the Big Family followed Morley. In mere weeks, two of Kirtland's disparate sects had turned themselves into Mormon churches.

The rush of two whole communities into Mormonism made news, the news brought more attention, and more attention added converts. Ohioan Tamma Durfee heard talk of the Book of Mormon in 1831, and when a missionary arrived in her neighborhood months later, she took the chance to see what the fuss was all about. She "became a Mormon in belief" and kept her conversion a secret until she was married.[22] Philo Dibble heard of the arrival of missionaries "with a Golden Bible" and then made it a point to "hunt up those strange men." He traveled a few miles to Kirtland and received baptism into the church.

That night, he felt a supernatural "sensation like fibers of fire" across his body and was confirmed in his belief.[23] In Ashtabula County, Ohio, John Corrill heard "every thing bad . . . reported against [the Mormons]," but on learning that Sidney Rigdon and his Campbellites had converted, Corrill eventually changed his mind.[24] Even Campbell's ally Walter Scott came to hear the new gospel, though he remained unconvinced.[25] Conversion to Mormonism in Ohio was not a matter of hearing one voice, or even both sides of an argument, but a part of an ongoing, multilayered cacophony of biblical interpretation, prophecy, bad press, rumor, and mystical experience. On occasion, some people actually managed to find new paths to salvation through all the noise.

Back in New York, Joseph Smith received a December revelation instructing all Saints to "assemble together at the Ohio." Smith and his family dutifully arrived there in February 1831.[26] Within months, dozens of New York Saints made the journey, along with hundreds of the curious and the converted from Ohio and elsewhere. The beleaguered Colesville Saints moved en masse to Kirtland. The influx of Saints strained Kirtland's resources. Some of the arrivals could stay on Morley's farm, but northern Ohio was, in Parley Pratt's words, "one vast scene of mud and mire."[27] The town's infrastructure was not ready for so many arrivals; one observer recalled that it seemed "as if the whole world were centering at Kirtland. . . . Every available house, shop, hut, or barn was filled to its utmost capacity. Even boxes were roughly extemporized and used for shelter."[28] Food shortages came with the crisis. Oliver Huntington remembered his mother going without food so her children could eat, even while making meals of "beech leaves, after string beans and sometimes a very scanty allowance of corn bread. Once in a while when we were most starved out we would kill a starved to death hen."[29]

Nor was Kirtland really intended as a final stopping point; the Mormons had in mind a third location, neither New York nor Ohio, but Zion. Smith had not forgotten God's commandment to establish a presence on the "border with the Lamanites." While Joseph Smith and the New Yorkers prepared to move to Ohio, the Mormon missionaries who had brought the faith to Kirtland had moved on to Indian Territory, crossing (illegally) into what is today Kansas in January 1831. The US government found them and forced them out, so the missionaries set up shop at a new town, just across the river in Missouri. Independence, founded four years previously, gained its first Mormons. In July 1831, God revealed to Smith that all the Mormons would eventually follow in the steps of the missionaries to the Lamanites, for Missouri was "the land . . . I have appointed and consecrated for the gathering of the saints."[30] Mormons began to call the place Zion, named after the hills of Canaan on which the Hebrew Temple rose. For most of its first decade, Mormonism would have two geographic centers. Maintaining the balance between two Mormon enclaves more than a thousand miles apart would prove one of the church's thorniest tasks.

The church had other problems in Ohio. The rush of converts in 1830 and 1831 had never met Smith when they joined, and, just as with Hiram Page, there were disagreements about what constituted the restored church. As in any new organization, membership could be fickle, with believers leaving if they objected to evolving aspects of a new church. Warren Foote in New York's Steuben County, for example, met Mormon missionaries named Landon and Orton, but when Foote tried to follow up with them, he discovered that Landon and Orton had been excommunicated because they did not accept a recent revelation.[31] Others remained in the church, but complained constantly. When Thomas Marsh was appointed to a leadership post, other Mormons objected, he wrote, "owing to my inexperience." Though Marsh had Smith's support, "my opposers never became reconciled to my presidency."[32] A number of Mormons received their own revelations from heaven, and "all manner of spirits were there made manifest," Dibble wrote.[33]

As always in early Mormonism, supernatural experiences could validate and challenge emerging church institutions. By 1831, the Kirtland church encountered "a woman by the name of Hubble who professed to be a prophetess of the Lord and professed to have many revelations, and knew the Book of Mormon was true; and that she should become a teacher in the Church of Christ."[34] "Hubble" was Laura Fuller Hubbell, a mother of three young children who came to Kirtland in 1831 to visit her brother and ended up becoming a visionary. John Whitmer, who recorded the incident, rejected Hubbell's claims about their church; she "deceived some, who were not able to detect her hypocrisy."[35]

Hubbell was initially accepted by the new church; Rigdon "gave her the right hand of fellowship, and literally saluted her," perhaps because she claimed visions rather than revelations and thereby offered more supernatural proofs of the authenticity of the golden plates. Moreover, Hubbell's claim to be a "teacher" implied that she sought an office below that of prophet or preacher. American sects were divided on the role of women in Protestant Christianity;

some congregations allowed women to preach, and others allowed them merely to "exhort." (The difference was linguistic.) The Disciples of Christ sometimes allowed women to serve as deaconesses, but other churches relegated all women to secondary roles. When Hubbell professed to be a "teacher"—a vague office referenced at the church's 1830 founding—she was seeking a position that "few members, if any, understood," as historian Mark L. Staker writes.[36]

Many women held similarly undefined positions of authority in the American sectarian explosion of the 1800s. Freedom of religion meant that women as well as men could begin preaching without institutional warrant. Harriet Livermore took to the pulpit unsanctioned by any organized church and became phenomenally popular as a speaker and writer. She twice preached to a joint session of Congress. Even though John Quincy Adams referred to her religion as "monomania," the Capitol was filled to capacity when she spoke in 1827.[37] Nancy Towle began as a Methodist and circulated through the Northeast and Midwest—even to Kirtland—as a traveling missionary. She was often accompanied by other women in a network of female preachers. Amy Post recruited Americans into the new religion of Spiritualism in the 1840s, while also arranging anti-slavery meetings and smuggling fugitive slaves across the border to Canada.[38] Not every woman who found new roles as leaders, preachers, and organizers achieved as great success or notoriety as Livermore, Towle, or Post—but thousands of women shaped and fashioned the theology and structures of new American religions.

Several women led their own religious revolts. Ann Lee was declared to be a Second Eve to Christ's Second Adam among the Shakers. After her death, men generally assumed leadership roles in the new religion—with the notable exception of Lucy Wright, who led the celibate community from 1796 to 1816 and oversaw its largest expansion, into Ohio and Kentucky. Rebecca Jackson, an African American, lived as an itinerant preacher before she too joined the Shakers and founded and led the urban Shaker experiment in Philadelphia. Jemima Wilkinson led a new sect based on the claim that she—the woman known as Jemima Wilkinson—had been resurrected as a new, genderless figure, the "Public Universal Friend." As the Friend, Wilkinson founded a new town called Jerusalem, but kept to fairly traditional Protestant teachings. The Friend's new sect, however, refused to acknowledge male or female among its leadership. Men and women assumed leadership roles, and so did other genderless prophets. Ellen Gould White in the 1840s assumed control of the burgeoning Millerite movement, eventually becoming the leader of a new group of vegetarian Christians who worshipped on Saturdays—the Seventh-Day Adventists.[39]

Hubbell's claims and theories about how women might lead and participate in this new religion were thus not unique or even terribly unusual in the 1830s. Indeed, one of the most enduring aspects of American religion is the presence and activism of women relative to men. With very few exceptions, women have formed the majority of participants in American religious activities and institutions.[40] In the nineteenth century, a growing number of American Protestants began to think of women as naturally more virtuous than men. Perhaps paradoxically, this assumed predilection for moral behavior tended to restrict women to leadership in the home and moral teaching rather than leadership in politics or the institutional church. As the novelist Catherine Maria Sedgwick wrote in 1812 to her father, "You may benefit a Nation, my dear Papa, I may improve the condition of a fellow being."[41] Thus, Towle, Livermore, and others had no official church roles, but Lee, Jackson, and White proved that "women's religious leadership, itself a dissent from prevailing norms," was "especially visible among dissident groups"—including the Saints.[42] Women were both leaders of dissident religions and the backbone of the most successful Protestant denominations.

Female Saints occupied an unclear space in the leadership of the new church in Kirtland. Officially, only men served as priests, bishops, and missionaries. Yet the church generated an outpouring of new offices and was constantly revising its ecclesiastical structures. When Joseph Smith Sr. was named the church's patriarch (an office that no longer exists), he pronounced official blessings and instructions for faithful Saints. More than one-third of these blessings were given to women. Emma Hale Smith, wife of the prophet, was specifically "ordained" in her blessing to expound scriptures and exhort the church. Emma also led the creation and codification of Mormon hymnody. Sarah Leavitt, meanwhile, received her ordination without a human intermediary; an angel appeared to her in the night and ordered her to heal her sick daughter: "lay . . . hands upon her head in the name of Jesus Christ and administer to her and she should recover." Sarah followed the instructions and her daughter recovered.[43]

Other Mormon women simply began teaching and preaching on their own initiative. At a meeting in New Salem, Ohio, a "woman preacher appointed a meeting" where she "read and repeated copious extracts from the Book of

Mormon."[44] The women of Kirtland invited Nancy Towle to visit and preach in Kirtland, and Towle used their invitation to stymie male efforts to chase her out of town.[45] Nor did female authority emerge only from this world. Women spoke in tongues, received visions, and experienced miracles—sometimes in direct defense of the church. Prescinda Huntington confounded a visiting skeptic when she spoke in tongues simultaneously with another Mormon worshipper.[46] In Illinois, Leavitt encountered Sally Ann Chamberlain, "who had formerly the gifts and now was in the dark." Leavitt read her a passage from the Book of Mormon, which Chamberlain interpreted: "What is more righteous than angels or what is truer than the Book of Mormon?" Immediately upon doing so, Chamberlain announced, "I have got my gift again." Both women rejoiced, and Chamberlain resumed her career of bearing the spirit. In 1830, a group of Mormon women proved their faith "on a cold winter day, lying under the bare canopy of heaven, with no couch or pillow but the fleecy snow."[47]

The snowbirds of 1830 were likely part of the infamous effusion of enthusiasm that emerged in the first days of Ohio Mormonism. Traditionally, Mormons and Mormon historians have dismissed this enthusiastic era—an upwelling of supernaturalism, glossolalia, and prophecies in Ohio—as a kind of collective misunderstanding. Indeed, the supposed excesses of 1830–31 ultimately required a revelation to put down; a February 1831 message from God announced that Smith alone was "appointed unto you to receive commandments and revelations" and that "if ye desire the glories of the kingdom, appoint ye my servant Joseph Smith, Jun., and uphold him."[48] Some historians have assumed that because a revelation condemned it, unsanctioned enthusiasm was a fleeting moment in Mormon life.[49]

It was more than that. The *Painesville (Ohio) Telegraph* noted that as soon as Rigdon and the Lamanite missionaries left—the missionaries for Missouri, Rigdon for New York to meet the prophet—the new Mormon communities witnessed "a scene of the wildest enthusiasm . . . exhibited, chiefly, however, among the young people." These Mormons apparently engaged in many of the behaviors seen at Cane Ridge, among Shakers, or at Methodist revivals across the country. Visitors found them "creeping upon their hands and feet &c." or chasing "balls of fire which they see flying through the air." They would "get upon stumps and preach to *imagined* congregations, baptize ghosts, &c."[50] They spoke in tongues. They would act out the dramas of the Lamanites in the Book of Mormon, caricature Native American behavior, and lead invisible Native American converts to water for baptism.[51]

This supernaturalism was endemic to Mormonism, even if it later incurred official censure. Indeed, the pantomimes of Book of Mormon events and tongues speaking marked a season of leadership by Mormons who, like Hiram Page, embraced an expansive church where many members would receive impressions and revelations from God. Unlike Page, these worshippers brought their case to the believers of Kirtland, and not to the church leadership. One leader of these events was truly an outsider in early republican Ohio: a former Virginia slave who had achieved his freedom and begun a quest for religious truth by joining the Morley Farm. We know him today only as "Black Pete."

Black Pete served as "a chief man" and "a revelator" among the early Ohio Mormons. Peter began life in the slave quarters, born as property in Virginia's Appalachian counties in 1775. Although the region on the Monongahela River where Peter was born became part of Pennsylvania in 1781, he did not automatically become free. Slavery was legal in Pennsylvania until 1782, when all slave owners merely had to provide evidence that they planned to emancipate their slaves at some future time. Indeed, Peter's town of Fallowfield executed a slave boy in 1788—an affair Peter would legally have been forced to watch.[52]

Peter brought the memory of forced labor and legalized terror with him to Ohio, where he arrived as a free man in the 1810s. Although some slaves adopted their owners' last names or gave themselves new patronyms, Peter never did—perhaps a sign of independence and defiance. He committed another act of self-determination when he joined the Family on the Morley Farm, and later converted with them to Mormonism. Peter appears to have been the only former slave we can name who joined the church, but he was not the only African American leader in early Mormonism. Off the coast of Maine, Joseph Ball preached to the Fox Islanders of Penobscot Bay A freeborn son of an Afro-Jamaican father and a Caucasian mother, Ball had helped found the mutual-aid African Society in Boston years before he became a Mormon. The African American Elijah Abel was born free and joined the church in 1832 in Ohio. Abel later became the first African American member of the Quorum of the Seventy At least eight other African Americans joined the church before 1847—less than 1 percent of all Mormons, but a significant number given the later priesthood ban, the doctrine that prevented anyone of African descent from holding a priesthood office among the Latter-day Saints. (The ban was revoked in 1978, and today "every faithful, worthy man" among the Saints will serve as a Mormon priest.)[53]

The religion of the enslaved has been called the "invisible institution" of antebellum America—"invisible" because much of the slaves' religious activity was carried on outside the gaze of white Americans, but also "invisible" to historians. It was a faith that grew and developed largely without the copious written records from which so much of church history derives. On large plantations, enslaved people would gather secretly at night at places known as "hush harbors" or "brush arbors." Kalvin Woods remembered he "would slip about from plantation to plantation" preaching to the enslaved who would carry wet blankets and rags to catch the sound of their voices and thereby remain hidden.[54] Worship in these places by the 1830s featured a Christian emphasis and style quite different from the Calvinist or Unitarian concerns of institutional white churches. Moses and the Exodus story took on a relevance close to that of the resurrection of Jesus, and ecstatic exercises like those at Cane Ridge were the norm. Dancing in circles, the use of drums, and leaping and rolling with the spirit were elements common to both Methodist and African traditional religious experience, and they formed a new form of worship in African American culture.

Gospel lessons rarely traveled from masters to the enslaved. Pennsylvania's slave owners paid little attention to the "spiritual welfare" of their human property. As one eighteenth-century traveler observed, the enslaved "live on in their pagan darkness" because whites did not want slaves "seeing themselves upon a level with their masters in religious matters."[55] But the enslaved and formerly enslaved converted each other to Christian practice. Peter and many other African Americans converted in a great wave of religious transformation among African Americans between 1750 and 1790. In the free states, this new form of Christianity began to assume institutional forms in the nineteenth century. Richard Allen and Absalom Jones, founders of the African Methodist Episcopal (AME) church, and James Varick, founder of the African Methodist Episcopal Zion (AMEZ) church, were near contemporaries of Joseph Smith Jr. Allen had no visionary experiences like Smith, but he had been personally thrown out of an Episcopal church on his knees for the church crime of refusing to wait to take communion until all the white Christians had been served. In an independent African American church, Allen ministered to free Blacks and the enslaved and helped push the conversation in American religion toward abolition and civil rights. "We do not wish to make you angry," Allen wrote to his fellow Philadelphians, "but [to] excite your attention to consider how hateful slavery is in the sight of God." Allen wrote this appeal as part of a 1794 self-defense after the newspaper editor Matthew Carey published essays perpetuating the rumor that African Americans had introduced and spread yellow fever in the city. Allen's terse rebuttal defended the Black Christian sects that had, in fact, undertaken personal risk to act as nurses, medical reporters, and gravediggers when almost no one else in the city would.[56]

A different form of religious expression also existed in the American slave community, one that bore a strong resemblance to some of the religious experiences of Smith, Page, the New Israelites, and the astrologers of New England. An African American magical tradition grew alongside European forms of magic and divination in the early United States. Known by many names—rootwork, hoodoo, conjure, and others—magic among free and enslaved African Americans drew upon ritual and prayer to acquire power. Henry Bibb attempted several conjure recipes while enslaved in Kentucky. None were effective, but it was still "hard for me to give up the notion," though he eventually did.[57] As a magical tradition, conjure combined European and African beliefs—and it inspired belief and disbelief among the enslaved, as Bibb noted.[58]

At other times, African American magic became woven into the violent arc of slavery itself. Frederick Douglass, as a young man, purchased a conjure charm to protect himself from overseers. Conjure was implicated in the Denmark Vesey rebellion in the person of Gullah Jack Pritchard, an Angola-born slave who apparently provided magical charms for the rebels that would render them invisible to whites. (Pritchard never admitted to this accusation; he was executed without speaking in his own defense.) William Wells Brown related the story of Dinkie, an enslaved man and conjure master in Kentucky. When a new overseer on his first day planned to whip Dinkie, Dinkie swore his power would keep him safe, and although the overseer took him into the barn to perform the deed, Dinkie was not touched. "Dinkie's got de power," Brown recalled a fellow slave saying. "He knows things seen and unseen, and dat's what makes him his own massa."[59] A fellow slave qualified that statement: "Dinkie is a power."[60]

Participants in conjure and other forms of magic shared another quality with the early Mormons: they all faced deep suspicion from others, as well as fears about how magic might affect the social order. Charles Colcock Jones assumed that Christian slaveholding was a positive good and that enslaved peoples would therefore naturally convert. By that logic, any time non-Christian beliefs flourished among the slaves, it implied a deliberate effort on someone's part at misinformation. "Their superstition is made *gain* of by the conjurers," Jones warned. He also indicated that this "superstition" could breed violence: "Ignorance and superstition render them easy dupes to their teachers, doctors, prophets, conjurers. . . . When fairly committed to such leaders, they may be brought to the commission of almost any crime." African American religious leaders faced numerous impediments, not least of which was the idea that non-Christian belief or enthusiastic worship was a deliberate hoax and therefore bred revolt.[61]

Peter faced similar accusations regarding his leadership among Mormons. "Among them is a man of colour, a chief man, who is sometimes seized with strange vagaries," wrote the *Cleveland Advertiser* in introducing its readers to the "miserable production" of Mormonism in 1831. Since there were only six African Americans living in Geauga County in 1831, it seems likely that Peter was this "chief man." Peter does not appear to have sought to displace or challenge Smith; rather, he assumed control over Ohio worship services for the young denomination, and was preaching from town to town with white companions. As Mark L. Staker has written, Peter played "a significant but heretofore unrecognized role, directing worship during Mormonism's earliest weeks" in Ohio.[62]

Peter seems to have emphasized the ecstatic and supernatural elements of worship. A Campbellite critic noted in December 1830 that "five or six weeks ago some of them began to have visions and revelations, and to prophesy," while others "act, they say, as the Indians did where they were carried by the spirit." There were outdoor prayers, visions of Native Americans accepting the gospel, and trance states.[63] The Mormons would have "fits of speaking all the different Indian dialects, which none could understand." Ohio Mormons ran through the fields, stood on stumps, and preached to imaginary congregations."[64] Physicality of worship—as typical in the African American tradition and at Cane Ridge—became a piece of Mormon worship, and despite efforts to tamp it down, it would continue to be a part of official and unofficial practice through the 1830s. Ohio believers leaped, capered, and were struck motionless on the ground. Peter himself ran furiously when worshipping and was reported to have leaped from a cliff bank to a treetop. One critic alleged that

Peter "fancies he can fly." A more charitable observer might have said that Peter believed God could perform remarkable acts through him.[65]

The religious opposition to enthusiasm and miracles swiftly emerged to condemn the Ohio Mormons. The radical Samuel Underhill declared that the "success of the New System of the Mormonites" came only from their ability to make believers "tremble like an aspen leaf." These feelings "are extensively witnessed among the Mormonites & there as every where supposed to be owning and wonder working display of supernatural power." The *Evangelical Magazine & Gospel Advocate* took the exercises as a chance to blast Kirtland as a "region of fanatics," even while focusing mostly on impugning Smith and the golden plates.[66]

Not all the supernatural events centered on Peter. Levi Hancock, while saying his evening prayers, had a profound vision of "a personage . . . with a small yoke in his hand. Said he, 'This is the yoke of Christ.'" Stephen Burnett's father refused to allow Mormon worship at his house, until he saw "the evidences of the spirit . . . so evidently shown" in his son, and then he consented.[67] One Mormon preacher commanded the winds to cease, and found they did. Several reports claimed that Mormons received divine scrolls from the sky, covered in writing that "they had only time to copy . . . before they vanished from their sight." The similarities to messages from Smith's and Page's seer stones are uncanny.[68]

On the other hand, many new American religions believed in written messages from the divine; it was a common supernatural claim in early America. Shakers experienced visions of divine scrolls and, in 1842, published the results of one such communiqué.[69] Julia Foote, the first female deacon of the African Methodist Episcopal Zion church, met an angel with a scroll who commanded her to become a preacher. Whitmer (the official Mormon historian in 1831) similarly wrote that Mormons in Ohio sometimes "think that an angel of God appear[e]d to them, and showed them writings on the outside cover of the Bible, and on parchment, which flew through the air and on the back of their hands."[70] It seems likely that Ohio Mormons did have these experiences of heavenly scrolls, as did other new sects. And these stories, circulating orally and in print, may have merged together and mixed into rumor.

At other times, Mormons and other sects were accused of attempting miracles they never actually tried. In 1834, the *Philadelphia Saturday Courier* reported that a Mormon "preacher"—the man was never named—had planned to walk on water, just as Jesus had in the New Testament. According to the story, the unnamed Mormon secretly laid wooden planks across "a thin sheet of water covering a common swamp mire" so that he could walk across the planks and appear to be walking on water. Some hooligans made plans of their own, however, and sawed the planks in two. When the Mormon stepped out on the planks, they gave way and the preacher was plunged into the muck, sucked down, and drowned. The *Saturday Courier* felt free to tell readers that the man had drowned *because* of his faith, "a victim to his imposture."[71]

Only this grim story never took place. Fabulous tales of early Mormons trying to walk on water circulated widely in the nineteenth century. Warren Foote (a Mormon) heard it said in 1835 that the prophet Joseph Smith Jr. had attempted it and failed; that story was eventually reprinted in the *New York Times* and *Chicago Tribune*. But no known Mormon of the 1830s was ever recorded as having actually attempted such a miracle *except* in newspaper articles. (The paper even declared that it did not know whether the story was true, though "we shall expect to see it authenticated by the western papers if it be true." It was not authenticated.) Similar stories circulated even before the Mormon church was founded. As early as 1821, the radical prophet Jemima Wilkinson was accused of setting planks in Seneca Lake in New York to fake a water-walking experiment. Stories of other new prophets faking a water-walking miracle could be found in the same era from as far away as Virginia, Britain, and Australia.[72]

Peter and the Ohio worshippers elevated social and political outsiders in their activities. Peter's companions and followers were described as the "*young men and women*."[73] A Gentile observer noted that the worshippers included "girls from twelve to twenty years old." One thirteen-year-old female Saint linked a score of biblical and Book of Mormon prophecies into a single theological whole; she riveted the attention of Mormons, and "they defy Scott or Campbell" to produce as thorough an exegesis.[74] The New York Mormon branches also tended toward social leveling—which partly explains why many of their early disciples were impoverished autodidacts—but the new Ohio Mormons exceeded them.

Old and new Mormons alike participated in these supernatural exercises and beliefs. Supernaturalism did not begin or end in Kirtland. Tongues speaking was widespread, as were other supernatural gifts. Before Mormons had come to the Ohio Valley, church meetings in New York in June featured worshippers swooning and collapsing. Joseph Smith Jr. cast a demon out of

Newel K. Whitney in 1830, with Whitney being thrown about the room violently. The Lamanite missionaries in Ohio openly discussed and practiced supernatural healing.[75]

In 1831, Smith received a revelation on good order in worship. John Whitmer later wrote that "the saints came to [an] understanding on this subject, and unity and harmony prevailed throughout the church of God." Most historians have followed Whitmer's lead and assumed that the revelation settled all the differences.[76] It was not so. Whitmer himself would realize that unity and harmony did *not* prevail in the church when he discovered that Ohio converts were having "some difficulty" because they "denied the truth and turned to fables."[77] Throughout this period, healings, ecstatic worship, and exorcism continued apace. Competing revelations and the authority of the supernatural in the church's first years were perpetual problems for Smith, and for the Mormon faithful as well. Hiram Page's dissention was an opening chapter, and the controversies over Hubbell and Peter followed that. No wonder ordinary Mormons had trouble and confusion in determining exactly how God could reveal himself in a new church emerging with a new (and shifting) ecclesiastical structure.

Official church positions were also a headache for the nascent movement. There were elders, deacons, and both a president and a prophet. No one was getting paid for their religious work in 1831. (To this day, all Mormon missionaries and almost all church functionaries serve on a volunteer basis.) The modern Mormon missionary apparatus was still a long way off; missionaries were not even required to take a vow of celibacy. (Future apostles Orson Pratt, Luke Johnson, and William Smith all met and married their wives while on early church missions.)[78] Nor was it clear how members seeking any particular office—priest, missionary, elder, or prophet—might obtain it. Benjamin Shattuck complained that Mormons in Chardon, Ohio, "chose Edson Fuller . . . as their *overseer* or *temporal* or *spiritual* superintendent." Shattuck "disliked very much the promotion of *such* a man." Edson Fuller was Laura Hubbell's brother.[79]

It is unclear how much about these supernatural and organizational issues Joseph Smith understood when he relocated his family to what had become the center of Mormon belief in Kirtland. He knew of the ecstatic worship, but he also had performed exorcisms himself. Smith likely knew of Hubbell, but her name does not appear in his papers or the revelations. In February, however, an unnamed woman visited Smith "with great pretensions to revealing commandments, laws, and other curious matters."[80] Some Mormons clearly still felt comfortable speaking the word of God to Smith.

There were other problems. Communal living proved difficult among the Family. When Shattuck tried to leave the Morley Farm, he did not know what, if anything, he could take with him. What did anyone actually "own" at a communal farm?[81] A host of rumors joked that Morley's Mormons simply stole from one another and called it sharing. Meanwhile, for those not on a communal farm, there was a housing shortage. The Colesville Saints had settled on land in Thompson, Ohio, owned by Leman Copley; when Copley left the church, the Colesville Saints lost a place to live. Joseph and Emma Smith split a house with the Whitney family. As late as 1835, Saints held worship at the printing office, and the faithful had to arrive at dawn to secure a seat.[82] In Missouri, quarters were even tighter, "about ten families in one log cabin, which was open and unfinished."[83]

In June 1831, Smith himself received a divine commandment to visit Missouri, "which is the land of your inheritance." When he arrived, Smith received a revelation that Independence would be "the center place"—the site of the future city of Zion, where all the faithful could gather. Previously, Saints had known only that the "city Zion" would be "on the borders of the Lamanites." Now that the location was set, plans immediately went into operation to bring Saints to what would be their new home. The churches of Thompson, Chardon, and Colesville headed west to the center place.[84] Mormonism was therefore spread pretty thin by the end of 1831, and it had geographical divisions, internal struggles over authority, and diverse theological positions on supernatural power.

A deep reorganization could address all these issues simultaneously. Here, Mormons did what they believed they alone could do: ask God for guidance through their prophet. On February 9, church elders gathered and directly requested a revelation from God to answer pressing questions. First, "Shall the Church come together in one place?" Furthermore, what would be "the Law regulating the Church in her present situation till the time of her gathering"? They also worried about the coming influx of residents: "What preparations shall we make for our Brethren from the East & when & how?"[85] The elders seemed to be echoing general Mormon unease over how to organize the church, whether Ohio was a permanent home, and, if so, what they would do with everybody.

The revelation Smith received answered each question in turn and, in so doing, began restructuring the church framework. Elders were to "go forth for a little season" rather than stay in Kirtland, and they would go "two by two" and "build up my church in every region."[86] Here was the beginning of the Mormon practice of sending missionaries in pairs, but it was also an answer to the question of Kirtland's centrality: the church was to be built up *every-where*. As for the law of the church, the revelation explained that all who would teach the gospel had to be ordained, and reaffirmed the offices of elders, priests, and teachers.[87] In June, the priesthood was further developed with the differentiation between the high (Melchizedek) priesthood and the lower (Aaronic) priesthood. Aaronic priests would deal with "outward ordinances"; the Melchizedek priesthood would receive "the key to the mysteries of the kingdom, even the key of the knowledge of God."[88] At this point, the term *elder* might refer to either those who held or those who did not hold this high priesthood. If that seems confusing, it was. "I did not understand it," wrote Levi Hancock, so he asked Lyman Wight, who was ordaining high priests, but Wight's explanation "could give me no light."[89] These offices were not intended to be streamlined, however; they were intended to be holy.

The elders also asked how their families would be supported while they missionized, and the answer to this question institutionalized some of the Big Family practices already in place among Ohio Mormons. The bishop—an office established days earlier—would "see that their families are supported out of the property which is consecrated to the Lord."[90] Here was the beginning of a broad Mormon effort at communalism—an operation that would eventually be known as the law of consecration. Mormons were to deed or "consecrate" their property to the bishop of the church, who would then return "stewardships" to each family based on their need. The surplus would be saved to buy land in sacred Missouri.

The Mormons could now move forward with a communitarian ideal, less radical than that of the Morley Farm, but radical enough. They were not the only American Christians to try to live by the maxim of Acts 4 and have "no needy persons among them." Between 1790 and 1860, efforts at religious communalism took place in New Harmony, Indiana; Economy, Pennsylvania; Neshoba, Tennessee; Brook Farm, Massachusetts; Oneida, New York; Bethel, Missouri; Aurora, Oregon; and elsewhere. Most of these communal groups, unlike the Mormons, purchased their property first and then initiated the order. Mormons were attempting to add communalism to an existing patch-work of private property. Of course, not all Saints participated in the system—another sign of early Mormonism's loose structure.

The law of consecration provided a neat solution that addressed the practical needs of the poor and the structural questions about the church while answering long-standing questions in the Mormon community about where and how they were moving—and it was done not by fiat, but by revelation in the form of dialogue. Throughout 1831, elders continued to map out questions, for which they received revelations from Smith, on punishments and consequences for violating church law and the structure of sacrament and confirmation. They also sought further arrangements for the displaced Colesville Saints.[91]

Occasionally, individual Saints requested and received revelations from God through Smith. In 1831, William McLellin beseeched the Lord to answer his questions, but he kept them secret, asking God to "reveal the answer to five questions through his Prophet." The resulting revelation answered the questions, and McLellin considered it "an evidence which I cannot refute."[92] McLellin became a convert, missionary, and elder. Revelations emerged not at random from the divine realm but in response to questions that faithful Mormons debated and composed. Some Saints asked God through Smith, and other Saints probably still believed that Mormons other than Smith might receive revelations. Of sixty-two elders who attended the June conference, twelve eventually left the church or were excommunicated. At least one of those men thought he, too, had the power to receive revelations and an independent authority. Northrup Sweet, ordained a high priest that June day, would leave later that year and found the very first Mormon schismatic group, the Pure Church of Christ. The schismatic and enthusiastic tendencies of January were still-powerful influences. Edson Fuller also left—but in June 1831 he remained a voting member of the council despite his exasperation with the Morley Farm and Smith's skepticism of his sister's gifts.[93] In June 1831, Sweet, Fuller, and all future apostates classified themselves as Mormons. The Saints had still not settled on the idea of a single source of divine revelation, and while those who dissented did not receive official approval or sanction, they still participated and added to the fluid context and creativity of early Mormonism. Indeed, there was remarkable enthusiasm among the Saints in the very weeks the law of consecration was revealed: "The work is here breaking forth on east west north and south," Joseph Smith observed.[94]

These June 1831 reorganizations were not merely ecclesiastic. "Some curious things took place," wrote Corrill. At the same time that Smith conferred the Melchizedek priesthood, "visionary and marvelous spirits" descended. "It threw one [Saint] from his seat to the floor." The coming of the Melchizedek priesthood was a supernatural event. Ezra Booth recalled that Harvey Whitlock twisted into a strange position during the conference, "his mouth . . . contracted in the shape of an italic *O*; his eyes assumed a wild ferocious cast, and his whole appearance presented a frightful object." Whitlock could not speak; neither could John Murdock. Saints hurriedly discussed whether this was a divine or diabolic appearance, but Smith and others determined it "to be from an evil source." Smith "commanded the devil in the name of Christ and he departed."[95]

Exorcism was serious business on the American frontier. For some twenty-first-century Americans, it still is. Exorcisms in the Christian tradition date back to the New Testament; interpreting these miracles (and determining whether modern-day Christians can also experience demonic possession) is a serious matter for the faithful. Films such as *The Exorcist* (1973) have conditioned American audiences to think of exorcism as a purely Catholic activity, but Protestants have their own tradition of the practice. Several observers worried that the ecstatic exercises at Cane Ridge in 1802 were actually demonic; as Adam Rankin wrote during the revivals, there were "two powers of working miracles, the miraculous power of God supreme, and the miraculous power of the prince of darkness, under divine controul." Comparing the Cane Ridge exercises to demonic possessions in the New Testament, Rankin discovered that both sets of victims fell, foamed at the mouth, were either struck dumb or "disposed to cry out as if pierced through with a sword." Rankin concluded the work to be diabolical, an effort by Satan and demons to install false worship and thereby drag believers down into hell.[96] The revivalist Lorenzo Dow noted in his diary that other Americans "thought I was possessed of the devil" when he preached. Harvey Rice, however, remembered Dow turning the tables on his accusers: "Taking a small testament from his pocket," Dow declared, "'I have a commission from Heaven to cast out devils, of which I fear some of you are possessed,'" and endeavored to save them from a "'realm of fire vastly broader and deeper than Lake Erie.'"[97] Tenskwatawa, the Shawnee Prophet, believed that witches had cut evil spirits into pieces and hidden them in medicine bags. Four people died in his 1806 witch hunt as he violently sought to eliminate this demonic influence in Indiana. How-to guides for preventing possession also circulated in the ever-expanding universe of cheap print. Among the spells John George Hohman included in his 1819 *Long Lost Friend* (which went through more than a dozen printings) was one intended to keep evil spirits out of the house.[98] Ebenezer Sibley offered a host of symbols to ward off demons (among other things) in his 1784 *New Illustration of the Celestial Science of Astrology*. The Smith family owned a copy.[99]

For churches that accept exorcisms as valid—and the Saints in the 1830s certainly did—exorcism serves a structural as well as a theological role.[100] For nineteenth-century Christians who believed in demons, the ability to compel them to flee the innocent was powerful proof of the divine sanction of the exorcists and their church. For those who did not believe in demons, exorcism worked the opposite way—proof of a charlatan making "miserable dupes" of "ignorant fanatics," as the anti-Mormon critic Joshua V. Himes put it.[101] In 1829, Bernard Whitman attacked belief in demons as antithetical to religion and the republic; if people believed "the devil works miracles, that witches exist," then "trials for heresy, blasphemy, and witchcraft would once more disgrace the annals of our nation."[102] His critique made little difference to the Mormons; the Melchizedek priesthood arrived in 1831 and dispossessed demons in the name of Christ.

The practice predated the hubbub in Ohio; Smith cast a demon out of Newel Knight prior to the first organization of the church. Like Whitlock, Knight had "his visage and limbs distorted" and was tossed about the room. Knight understood his condition as possession and begged Smith to cast the demon out of him. Smith declared, "If you know that I can, it shall be done." Knight was levitated and tossed about the room, but eventually the demon was rebuked. Knight received "the visions of heaven" and an outpouring of prophecy.[103]

Other Mormons gained reputations as exorcists. William McLellin was called upon to cast out demons four times in March and April 1833. In Maine, Orson Hyde laid his hands on "Mr. Lawrey, who at times was possessed with the Devil."[104] Jared Carter tried and failed several times to dismiss a demon, and when he finally succeeded, he had "proofs of the divine origin" of the revelations to Smith.[105] David Patten met a "very remarkable personage" in 1835; it was Cain—son of Adam, murderer of Abel. Patten found Cain something like a demon, covered with thick hair, over seven feet tall, and dedicated to corrupting souls. Patten "rebuked him in the name of the Lord Jesus Christ and by virtue of the Holy Priesthood."[106] Cain left. Patten and the other Mormons commanded demons to go in the name of Christ and the restored priesthood of the Latter-day Saints. When the demons left, they thus left in the name of the restored church. Church structures and supernatural power validated each other; they were part of a single phenomenon.

Saints worked other Mormon miracles. Mormons continued to speak in tongues, as they had almost from the very beginning. John Whitmer wrote of people speaking in tongues in Missouri in 1833 as "gifts . . . breaking forth in a marvelous manner."[107] An eighteen-year-old Mormon reported from a New York meeting that God confirmed Saints' decisions by "imparting the gift of tongues to us."[108] Brigham Young began speaking in tongues shortly after his conversion—"an electric shock to speak in an unknown tongue." Far from condemning this supernaturalism, Smith and the elders joined in; at a church council in 1833, "all the Elders obtained the gift together with several members of the Church both male & female."[109] In 1842, Joseph Smith would explain Mormonism in part by saying, "We believe in the gift of tongues, prophecy, revelation, visions, healing, interpretation of tongues, and so forth."[110] Early Mormonism was far more inclusive than exclusive in dealing with myriad forms of worship in Ohio.

Healings and reports of healings also proliferated. Jared Carter claimed to have healed twenty-four people in 1831–32 and believed "members of the church might come to the privilege of standing clear of all diseases or fevers."[111] John Murdock believed he had cured "2 brothers and 2 sisters" of smallpox.[112] Patten's journal listed ten healings, including his own. In one case, he encountered a dissenter who accepted the Book of Mormon but had "so menny notions of his own." Patten then healed the man's ill wife and child, and the dissenter became a full church member.[113] Mormon healings functioned much like exorcisms; they validated the divine power in whose name they were performed.

And yet these supernatural events did not convince everyone, even among the Mormons. The announcement of the Melchizedek priesthood, and its attendant exorcisms, still met with "some doubting . . . among the elders, and considerable conversation was held on the subjects," according to John Corrill. "It took some time to reconcile all their [the elders'] feelings."[114] Supernaturalism joined with discussion and debate; it did not circumvent them. Indeed, some Mormons never reconciled themselves to the Melchizedek priesthood, whether it came with signs or not. When Ezra Booth left the church, he wrote extensively on the June 1831 meeting, mocking the exorcisms and noting that Smith had also tried and failed to heal a withered arm at the same time.[115] Even Harvey Whitlock left the church, his own exorcism notwithstanding.[116] After all, for exorcisms to be valid, believers had to presuppose the existence of demons. If there were no demons—as anti-Mormons often pointed out—then exorcisms were proofs of deception, not of devils.

Even as Mormons were criticized for performing miracles, they were also criticized for *not* performing miracles. E. D. Howe sneered that the Mormons had no miracle to restore their lost 116 pages.[117] McLellin met "a little arrogant Methodist" who offered to let McLellin poison him so that McLellin could cure the poison and prove his divine bona fides. Levi Jackman remembered preaching to the Marten family, a "hard unbelieving people" who "requested a sign to make them believe." In this case, Jackman had no sign to give, and the Martens did not join.[118]

In May 1831, questions of revelation, supernaturalism, and church organization came together in the Mormon mission to the Shakers. This time the Mormon bringing questions to Smith was Leman Copley, "formerly a shaker-quaker," who was "anxious that some of the elders should go to his former brethren and preach the gospel." He also annoyed Smith with requests for his own ordination.[119] As before, once Mormon membership set the question, a revelation clarified matters; the revelation permitted Copley's ordination and sent Copley, Rigdon, and Parley Pratt to preach "unto the Shakers" who "desire to know the truth in part but not all."[120]

Copley's brief time with the Mormons had an outsized impact; like many Americans in the sectarian maze of antebellum America, he moved from group to group, asking hard questions. He was fifty in 1831 and had been around twenty when he encountered a Shaker mission to Vermont. Copley and several other Vermonters seemed to accept Shakerism, but even as a member, Copley apparently could not help complaining about Shaker theology. At some point he left the sect and became a significant landowner in Thompson, Ohio, where he met the Saints. When he joined the Mormons, he pledged more than one hundred acres of his land to provide living space for the incoming Colesville Saints. But as with Shakerism, Copley again wanted to add his own suggestions and axioms to Mormonism; he insisted "that the Shakers were right in some particulars of their faith."[121] The revelation of May pointedly reminded Copley to "reason with them [Shakers], not according to what he has received of them, but according to that which shall be taught him by you, my servants." Clearly, Copley believed himself a Saint but possessed or retained a number of ideas that diverged from Mormonism as Smith understood it.[122]

It made sense for Saints to preach to Shakers. The Shakers practiced communitarian living like the Morley Family, whose members had converted en masse to the Mormons, and the North Union Shaker community was only a stone's throw from Kirtland. Yet making the actual decision to go was complex; Mormon missionizing had not yet assumed a streamlined (or even organized) structure—there had to be discussions, complaints, a revelation, and an ordination.

Ashbel Kitchell, presiding elder of the North Union Shakers, kept "occasionally hearing" in the 1830s that the Mormons "expected to come after a while and lead us into the water." Parley Pratt had preached at another Shaker village, and Oliver Cowdery had already visited North Union, explaining how he had "been an assistant in the translation of the *golden Bible*, and had also seen the Angel," as Kitchell wrote. Cowdery asked "to leave some of their Books [of Mormon] among us, to which we consented, and they left seven, which we distributed among the people."[123]

Kitchell described the Book of Mormon "as not interesting enough to keep them awake." Richard McNemar, the former Cane Ridge partisan turned Shaker stalwart, also read the Book of Mormon. He compared it to "Persian tales which I used to read as a boy . . . its endless genealogies & Chronologies, afford no light to a believer."[124] Kitchell himself found the Saints "very ignorant of Christ or his work; therefore I treated them with the tenderness of children." He also assumed that Copley "had taken up with Mormonism as the easier plan," not wishing to live a celibate life as Shakers did.[125]

Kitchell, McNemar, Copley, Rigdon, Pratt: all these men had left the church of their youth (and sometimes another church as well) and all had become leaders in their new sects. On what basis could they come together—or even have a discussion? Despite his aversion to Copley and the Book of Mormon, Kitchell still held out the possibility that miracles and the supernatural could provide an answer. He prayed that "if God had any hand in that work, he would inform me by some means, that I might know what to do," perhaps "by letting me have an interview with the angel." In conversation with another Mormon, Kitchell noted that "if the words he had spoken had come from a man of God, they would have caused my knees to smote together like Belshazers"—obliquely referring to the miraculous "writing on the wall" in Daniel 5.[126]

Kitchell "found that the life of self-denial corresponded better with the life of Christ, than Mormonism," but he was willing to listen, and he and Rigdon had a sociable chat. Rigdon consented to attend Shaker worship the next day.

Both men were engaged in a mutual evangelization, with Rigdon trying to convince Kitchell, and Kitchell hoping Rigdon "might desire to find a resting place—something substantial to place his feet on" in Shakerism.

When Rigdon gathered with the North Union Shakers for worship, however, Pratt barged in with the text of the revelation Smith had dictated and obliterated Rigdon's delicate diplomacy. Pratt demanded that his fellow missionaries ignore Kitchell, "for they had come with the authority of the Lord Jesus Christ." Rigdon accordingly rose, addressed the North Union community, and read the text of the revelation. (The revelation informed the Shakers bluntly that celibacy was not divine and that Ann Lee had not possessed the Christ spirit, for "the Son of man cometh not in the form of a woman.")[127] Kitchell was unmoved, dismissing "their Christ" as a false Christ and asking them to leave. Seeing no takers for the Latter-day Saint message, Rigdon apparently sat, but Pratt arose and shook the dust of his garments as a condemnation of the Shaker community.

Kitchell exploded. "You filthy Beast," he shouted, coming face to face with Pratt, "dare you presume to come in here and try to imitate a man of God by shaking your filthy tail." He then turned on Copley: "You hypocrite, you knew better—you knew where the living work of God was, but for the sake of indulgence, you would consent to deceive yourself and them." As Kitchell remembered it, Pratt sat back in a stunned silence. Copley began to weep. Pratt soon dashed out of the service, jumped on his horse, and lit out for Kirtland. "We fulfilled this mission," he wrote tersely in his autobiography, "as we were commanded."[128] Rigdon, however, stayed for dinner.

The Saints' mission to North Union had not netted a single convert; in fact, the opposite proved true. Kitchell's admonition shook Copley out of Mormonism; he eventually "came back to us and begged for union" with the Shakers. Kitchell took him back and then journeyed with Copley to Kirtland, where he returned the Mormons' favor and preached to *them*. "They appeared to be struck with terror and fear lest some of them might get converted," Kitchell wrote. But he left Kirtland with only Copley in tow.[129]

Losing Copley was a severe blow. He had consecrated his lands for the Colesville Saints, but now that he had rejoined the Shakers, he withdrew the offer, "which thing confused the whole church," Whitmer wrote.[130] Copley's decision meant that the incoming Colesville Saints had no place to stay; plenty of Mormons in Thompson had also been residing on Copley's holdings. Joseph Knight was one of the Saints kicked off Copley's land; Copley "took the advantege of us and we could not git anything for what we had done." With no land immediately available, the Colesville Saints moved ninety miles away to Wellsville, then headed for Missouri.[131]

John Whitmer and others chalked up Copley's actions to "rebellion," but the Shaker crisis of May 1831 suggested issues larger than Copley's indecision. It indicated the widening gyre of sectarianism; in one sense, it proved Smith had been right when he worried that American Christianity had become "Lo here!" and "Lo there!" When Shakers and Mormons met in 1831, they each tried to convert the other; they could see similarities in their approaches, but in the end, they were each trying to form a *new* church, rather than collect and combine existing churches. Trying to solve sectarianism bred sectarianism. Proselytizing in antebellum America was a zero-sum game.

Sometimes faiths lost this battle for existence. The antebellum world was filled with churches that shone brightly in the heat of the Second Great Awakening only to perish. Osgoodites. Wilkinsonians. Babcockists. Cochranites. Shakerism survived with a missionary approach like Kitchell's until the twentieth century, when missionizing fell off and—with no natural increase from the celibate Shakers—the sect dwindled to a few members. Twenty-first-century Protestantism can have a certain denominational slipperiness; often churches of many denominations may be seen as "Christian" or "evangelical," and religious choice is sometimes caricatured as one between belief and unbelief. The nineteenth century was much more transparent as to how "religious belief" is not a uniform phenomenon.

Copley's apostasy highlighted the Mormon church's endemic organizational struggles, which in turn reflected the problems of dozens of new churches in the United States. In a world of religious freedom—where no state power could stop anyone from calling themselves a minister and heading off to preach—building institutional power and clear lines of authority was a challenge. Even America's Roman Catholics (heirs to a very old institutional church) had breakaway parishes and renegade priests in the 1820s.[132] Mormons, often characterized as extremely hierarchical, had perpetual problems with institutional authority in 1831. Page, Hubbell, and Copley had all challenged the centralized role of a single prophet; intense supernatural worship continued both with and without tacit approval, and while supernatural proofs could establish authority, they did not always do so. In a religious environment where no church could *make* anyone do anything they did not consent to, leadership, even braced by divine powers, had to negotiate and cajole believers. Mormons were simply not going to be told what to do. This dilemma placed practical as well as spiritual strains on the church.

The problems with organization and authority persisted. At a November church conference, Smith and ten elders decided to publish the Book of Commandments, a collection of all the revelations Smith had received from God to that point. It was an important step. Without a published source of revelations, Mormons could access these sacred texts only through word of mouth or handwritten copies of copies. Non-Mormons had the same limitations, which explains in part why an Ohio newspaper could claim that Smith had given a divine commandment for the Saints to "build him an elegant house, and give him 1000 dollars." (Neither commandment is found in Smith's revelations.)[133] A published record might inhibit misinformation.

When Smith asked the council whether it would attach a testimony to the Book of Commandments affirming that the text was "of the Lord," however, not everyone agreed. That brought the council to a standstill: How exactly could anyone *prove* a revelation divine? Did each elder need a personal divine assurance, and, if so, why had some elders received it but others had not? The issue was not whether the prophet spoke with God's authority, but how and in what way it could be known.[134]

A new revelation suggested a radical solution: those who could not consent to the testimony should take any revelation from the Book of Commandments, "appoint him that is the most wise among you," and see if he could "make one like unto it."[135] If an elder tried and failed, then the Saints would be "under condemnation if ye do not bear record that they are true." It was, to put it crudely, a kind of revelation-off. The failure of an opposing prophet would be the very supernatural validation the dissenters were looking for.

William McLellin offered to try. A newly appointed elder, McLellin had met Smith just a few days before and spent the night at his house. He was hardly a rival prophet, and probably intended his efforts as an honest means to seek light, rather than an effort to depose Smith. McLellin has received a great deal of opprobrium in Latter-day history for his efforts, perhaps because he later left the church in a huff over Smith's leadership. Smith later described McLellin as "having more learning than sense" and engaging in a "vain attempt . . . to imitate the language of Jesus Christ," but as historian Mark R. Grandstaff has pointed out, these accusations are not found in the documents of 1831.[136] In fact, no contemporary diary—not even McLellin's own—mentions the competing revelations. McLellin may not have been "challenging" Smith's leadership but rather serving as a guinea pig to see if organizational and theological problems really could be solved through supernatural means.

McLellin tried to produce a revelation; he failed. There is no official record of what he produced, but there is an extant copy of McLellin's transcription for Doctrine and Covenants 22 (a revelation on baptism), which does contain a few changes in language that were then crossed out. If that commandment was indeed the one McLellin tried to rewrite, he didn't get far. McLellin moved some words around, changed the existing "even as in the days old" to "even that which was from the beginning," and then gave up. (It's also possible that this error was a routine transcription error from later in November, when McLellin served as Smith's scribe.)[137]

Either way, the elders had participated in the divine test, and they were now obligated to affirm the divinity of the Book of Commandments. As Grandstaff points out, technically this effort was charismatic rather than supernatural—the Holy Ghost had affirmed the reality through actions and feelings, rather than through a suspension of natural laws.[138] All the elders, including McLellin, "bore witness to the truthfulness of the Book of Commandments."[139]

After all was said and done, there was even a carrot offered to the dissenters; Smith accepted the conference's request that he "correct those errors or mistakes which he may discover by the holy Spirit while reviewing the revelations." Both sides got something. Leadership was not precisely collaborative, but it was participatory—perhaps the best any voluntary church could hope for in the age of disestablishment.[140]

McLellin was not punished for his efforts, either. Just after the prophecy contest, Smith received a revelation that included McLellin as one of the "faithful elders," and he continued to do church work. He even continued to lodge with the Smiths. In an 1832 letter, he praised Smith as "a true Prophet or Seer of the Lord" who "*has* power and *does* receive revelations from god."[141] Later in life McLellin became disillusioned with the church, but later apostasy cannot explain the workings of the early church. After all, nine of the ten elders at the Hiram conference broke with Smith at one time or another between 1831 to 1839.

Other people left, too. One-sixth of the attendees at the June 1831 conference eventually left; so did some of the Colesville Saints, pushed off one plot of land and then another.[142] Jesse Gause, a former Quaker and former Shaker who spent much of 1832 as Smith's church counselor, simply abandoned his missionary companion on August 20, 1832, and was never heard from again.[143]

Laura Hubbell, as well, vanished from the record. Somewhere between 1831 and 1833, Black Pete left Kirtland and did not return.[144]

These disaffections, schismatics, and deserters did not necessarily harm the new church, but they did form a theme of Mormon history. There were *always* dissenters and schismatics in the church; Smith and other leaders were perpetually dealing with some kind of internal squabble, and their leadership positions were therefore, in some sense, always vulnerable. Supernatural events could create believers, and they could create authority, but they could not create unanimity. Mormons were not a pliant, happy group, eager to do whatever Joseph Smith asked. Especially in their first decade, they were prone to bickering and argument. That meant, in turn, that anti-Mormons had a reliable supply of disgruntled Saints to draw on for scuttlebutt on the prophet and his people.

Two defections in particular had pernicious consequences. Symonds Ryder and Ezra Booth each spent less than a year in the church, but they left with a flourish. Ryder (another former Campbellite) had received a commission at the June conference where the Melchizedek priesthood had been announced. In later years, a story would circulate that Ryder left the church when his name was misspelled in the handwritten version of a revelation ("Simonds Rider"), but there is little evidence from 1831 to indicate Ryder's difficulty with that document.[145] Ryder's recorded worries concerned the law of consecration. He apparently ran across these revelations about redistribution of wealth in the summer of 1831; by September, he had taken the handwritten text and published it in a local newspaper, where it was labelled "SECRET BYE LAWS OF THE MORMONITES."[146] With no official account of Mormon revelations yet printed, Ryder's reports gave rise to rumor and exaggeration. Tensions increased.

Shortly thereafter, Ezra Booth began publishing his exposés of Mormonism, bolstering the claim that Mormonism was a "deep-laid scheme . . . designed to lure the credulous and the unsuspecting into a state of unqualified vassalage."[147] Americans had been warning each other for years about the dangers of superstition; as Whitman wrote in his essays on superstition, "superstition . . . turns your attention from God to fate and chance and devils."[148] Or, as James Thacher wrote in his 1831 essays on demonology, the "mind that is imbued with a superstitious temperament, is . . . prepared to inflict the most atrocious evils on mankind; even murder, suicide, and merciless persecution."[149] Mormonism was a threat to souls, property, and civil peace.

Anti-Mormon feeling had already heated up. What had begun with the laughter of newspapers and the theological denunciations of Campbell and other ministers was beginning to become more violent. Shouting down the religion was apparently not enough. Threats became more common. Charity Ames met a Methodist minister who said the best way to deal with her Mormon relatives was to "have cracked their heads together."[150] Ames subsequently headed to Kirtland with her husband. William McLellin's preaching was broken up by a stink bomb, an "odious smelling thing . . . that raised confusion in all the house."[151] While John Murdock was leading a Latter-day Saint service in Cleveland, people threw books and inkstands at him.[152] Orson Hyde reported a crowd a hundred strong that intended to tar and feather him for preaching Mormonism, a fate he avoided when a child misled the mob about Hyde's location.[153]

As 1831 turned to 1832, the Mormons tried to respond peacefully to Ryder and Booth. Rigdon challenged both men to a public debate at a local schoolhouse often used by the Disciples of Christ. Ryder wrote back a terse response asking Rigdon to debate in private. Rigdon instead showed up at the schoolhouse and lectured for two days on Mormonism. He likely thought Ryder's refusal to appear settled the matter. It did not.[154]

On the cold evening of March 24, 1832, a group of men gathered in Benjamin Hinkley's backyard in Hiram, Ohio, where they boiled tar and passed around alcohol. In the small hours of the night, they moved out to the houses where Smith and Rigdon lived—only about a thousand feet from Ryder's own home.[155] The men smashed open the doors, pulled Smith and Rigdon out of bed, and gave them a tar and feathering.

Tarring and feathering can seem comic or quaint today, but it was deadly serious in the nineteenth century. The practice dated at least to the 1300s, but it took on a special meaning for Americans as they passed through the Revolution. Patriots frequently resorted to tarring and feathering colonial officials and clergymen who opposed them. Hot tar was poured on the victim, resulting in severe burns, and then the feathers were added for humiliation. The mob would then beat the victim, fill his mouth with tar (potentially killing him), and sometimes take more drastic measures. In 1776, patriots tarred and feathered a loyalist minister in Charleston, then hung and burned his body for good measure. In 1775, Carolina patriots tarred a loyalist, burned off two of his toes, and partially scalped him.[156] Tarring and feathering had connotations of liberty, but it was meant as violence—the preferred way for patriots to get rid of Tories, real or metaphorical. In the Age of Jackson, the ritual violence frequently got out of hand. Tar and feathers have had a long and dark history; the tactic was used by the Ku Klux Klan into the twentieth century.[157]

Smith and Rigdon survived, but not by much. Both men were badly beaten; Smith had a vial of acid thrown in his face. Rigdon fell unconscious. The crowd stripped Smith naked and forced tar down his throat, breaking some of his teeth. Someone raked Smith's naked body with nails and cried, "*God damn ye, that's the way the Holy Ghost falls on folks!*" Luke Johnson later reported that the crowd had intended to castrate Smith but opted for mercy at the last moment. Ryder's participation was never proved, though he wrote a letter in 1868 that contained a suspiciously accurate list of details. Chillingly, he wrote that the attack "cleansed" his community.[158]

Although the mob showed mercy on Smith, the tarring and feathering nevertheless took a victim. Smith had been sleeping next to his adopted son, a baby also named Joseph who was sick with measles. Breaking down the door and pulling Smith away from the infant left the child exposed to the deep cold of the March night. The child died four days later.[159] If the child did indeed die from complications involving the mob, then he was the first Mormon martyr.

It was a wake-up call to the Saints. They had been taunted and bullied and had seen fellow Americans brandishing weapons. Preachers had fistfights and close calls. Still, most Mormons likely thought that American republicanism and freedom of religion would keep the discussions civil—making cruel jokes in papers or snubbing public debates. "The American people boast of republicanism and . . . speak very contemptuously of the dark ages of persecution," McLellin wrote when he heard about the attack on Smith. But Americans did not follow their own beliefs: "They rise in mobs, black themselves, waylay houses and even break in and drag the servants of god from their beds, and families into the streets, and abuse and torture them for no other reason only their religion differs from the popular."[160]

Smith's wife and friends spent the night scraping tar off the prophet. Smith managed to appear in public to preach the next day, covered in his wounds from the night before, "my flesh all scarified and defaced," Smith wrote.[161] Now the Saints understood that American law would not protect them from neighbors who wished to silence them in the name of God and country. Smith blamed the violence directly on the sects he wanted to replace: "mostly Campbellites, Methodists, and Baptists, who continued to molest and menace Father [Luke] Johnson's house for a long time."[162]

Smith did not stick around Ohio for another battle; within a week, he headed west to visit the Mormons in Missouri. This decision to preach and then leave the area was a peaceful response to open violence. Even in 1832, even after the loss of his son, Smith was still upbeat about the promise and possibility of American freedom. He did not realize then, as McLellin did, that when mere popularity determined which religions rose and fell, mere popularity could also dictate when violence could happen. And neither man could know that the Mormons' perpetual problem with apostates—another byproduct of religious freedom—was going to add fuel to the fire. And so Smith went off, perhaps hoping for a different response in Jackson County, Missouri. Jackson County had other ideas.

# 4

## "Their God Is the Devil"

KIRTLAND HAD COME TO THE SAINTS. An organized flock had fallen into the Mormons' collective laps, complete with known theologians, preachers, leaders, and land, in a boomtown stocked with other ex-Yankees. Kirtland pulled the Saints in. Missouri seemed selected almost at random, with precious few points of connection with the haggard and pious lot in Ohio.

Yet Missouri had long called out to people across the world—French, Comanches, Osages, Spanish, Otos, and others. The confluence of the Mississippi, Ohio, and Missouri rivers had brought people, weapons, and viruses together over the centuries, and these rough combinations had produced fractures. The great city-state of Cahokia emerged and dominated the region in the eleventh century, and when it declined, the people of the region retreated behind palisades and moats. The Spanish arrived in the 1540s and were quickly chased out. By the sixteenth century, Native American city-states and confederacies on the Mississippi contrasted with an emerging Plains Indian culture to the west that had become more adaptable. As the Comanches, Sioux, and other Plains nations adapted to the horses the Spanish introduced, new geopolitical possibilities spread across the plains and into the heart of the continent.[1]

The region was still a site of conflict between Osages, Spanish, Shawnees, and British when the American Revolution broke out. The Americans invaded Kaskaskia in 1778, in what is today the Mississippi River border of Illinois and Missouri. British-backed Indian nations struck the Spanish redoubt of St. Louis in 1780. In 1785 the Osage nation fractured into several groups, and in 1793 the Spanish empire declared war on the Osage nations. The Spanish lost.[2] When the United States took control of the region following the 1803 Louisiana Purchase, territorial governor Meriwether Lewis had to order white squatters off Shawnee and Delaware land. As recently as 1818, the Shawnee, the Kickapoo, and other Indian nations were planning a campaign against the Osages for parts of Missouri.

Shortly thereafter, the famed Missouri Compromise of 1820 put the state in the American union with slaveholding intact. The Compromise solidified the position of white slave owners in central Missouri (known as "Little Dixie"), and thousands of enslaved Africans were forcibly moved west into these regions from Kentucky, Tennessee, and elsewhere. Meanwhile, Yankees attached to commercial firms in New York and Boston headed to the north of the state, displacing traders who had long cultivated family and cultural connections to the Indians of the confluence region. The only constant in nineteenth-century Missouri was change.

White Americans poured into the state after 1820, bringing with them a new weapon in these ongoing exchanges: popular democracy. Leaders selected to carefully balance competing interests were out; leaders who would enact the will of the majority were in. The new white Missourians wanted Indian land, and they wanted it as cheaply as possible. William Clark (of the eponymous 1803 expedition with Lewis), who had spent years negotiating white and Indian claims for the federal government, lost his bid for governor to Alexander McNair. Taking the reins of state power and militia control, McNair spearheaded a series of treaties expelling Native Americans from the state. Shawnees, Osages, and the Sauk and Meskwaki nations all were forced to surrender their lands in the 1820s. Local Native Americans were marched out of Missouri and into Kansas. Missouri's Shawnees were forced off of Apple Creek in 1825; the Osages in western Missouri were removed piecemeal between 1825 and 1830. The land on which Independence was built in 1827 had been Osage territory in 1824. White Missourians who claimed that Mormons had no right to live in their towns had moved into the area only six years previously. The conflict that emerged was not old-timers versus new arrivals but newcomer against newcomer.[3]

Indian removal also conditioned white Americans to accept forcible exodus as something both possible and natural, rather than as a specific political choice.[4] In 1829, Jacksonian policy on Indian removal sent Native American nations from across the United States into Indian Territory, so that even as Indians were removed *from* Missouri, they were also removed *across* Missouri into Indian Territory. White Missourians of the 1820s and 1830s saw and heard about the forced transfer of population. Even in the years before the infamous Trail of Tears, numerous Native Americans suffered their own long marches. Groups of Shawnees, Senecas, and Ottawas were forcibly marched from Ohio across Missouri into Kansas between 1827 and 1833. North of the border, the Sauk leader Black Hawk remembered how white settlers blamed him when they attempted to settle on land he had never relinquished: "The whites were *complaining* at the same time that *we* were *intruding* upon *their rights!* THEY made themselves out the *injured* party, and *we* the *intruders!*" It was a sentiment the Mormons would soon become familiar with. Indian removal indicated a social willingness to expel people from their homes, as well as a political tolerance for this idea. The practice of signing perfidious treaties and then enforcing them by gunpoint would not be limited to Native Americans.[5]

So the idea of ethnic cleansing was an established Missouri tradition by 1833, when a self-appointed mob of Jackson County's Gentiles applied it to the immigrant Mormons. The Saints were given the choice to move or die: if, "after timely warning . . . they [Mormons] refuse to leave us in peace, as they found us," then the anti-Mormon Gentiles would "use such means as may be sufficient to remove them." They promised to perform this act "peaceably if we can, forcibly if we must." The Missourians openly declared that they undertook these actions because the Mormon faith was a threat to democracy: "The lives and property of the other citizens would be insecure, under the administration of men who are so ignorant and superstitious as to believe that they have been the subjects of miraculous and supernatural cures." They concluded their affidavit by echoing the Declaration of Independence, pledging to one another "our lives, fortunes, and sacred honors" to justify the forced removal of "these fanatics." It was signed by more than a hundred Americans, including the Jackson County jailor, judge, clerk, and two militia colonels.[6]

The Mormons dithered on how to respond, and the mobs came. Riots broke out against them in the town of Independence. The Mormons initially approached the Missouri state government for help in protecting their faith and property, but they found scant help from a governor with little stomach for taking political risks to ensure domestic tranquility. After all, the anti-Mormon mobs in Jackson County were not a random, disorganized group. They were "composed of lawyers, magistrates, county officers, civil and military," wrote Parley Pratt.[7] David Pettigrew noted the presence of men and women attending an anti-Mormon meeting, and thought the women "seemed more interested in mobbing" than the men.[8] It was a mob that cut across social classes and had a clear organizational structure. Its membership was formed by compacts signed by local leaders and prepared not just to humiliate or insult Mormons but to terrorize or eliminate them. The "mobbers," as the Mormons called them, acted more like an extralegal military force than a spontaneous uprising.

How did things get so bad so quickly? Why was the response in Missouri more intense than that in Ohio? The answers are not always clear, but once again, the combination of Mormon supernatural claims, sectarian demands, and the swirling rumors of the printed word all played their part. And those who initiated the violence against the Mormons and spread the rumors in 1833 were "not what is termed 'rabble' of a community," remembered Alexander Majors, a Gentile participant in the mob. The people who wrecked houses, tarred and feathered Mormons, and chased unarmed Saints from horseback "were respectable citizens and law-abiding in every other respect, but who actually thought they were doing God's service to destroy, and if possible, obliterate Mormonism."[9]

Once again, the Mormons were not alone. The expulsion from Jackson County was part of a string of violence across the country in the 1830s, including the Black Hawk War, the Second Seminole War, the Texas Revolution, and the anti-abolitionist riots in New York and Illinois. Sometimes, as in the Nat Turner rebellion, the violence was explicitly religious. Other times it bubbled up from religious tensions—as when Protestants sacked and destroyed the Ursuline convent of Massachusetts in 1834, or when a Protestant fire brigade ran into a Catholic funeral procession in 1837 Boston and sparked a riot involving fifteen thousand people. Still other times it was just a free-for-all, as in 1826, when a disappointing display of fireworks set off a riot in New York. Violence and democracy lived together in the Age of Jackson.[10]

In January 1831, during this age of violence, the missionaries to the Lamanites arrived in Missouri. Cowdery crossed the border into Indian Country.

"Indian Country" was a new designation—one discussed and encouraged by previous presidential administrations and made a terrible reality by Andrew Jackson. Jackson's Indian Removal Act (1830) *required* Native American nations to forfeit all lands east of the Mississippi and relocate beyond the Missouri border. Jackson encouraged nations to relocate peacefully, but he intended to use force if necessary. His threats would be carried out in later years, creating the Trail of Tears among the Cherokees, Creeks, and other southeastern nations, the Trail of Death among the Potawatomis, and countless other unnamed tragedies in the 1830s.

Yet another prophet had settled across the river from Independence. The Shawnee nation had long been split into distinct political groups, living (by 1825) in Ohio, Missouri, and Texas. Some would be removed under Jackson's auspices—crossing Missouri in 1832–35 en route to a Kansas reservation that would subsequently be taken from them in 1869. Another group of Shawnees had moved by choice even before Jackson came to power. They had done so under the leadership of Tenskwatawa, a prophet of the Master of Life—a traditionally distant deity in Shawnee cosmology. In 1806, the Master of Life granted Tenskwatawa a vision and a new dispensation to gather all Native Americans into one monotheistic nation. As part of this mission, Tenskwatawa had established a Native American city in the Indiana Territory known as Prophetstown; the place had thousands of residents and was an active theater in the War of 1812. The famed Native American general Tecumseh was Tenskwatawa's brother and later commanded the movement, but well into 1811, American officials referred to Tecumseh as "the Prophet's brother," suggesting that it was Tenskwatawa and not his elder brother who led the resistance. Like Smith, Tenskwatawa preserved the content of his visions, though his descriptions of God, divine law, and the afterlife were transmitted orally rather than in writing. Tecumseh's death at the Battle of the Thames in 1813, however, largely ended Tenskwatawa's religious program.[11] Violence disrupted and weakened this religion.

After the war, Tenskwatawa lived as a refugee in British Canada; when he returned to the United States in the 1820s, he advocated for voluntary removal. Eventually a few towns of Shawnees joined him, and Tenskwatawa once again became a leader in his nation. These Shawnees were relocated to Kansas, and although Tenskwatawa was far from the paramount Shawnee leader in 1831, he had by then built another community called Prophetstown in what is today the Argentine district of Kansas City—just fifteen miles from Independence.

It was the Shawnees and Delawares who first received Cowdery as a Mormon missionary.[12]

The choice could not have been coincidental. Cowdery selected as his first cross-border audience two nations that had religious connections to mono-theistic prophets. (Neolin, the Delaware Prophet, taught a similar doctrine in the 1760s.) So Cowdery was visiting Indians who knew prophets as he spread the word of the Mormon prophet. On the other hand, Cowdery did not meet with Tenskwatawa; he met with Kit-Tha-We-Nund, the Delaware leader known among Anglophones as William Anderson. After some initial diffidence, Anderson agreed to call a council of the nation to listen to the missionaries, and received the Book of Mormon.[13]

Cowdery's initial reports brimmed with confidence. "There are many among the Shawnees who also believe," he wrote, "& we trust that when the Lord shall open our way we shall have glorious times." Cowdery took heart, too, from a landscape he saw as evidence of Book of Mormon history, noting shattered rocks he thought fulfilled a prophecy in the Book of Helaman. Although the Shawnees did not convert as he hoped, by May 1831, he informed the Ohio Mormons of the need to evangelize the Navajo nation—a people the Mormons were wholly unfamiliar with and who lived a further thousand miles from Missouri. Cowdery was beginning to sense that this mission might need more than four people. "Much is expected from me in the cause of our Lord," he wrote.[14]

Unfortunately, American officials expected trouble from the Mormons. Federal Indian agent Frederick Cummins had Cowdery thrown out of Indian Territory for preaching without a license. Cowdery initially wrote to Cummins explaining that "I have been appointed by a society of Christians . . . to superintend the establishing Missions among the Indians" and for the purpose of "teaching them the Christian religion." Cowdery's creative omission of any Mormon references did not fool Cummins, who wrote to his supervisor that "they have a new Revelation with them, as there [sic] Guide in teaching the Indians, which they say was shown to one of their Sects in a Miraculous way, and that an Angel from Heaven appeared to one of their Men."[15] Cummins seems to have learned something about the Mormons from swirls of rumor rather than direct report. The US government likely grew anxious over the idea of any "very strange" prophets preaching to Native American nations that had so recently fought the Americans in the name of prophecy. Most whites assumed that Indian prophets were deliberate hucksters; Charles Augustus Murray wrote that the Kickapoo prophet Kenekuk had "grafted the knowledge" of Christianity "upon his Indian prejudices and superstitions" to create a religion "as an engine of personal aggrandizement."[16] Much the same was said about Joseph Smith Jr. While Kenekuk, Tenskwatawa, and Smith were very different men with very different religious programs, they all faced the same popular proclivity to condemn novel religions as delusion and imposture.

It is fascinating to wonder how Mormonism might have developed differently had Cowdery remained in Kansas, and had the Shawnees and Delawares truly been as receptive as he claimed. But the US government did not grant the license, and the Shawnees and Delawares did not yield any converts. Cowdery and his missionaries crossed back into Missouri and began preaching to whites.[17]

That did not go well, either. Missouri appeared to be stony ground for Mormons, even though the state had the same sectarian shockwaves that rattled New York and Ohio. Timothy Flint (an advocate for Indian removal) found Missouri filled with Presbyterians, Lutherans, Baptists, Cumberland Presbyterians, Methodists, and Catholics; he also found religious enthusiasm: "frequent meetings, spasms, cries, fallings, faintings," and a kind of "holy laugh" that Flint found "idiot and spasmodic" and unlikely to affect true conversion. Much the same thing was said about Mormon exercises in Ohio.[18] The western town of Millport—where Mormons later settled—was known as "Methodist Campground" before 1836.[19] Majors noted the presence of "Methodists, Baptists of two different orders, Presbyterians of two different orders, and Catholics, and a denomination calling themselves Christians."[20] Cowdery found even more sects in western Missouri, which he described as flooded with "Universalists, Atheists, Deists, Presbyterians, Methodists, Baptists, & professed Christians." Unfortunately, he also found that *all* of those sects "with all the Devels from the infernal pit are united and foaming"—presumably against the Saints.[21]

Missouri apparently had much the same religious makeup as the rest of Jacksonian America, but whether all those sectarians were "united and foaming" against the Mormons is another matter. As in Ohio, newspapers in Missouri plied their readership with truth and rumor about multiple religious groups. The *Missouri Intelligencer* (Columbia), for example, featured articles and news stories condemning Universalism.[22] The *St. Louis Observer* routinely published anti-Catholic items. It is not surprising, therefore, that most of the (few) news articles about Mormons published in Missouri prior to 1833 were either derogatory or filled with rumor. The *Intelligencer*'s first reference to a

Mormon newspaper noted that Mormonism "will have an advantage not enjoyed by other denominations: no one will think it necessary to controvert their creed," because Mormonism was, in the editor's eyes, too foolish to require refutation.[23] In 1832, the paper reported a rumor of famine among the Mormons; the next year, it described them in want of necessities. LDS printer William W. Phelps had to publish a rebuttal to these "false reports," insisting that the Saints, "in general, enjoy good health."[24] These were not devastating rumors, but they do indicate the way in which rumors—damaging or not—circulated on the American frontier.

In some ways, these rumors and dismissals of Catholics, Universalists, and Mormons said less about specific faiths than about a larger pattern of an idealized America. American newspapers of the Jacksonian Age routinely imagined a perfect country and described any and all critics as enemies of democracy. "A spirit of dissension has been generated between the people of the United States that is tearing their vitals," wrote the *Intelligencer*, and "the persons who gave rise to this spirit, are actuated by motives that are impure . . . very many worthy men within the United States, have been grossly deceived." To challenge the powers that be or to raise questions was to tear the country apart. There was no such thing as a loyal opposition. In Jacksonian democracy, as historian Harry Watson writes, political opponents were considered "parasitic minorities"; the will of the majority could never be wrong. That attitude shaped newspaper responses to the Mormon crisis and turned the Mormons from an odd religion into a threat to democracy.[25]

In later years, Mormons and Mormon historians laid the blame for the rough reception of Mormonism squarely at the feet of the Gentiles. In 1837, Joseph Smith described the residents of the state as possessing "the degradation, leanness of intellect, ferocity, and jealousy of a people . . . without civilization, refinement, or religion."[26] Other reports of bad behavior by white Americans in Jackson County seemed to back this assertion, especially one account of ne'er-do-wells who came to Missouri to commit crimes and then fled across the river to avoid lawmen.[27]

And yet things started out well. Josiah Gregg, a Santa Fe trader who drifted through Independence in 1833, held that "the Mormons were at first kindly received" by the old settlers—most of whom had immigrated to Missouri only a few years previously. "We found our selves among strangers," remembered Mormon Joseph Knight. "But the people seemed to be friendly with us."[28] In 1833, even as a Mormon resident of Independence scorned his persecutors as "enemies to the cause of Christ," he also noted that the Gentiles "have been very friendly with us till within six months."[29] Similarly, William McLellin found in 1831 that locals thought the Mormons "a very honest people but very much deluded."[30] Titus Billings worked for his Gentile neighbors in 1832 and "always had a good understanding" among "the People of the County."[31] Another Gentile described the Mormons as industrious, and Mormon women in particular as "quite intelligent."[32] Indeed, when the Mormons later petitioned for redress of grievances, they described the actions of the mob as "so unexpected" that they needed time to consider what they should do.[33]

Gentiles also seem to have tolerated the Mormons at first. "The conduct of the Mormons for the three years" in Independence, wrote Alexander Majors, "was that of good citizens." Majors noted Mormonism's "tantalizing tales"; they were "clannish . . . and carried with them a melancholy look." A Gentile, Majors wrote, "could tell a Mormon when he met him by that look."[34] If the Missourians did not initially fear the Mormons, they had begun to make distinctions. It seems as though some in Missouri *chose* to fear the Mormons.

The distinction may seem too fine, but these kinds of choices were becoming increasingly frequent in 1833 America. US Catholics had carved out realms of influence and prestige despite an undercurrent of anti-Catholic vitriol. By 1831, Catholics served in Congress, and Catholic Roger Taney had become United States attorney general. (By 1835, he would be chief justice of the Supreme Court.) Priests sometimes toured with Protestant ministers in public debates on the Bible and doctrine without incident. The Ursuline convent of Boston opened a private school that attracted numerous Protestant students. John Carroll, America's first Catholic bishop, rejoiced that America's "public protection & encouragement are extended alike to all denominations." John England, bishop of Charleston, South Carolina, so loved the American system that he ran his diocese with a kind of two-house legislature modeled on the US Constitution; he consulted a House of Laity elected from the churches in his district, and a House of Clergy made up of the priests. But England was not naïve about the challenges facing American Catholics. In 1826, he wrote that it was normal for Protestants "to vilify the Catholic religion, and to use the harshest and most offensive terms when designating its practices, but that if a Catholic used any phrase . . . which even insinuated anything derogatory to the Protestant religion, he was marked out as a shocking bigot."[35] American Protestant newspapers routinely printed articles condemning the Catholic Church, laced with innuendo and rumor—or, as an American Catholic council put it in 1829, they "repeat the hundred-times-refuted calumnies of the days of angry and bitter contention in other lands" and "even denounced . . . us as enemies to the liberties of the republic." (Things had, the bishops noted, "within a few years become more unkind and unjust.")[36]

In the 1820s, a series of salacious novels portrayed Catholic nunneries as dens of sin, fornication, and infanticide. Abolitionist hero Lyman Beecher began railing publicly about plots by Catholics to overthrow the United States. In 1834, these threats turned violent. A mob sacked and burned the Ursuline convent, and armed Americans went about in Massachusetts to guard surviving nuns and their churches. Beecher was unrepentant: It was "treason" to allow American children to be taught by "Jesuits and nuns, educated in Europe, and sustained by the patronage of Catholic powers in arduous conflict for the destruction of liberty." Anti-Catholic riots plagued the United States through the Civil War.[37]

Collectively, the United States saw thirty-five major riots between 1830 and 1860; abolitionists counted 209 discrete examples of racially motivated or anti-abolitionist violence in the same period. In the United States, "the arm of the law," wrote an English visitor, "is feeble in protecting life and property."[38] In 1838, a mob burned down Philadelphia Hall, an abolitionist meeting place. Fire companies refused to put out the blaze. Abraham Lincoln—across the Illinois border from the Saints—warned in 1837 of "the increasing disregard for law which pervades the country—the growing disposition to substitute . . . the worse than savage mobs for the executive ministers of justice." It was, Lincoln wrote, common to all parts of the country.[39]

Missouri had particular jitters. Indian removal policies ignited an open war in Iowa in April 1832. Black Hawk denied the validity of the spurious federal treaties signed with pliant chiefs, and he denounced the federal government's decision to lease Native American lead mines to white Americans. Black Hawk crossed the Mississippi to reoccupy his former tribal lands, and the governor of Illinois called out the militia. While the fighting was largely confined to Illinois and Iowa, the Sauk and Meskwaki (Fox) nations often traveled from Kansas across Missouri, and federal troops marched from Missouri to meet them. Missouri's newspapers passed along reports, rumors, and alarm: "This is no longer a joke," the *Intelligencer* wrote as the Black Hawk War broke out. It would be a "whole season" before "the frontiers [are] left in a safe condition," the article opined, and then repeated a rumor that "Winnebagoes and Potawatomies have become unusually saucy and turbulent," suggesting they

**Destruction by Fire of Pennsylvania Hall,**
On the night of the 17th May, 1838

"Destruction by Fire of Pennsylvania Hall, on the night of the 17th May, 1838." This image of the 1838 burning of the abolitionist hall in Philadelphia pointedly showed fire companies refusing to put out the blaze. The Library Company of Philadelphia

would join Black Hawk's forces. (They did not, nor was it clear what "saucy and turbulent" meant in this context.)[40] Reports of Indian wars and rumors of wars made little effort to calm nerves or stifle panic. "We shall not be surprised to hear any day of massacres on our borders," ranted one Missouri paper.[41] Federal troops travelled from New York to join the fray, but they were struck down by cholera, which they brought west with them. The *St. Louis Beacon* reported that the US troops could do little against Indian forces, despite the "critical situation of things."[42] Little wonder that new militia units were mustered out from Independence; the existing forces were dubbed "insufficient for the protection of our own frontier," especially a frontier now crawling with cholera.[43]

None of this violence stemmed the continued illegal occupation of Indian lands by whites, which continued until the federal government bowed to white demands and opened all Indian territory in Missouri to white settlement.[44]

Anti-Catholic riots, 1844. Days of Catholic-Protestant rioting convulsed Philadelphia in July 1844. Fifteen people were killed and a Catholic church destroyed. Image from John B. Perry, *A Full and Complete Account of the Late Awful Riots in Philadelphia* (Philadelphia, 1844). The Library Company of Philadelphia.

Anti-Mormon writers openly played on this fear, informing readers that Mormons planned to exhort Native Americans to violence; Mormons encouraged Indians, these reports claimed, to "expel the white inhabitants."[45] When E. D. Howe wrote of Mormons combining with Native Americans against Missouri's whites, he suggested that "Gen. Black Hawk" would join them. An eastern newspaper noted that "the same spirit of injustice which impelled the borderers to destroy the property and seize upon the possessions of the Sauk Indians, has now induced a series of attacks upon the unoffending Mormons." Fears of Mormons became attached to anti-Indian rhetoric on a violent frontier crisscrossed by soldiers and refugees.[46]

Missouri was also slave territory, and slavery entailed all sorts of daily violence. The state established slave patrols in 1825, which institutionalized a vigilante corps to hunt down escapees. In Westport, a stone's throw from Independence, Esther Easter recalled seeing a runaway punished, chained in public, and whipped until his body swelled "like a dead horse." Easter's owner reinforced the lesson to her: she could not run away, he said, because of "the whips."[47] Elsewhere in the state, William Greenleaf Eliot saw a young enslaved woman tied by her thumbs, stripped to the waist, and lashed because she would not "'submit to the wishes' of her master," a nineteenth-century euphemism for rape. The violence did not end at the state border; as Flint observed, when escaped slaves reached the free states, "the people amongst whom they seek refuge, do not always show much anxiety that the owners shall recover their property." Therefore, "pursuers of slaves adopt forcible means instead of . . . legal redress," and "peaceful communities are thus invaded by small parties of armed men, who carry off blacks without certifying their right to them."[48]

The slave system necessitated violence and vigilante action in its very operation. Violence could also rise from enslaved communities. In 1831, Nat Turner led a revolt in Southampton, Virginia. Turner saw himself as a prophet who had knowledge of events prior to his birth, saw the Spirit of God and visions, and "wrapped myself in mystery, devoting my time to fasting and prayer." His short-lived rebellion, justified in Turner's words by "the blood of Christ . . . shed on earth," resulted in the death of dozens of Americans—enslaved and free—and ended in a bloody suppression of the enslaved rebels after a three-day siege.[49] In response, the Virginia legislature tightened the state's and masters' control over slaves and instituted strict regulations over what kinds of religious teaching could legally be taught to slaves. The strictures likely did little good in altering the diverse beliefs of enslaved Americans, but the revolt and its aftermath surely spread fears of heterodox religious teachings across America, even all the way to Missouri. Indeed, the very first reference to Mormons coming to Missouri in the *Intelligencer* occurred in the same issue that bore news about Turner's insurrection. As readers read the "horrible tale" of the "savage ferocity of demons in human shape"—Turner's allies—they also read, on the very next page, that the "deluded, insane enthusiasts" of Mormonism were headed to Jackson County.[50] Missourians and Americans of many backgrounds had a stomachful of worries about religion, politics, and violence in 1833.[51]

Mormon settlement began in earnest in July 1831. About one hundred Mormons arrived to settle in Kaw township, outside Independence.[52] By October, some four hundred had arrived; one newspaper described the Mormon settlement as "squalid."[53] Most of these Saints came from Colesville—the same Saints who had already moved from New York to Ohio earlier that year. The Colesville Saints became the first sizable group of Mormons to migrate to Missouri, a place that, Rigdon said, "God by his own commandment has consecrated to him self . . . best adapted, for his children, where Jew and Gentile might dwell together."[54]

Independence had its drawbacks as a homeland. The wind could blow "with a keenness which would almost take the skin off the face." Missouri had deep snows in winter, which meant that spring left "the whole country . . . inundated with mud and water."[55] By 1831, the town had around twenty houses, a courthouse, and a few stores; it served as the eastern terminus of the Santa Fe trail, the major trade route between the United States and Mexico. Independence was also home to a few "pale-faced invalids" seeking the "sanative effects" of the prairie to cure long-term disease.[56] West of the town, American carriage roads ceased and "one deep black trail only" extended into the plains, all the way to Santa Fe.[57] Washington Irving, on a visit, described Independence farmers as leading "a lazy life in this easily cultivated & Prolific country." Venison, turkey, squirrel, crabapple, pawpaw, and honey were plentiful wild foodstuffs. The northern section of Jackson County was heavily wooded, while the plains stretched away to the south, coated in sagebrush and peavine.[58]

Several church leaders, including Smith, Rigdon, and Harris, arrived alongside the Colesvillians. They dedicated a spot for a temple to the Lord and began construction of houses. On August 4, the Saints had their first conference in Missouri, and in Whitmer's words, "rejoiced together upon the land of Zion."[59] For Mormons of the 1830s, the land dedicated for this first temple would not be known as Independence, or Kaw, or even Missouri. It was Zion— the promised land. When Reynolds Cahoon arrived, his "eyes beheld grate and marvelous things such as my eyes never even contemplated of seeing in this world."[60] Simeon Crandel traveled there in 1832 with the "intention to Settle for life."[61] Phoebe Lott told her sister that God had "brought her safely to this land where I shall spend the remainder of my days."[62]

Neither Crandel nor Lott managed to live out their intentions, but the Saints clearly had big plans for Independence. In a July 1831 revelation, God named it "the land which I have appointed and consecrated for the gathering of the saints . . . the land of promise, and the place for the city of Zion." Independence itself was "the center place," and God ordered the Saints to raise a temple "not far from the courthouse." The Mormons purchased the land from Jones Flournoy, who later became a leader of the anti-Mormon mobs.[63] Smith and Cowdery laid a cornerstone on the spot, though they did not have the resources to begin building. Nevertheless, Hiram Rathbun recalled that the enthusiasm for the location was such that Independence Saints held religious meetings in the lot's uncleared woods, weather permitting.[64]

Mormons revamped the landscape of Independence in other ways. In 1832, William W. Phelps began publishing a Mormon newspaper there—the *Evening and Morning Star*. He printed biblical exegeses, revelations received by Smith, and occasional odds and ends. Mormons constructed a two-story printing house near the courthouse, a "building belonging to our people occupied as a dwelling house and a Printing Office," as one Mormon widow described it.[65] By June 1833, the church presidency had designed the "Plat of the City of Zion"—an urban plan for a holy city that divided the town of Independence into lots, with farmland on the periphery. Mormons would live in the center of town—where the temples and meetinghouses would be—and head out to their farms in the hinterlands. The Missouri Mormons revised the plan soon after, but they too sought to have an equitable distribution of access to farmlands, schools, and worship. The Saints seemed to have expansive dreams for Missouri.[66]

Ezra Booth had the opposite reaction to Independence; his experiences in Missouri ushered him out of the church. A former Methodist minister, Booth joined the Latter-day Saints in May 1831 and left by September. Booth sought out supernatural proofs and hurried to Missouri expecting Saints to be speaking in tongues and "communicating to the Indians in their own dialect." Booth arrived in Independence and heard Saints speaking only in English. He wrote that Smith had prophesied that "a large church" would already be built in Missouri; when Booth arrived, he found the mighty church consisted of only "four females." Booth took that to mean "*prophecy* and *vision* had failed." He found the temple to consist of a simple stone for the cornerstone and a shrub oak laid on top of it, "the first stone and stick" of the "splendid city of Zion." And the church conference he attended there dealt not with mighty matters but only with the sexual indiscretions of one elder. Booth was not impressed.[67]

Yet over the same few months in 1831, as Booth lost his faith, John Whitmer found "many mighty miracles were wrought by the Elders" in Ohio. Whitmer himself healed an old woman, who then joined the church.[68] It was not that Booth somehow missed these miracles. Rather, he ceased to believe in miracles as a source of religious truth or authority; he replaced his earlier trust in miracles as a sign of the true church with a belief in consistency as that sign. He condemned Smith and Cowdery as inconsistent; they would, Booth wrote, "turn and twist the commandments to suit their whims."[69]

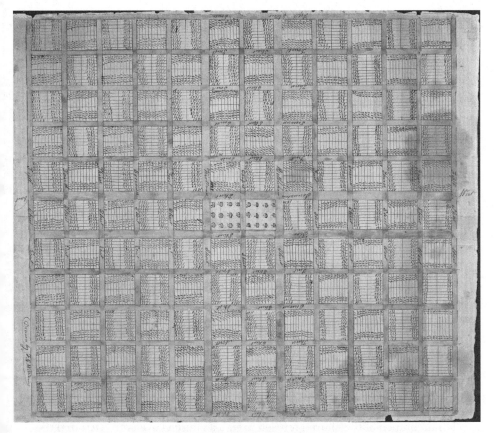

"Plat of the City of Zion." An idealized Mormon view of Independence's future as a holy city. Some of these urban designs would be brought to fruition in Mormon Utah. Church History Library, Salt Lake City

Booth was particularly irked when a divine commandment to take a boat to St. Louis was superseded by a commandment to travel by land. Booth disregarded the second commandment and took the boat. When nothing untoward happened, he wondered whether Smith was really a man "to whom the Lord has intrusted the mysteries, and the keys of his kingdom?" Booth answered no: God did not change his mind but was instead "a God of consistency and wisdom."[70] Booth swung back to Methodism; like many American Christians in the sectarian sea, he moved from shore to shore.

When the Saints returned to Ohio, Booth confronted Smith with his concerns. Records of that meeting do not survive, but by September, Booth had publicly renounced Mormonism at another sectarian event—a camp meeting—in Shalersville, Ohio.[71] If there were Mormons abroad on the frontier who expected "a desire for spiritual gifts," in the words of historian Richard L. Bushman, there were also Mormons who lost that desire.[72]

The disaffection spread. In Missouri, Booth's concerns resurfaced in the anxieties of Edward Partridge, Mormon bishop of Independence. Booth wrote an open letter to Partridge recalling a shared frustration: "You complained that he [Smith] had abused you." Booth reminded Partridge of his own struggles with Smith's prophecies; Partridge had apparently once told Smith "not to tell us any more, that you know . . . by the spirit when you do not.'"[73] Partridge too may have wondered whether consistency superseded prophecy. A September revelation condemned both Partridge and Booth, though Partridge received forgiveness.[74] The bishop remained a faithful Saint the rest of his days.

Others did not. The fledgling Missouri branch of the church "silenced" several members. Whitmer recalled those days as having "much trouble and unbelief among those who call themselves disciples of Christ: Some apostatized, and became enemies to the cause of God."[75] Edson Fuller and William Carter were "silenced from holding the office of Elders" on September 1, 1831; Fuller seems to have remained for a while, but both men eventually denied the faith.[76] A few days later, in Ohio, four more members (including Booth) were silenced.[77] Reynolds Cahoon visited branches outside Kirtland and found again "the church lifted their hands against some members." In April 1832, the Hiram branch of the church refused to sign a church covenant.[78] Around the same time, McLellin's faith foundered as he wondered in midwinter whether his call to preach had come from heaven or from earth and he "determined to cease proclaiming until I was satisfied in my own mind."[79]

Unusually detailed minutes of an October 1831 conference of elders recorded how some average Mormons confronted the tide of apostasy. Simeon Carter said he "mourned because of the falling away since he took his journey to the land of Zion"; Major Ashley's "greatest fear was for those who were weak in the faith."[80] Ashley himself was later excommunicated. One month later came the hubbub over the Book of Commandments. Disaffection was in the air; Booth speculated that it grew out of the efforts of Laura Hubbell earlier that year: "the barbed arrow which she left in the hearts of some, is not yet eradicated."[81]

It is possible that the dissents of Hubbell and Booth merged to form this particular uprising within Mormonism; it is also possible that dissent and rumors of dissent shaped the contest between Smith and McLellin to produce a revelation in November 1831. On the other hand, claiming the right to receive revelations or independent confirmation of the right to teach was endemic to a Mormon movement that solved sectarianism through appeal to personal experience and revelation. The rising and falling of new prophets, or the rejection of old ones (including, in Booth's case, Smith himself), were always roiling the Saints. In 1833, a Mormon with the unlikely name of Broth Lake returned to Kirtland "professing to have received revelations." The Kirtland Council "unanimously agreed that said Lake was under the influence of an evil spirit" and revoked his preaching license.[82] In December 1832, Thomas Mils was "preaching much" and issuing prophecies of his own. He was "silenced" by the Missouri Council and told "if he would still persist in his foolish doctrine to withdraw from the Church and save us the trouble of excommunicating him from the same, which he did."[83] Schisms, and dealing with schisms, were standard for early Mormonism.

Ezra Booth thus did not create the dissent within the church, but he certainly added to the clamor surrounding it. In 1831, Booth wrote nine letters to the local newspaper, the *Ohio Star*, accusing the Mormons and the prophet Joseph Smith of purveying a false Christianity.[84] Booth included myriad details of the Missouri trip that cost him his faith, but he framed his story as a political argument. Saints, Booth wrote, really wanted temporal dominion: "the establishment of a society in Missouri, over which the contrivers of this delusive system, are to possess unlimited and despotic sway." The threat was political as well as religious.[85]

It was not the first anti-Mormon harangue to be published, but it was the first from a former member, and that likely gave weight to Booth's words, even when Booth was reporting rumor and hearsay. At the very least, Booth related events not recorded in other Mormon sources, including the claims that Smith had a revelation for the church to give him a thousand dollars and that the church tried and failed to resurrect a dead child.[86] Booth explicitly wrote that he took his information from reliable sources or from his own experience. He did not deliberately lie, but he may have passed along urban legends, hoaxes, and frauds. Just as with modern social media, exaggerations and rumors circulated freely in the newspapers and conversations of the frontier, with similarly caustic effects on discourse and political behavior.

How did rumor spread in the world of newspapers and frontier tales of the 1830s? Booth's letters to the *Star* first appeared in October 1831. Just a few months after the letters were printed, Mormon preacher Reynolds Cahoon heard "the discussion of Booths letters" in response to his preaching.[87] Smith and Cowdery began a preaching tour in December 1831 specifically to respond to the letters. In 1832, an Ohio resident sent a copy of Booth's letters to his relatives back east to educate them about the Mormons. He added his own opinion of the Mormons: "Their god is the Devil."[88] A report of Booth's letters on the "diabolical pretensions and impositions" of Mormonism was printed by the *New York Baptist Register*, which was then borrowed and reprinted for readers in eastern Missouri by the *St. Louis Beacon*.[89]

Booth's letters were reprinted in E. D. Howe's 1834 *Mormonism Unvailed*, the same book that mercilessly lampooned the Book of Mormon. *Unvailed* took root among preachers and everyday Americans. Lorenzo Barnes's 1836 missionary tour had trouble near Youngstown where he discovered "the book Mormonism unveiled & found that many of the people in the place were making a refuge of it to hide themselves under."[90] When Parley Pratt heard a New Englander spouting lies about Mormons, he "told him that I was astonished that people should be led away with such strange stuff." The man responded, "if you will get the anti-Mormon book, it will tell you all about them."[91]

Rumors and reports could take a darker turn. Joseph Antrim wrote from Illinois in 1832 that "we have a new sort of people in our Country who call themselves Mormonites" and who intended "to build a new Jerusalem away out in the plains. . . . It is suspected that their new Jerusalem is a fort & they themselves are british spies." He also wrote that he had heard that the Mormons had boxes and coffins full of guns and planned to arm and support Native Americans in an uprising. Antrim explained that he thought the news about the guns was not a fact, and yet he wrote it was "too true to be made a Joke of."[92] In 1833, the same story cropped up in Illinois and Ohio. W. W. Phelps had to explicitly declare in the *Evening and Morning Star* that "no coffins filled with arms and ammunition have arrived" in Independence.[93] Evan Green was stopped and searched in 1833 by authorities "calling us impostors, counterfeiters, pick pockets &c."[94] Arms, ammunition, and Indian uprisings were associated with Mormons by 1832. These rumors reinforced Booth's charge that Mormons sought "despotic sway."

The Mormons did own some firearms; they were not pacifists. And if Mormons never tried to resurrect a dead child, they did claim many other miraculous feats that Booth recorded. So begins rumor: a cache of items related to facts and in keeping with general notions and widely held suspicions that imports nonspecific claims, usually intended to produce outrage or fear. Indeed, rumors are often believed because they match expectations better than reality. (Reality has a habit of defying stereotypes.) The collapse of Gentile-Mormon relations in Missouri has many causes, but the collection of rumors deployed about the Saints on the tense frontier of 1833 has to be one of them.

People also spread rumors deliberately. Baptist minister Benton Pixley had been fulminating about his Mormon neighbors in Independence. He wrote several letters to newspapers, and his words were reprinted from Missouri to Massachusetts, lambasting Saints' accounts of miracles. To make sure his Jackson County neighbors got the point, Pixley physically went from house to house "to incense the inhabitants against the church to mob them and drive them away." Indeed, John Greene pointed to the clergy as instigating trouble through both "the press and the pulpit."[95] Individuals raised the alarm about the new religion, as when Pixley wrote that Mormons were liars or at least rumormongers: "Miracles . . . are not *seen* to be done, but only *said* to be done." Pixley added a number of other theological objections, claiming that Mormons rejected the Bible, that they conversed with angels, and that they were in general the kind of "false Christs and false Prophets" whom good Protestants could expect in the latter days. Pixley shared one of his own half-heard claims— that Mormons claimed to know the location of the Ark of the Covenant and a "Pot of Manna"—and this rumor got reprinted across American newspapers.[96] Mormons were made up of "people of every sect and kind, Shakers, Baptists, Methodists, Presbyterians, and Campbellites, and some have been of two or three of these different sects." Such heterogeneity "must at length produce an explosion," he wrote. Pixley would later play a significant role in the mobbing of the Mormons, but he would lay exclusive blame for their fate at the feet of the Saints.[97]

In January 1832, Missouri's Saints did not yet know how these conflicts would work out, but they were trying to make the best of their situation. They had purchased more than a thousand acres of land at the junction of Brush Creek and Blue River, where they spent a miserable first winter.[98] "Provisions are scarce & dear," wrote one Mormon. They had not opened their own store, and goods therefore cost "nearly double what they were a year ago." Nor were the Missouri Saints prepared for more brethren to arrive: "We are not in a situation," Partridge informed Kirtland, to even purchase "provisions & cows for those who are coming."[99] Phoebe Lott called her life in Missouri "days of rejoicing and also days of mourning."[100] Movement of Mormons to Missouri in these years was haphazard; Smith had authority (by revelation) to determine who would go to Independence and who would stay in Kirtland, but in practice Mormons moved as they wished. The Mormons at Kaw requested skilled laborers in January 1832; six months later, they wanted all migration to stop. The *Evening and Morning Star* asked that all those who wished to emigrate first procure recommendations from the bishop of Ohio or Zion, for the new settlement was already "labor[ing] under many disadvantages."[101]

Mormons also sought to implement the law of consecration in both Missouri and Ohio, pledging money collectively to the bishop, who then redistributed the money in the spirit of the Book of Acts. Smith ordained Jesse Gause (the former Shaker) to high office in the church, perhaps because his experience in a collective utopian community would help them achieve their goals.[102] Under the law of consecration—also called the United Order, Order of Enoch, and other names—Saints pledged their goods to the bishop but received some or all of those goods back. The Saints then became trustees rather than owners, and in this way, the Mormons managed to develop a communitarian movement without collective ownership.

Establishing the order was not easy. The tiny Mormon community of Richmond, Indiana, nearly split over differing interpretations of Acts 5; Cowdery and John Whitmer spent over a week working out these differences among the faithful and succeeded only "with much caviling."[103] A Mormon named Bates sued to get his money back; the court sided with Bates. Baptist minister Pixley passed along the rumor that "several other members are ready to make similar demands upon the good bishop."[104] By the start of 1832, Partridge and the Missouri Saints began to get snippy about money, especially regarding the payment of expenses for leaders traveling from one enclave to another.[105] Partridge and Rigdon had a falling out over church funds; Partridge and Smith clashed over lands purchased in Missouri.[106]

Critics seized on the United Order. Howe wrote that it was proof that Smith was "robbing them [Mormons] of their worldly possessions."[107] The *Christian Watchman* similarly predicted "some feeling and some dissention" from the effort.[108] Critiques of the Order merged with Booth's concerns about authoritarianism. Booth flippantly suggested that "should any refuse [to contribute], they are sure to be hung for rebellion."[109] Here again was the language of tyranny: Mormons (according to their critics) *hanged*, rather than *expelled*, the disobedient. In fact, not all Mormons in Independence chose to participate in the United Order; some purchased their lots privately.[110] Others simply lost interest—including Gause, who was supposed to run the thing. It's not clear why Gause left—he simply walked away during a mission trip—but clearly he felt no real concern about the United Order.[111]

In January 1832, the Missouri conference attempted to heal the breach between Partridge and Rigdon. The Missourians suggested Partridge write "a friendly humiliating letter advising that this difficulty be settled and thereby the wound in the Church be healed."[112] The letter was composed and sent. In response, Rigdon brought the Zion branch up on ecclesiastical charges.

Then, in March 1832, the Kirtland mob attacked Rigdon and Smith. Independence became a refuge for both men, and the contending parties took a deep breath. Partridge convened a council in which "all differences [were] settled & the hearts of all run together in love."[113] Phoebe Lott described the visit of Smith and Rigdon as a time of "joyful meetings" with "many mysteries unfolded . . . which gave me great consolation."[114] By July 1832, however, Smith (back in Ohio) was fuming at the Missouri branch, condemning their "unorganized & confused state" and the "neglect of duty" they had shown. Smith wrote that he had gone to Missouri, "leaving our families in affliction amidst of death upon the mercy of mobs," but found the Missouri Mormons all too ready to criticize him after his visit: "raking up every fault . . . bringing up those things that had been settled & forgiven & which they dare not bring to our faces."[115] Letters described a spirit "like a pestilence" in Zion. Smith saw a "conspiricy" among the Missouri Saints.[116] For their part, the Zion branch chastised Oliver Cowdery in council and accused "Bro Joseph in rather an indirect way of seeking Monarch[ic]al power." Phelps wrote to Smith with a "*lightness* of spirit" that did not play well in Kirtland; Sidney Gilbert wrote to Kirtland with "low, dark, & blind insinuations." Smith in turn blamed Zion for its "sensorious spirit."[117]

As these troubles brewed, Sidney Rigdon complicated things by bursting into a prayer meeting at Kirtland and declaring that "the keys of the kingdom are rent from the church." He also apparently said that the keys would not be restored until the Saints built him a new house. Neither claim was true—or at least, no other Saints had heard such messages from God or any other source. Rigdon had to be suspended from leadership for a short time.[118]

In January 1833, Smith offered Phelps "an Olieve leaf" but also warned him to "repent, repent . . . lest Zion fall." The Missouri Saints, Smith wrote, had hard feelings toward their Kirtland brethren, but for Smith that was secondary: "The Lord approves of us & has accepted us & established his name in

Kirtland." This letter came just a week after a revelation declared that Mormons must build a temple to the Lord in Kirtland—meaning that the planned temple in Missouri was *not* going to be built for some time, no matter how many Saints went there. The icy state of relations between Ohio and Missouri seems clear.[119]

These kinds of internal religious conflicts were not unusual in antebellum American religion, especially among the new sects. Among the Shakers of Ohio, for example, a leadership struggle in 1839 led to the brief expulsion of Richard McNemar, leading theologian and perhaps the most prominent Cane Ridge revivalist. Charles Grandison Finney became the most famous revivalist across upstate New York—but, though nominally a Presbyterian, he publicly admitted he could not name any points of their doctrine. Jemima Wilkinson never officially designated a successor to the Wilkinsonian church or their community of around four hundred in upstate New York, so when Wilkinson died in 1819, legal arguments over land and leadership helped scuttle the movement.[120] American church members, already prone to sectarianism and division, often spent as much time fighting one another as they did fighting the devil. If the idea of an Edenic age of Mormonism when the Saints all got along and dutifully followed Smith without question is mostly an illusion, then Saints can at least take comfort that almost no American religion ever had any such a golden age.

Still, the internal strains of 1832–33 came at a bad time. Anti-Mormon feeling had grown among some Gentile neighbors. Josiah Gregg believed relations soured because of the "immorality of their [Mormons'] lives" and because the Mormons published "a little paper" (the *Evening and Morning Star*) that exacerbated tensions.[121] Alexander Majors, another Gentile resident, recalled that "their church literature . . . was very distasteful to the members and leaders of other religious denominations."[122] Emily Austin recalled hearing when she was a teenager "that the inhabitants of Jackson county were displeased at the idea of so many coming into the county . . . and they boldly declared they would not suffer this to be so."[123] Isaac McCoy noted a more concrete problem: cholera had broken out in Independence in the summer of 1832, and McCoy heard that Mormons thought the disease "was for the destruction of the wicked, whilst they, the righteous, would escape."[124]

The anti-Mormon animus was undoubtedly pushed forward as well by specific actors; Pixley and others were circulating and writing their anti-Mormon letters and openly calling for the expulsion of Mormons.[125] The crisis may have evolved not from Mormon behavior but from the specific work of anti-Mormons spreading panic and advertising expulsion as a reasonable alternative. Neither hatred nor respect are naturally occurring materials; each can be built or forced upon populations by individuals.

Indeed, even before the cholera outbreak, in March 1832, local Gentiles "held a council in Independence" to discuss evicting the Mormons or, as they put it, "this tribe of locusts." The council was convened by those "very desirous to expel our people," but at this particular meeting, John Corrill noted, other Gentiles attended "with a view to prevent any violent or unlawful acts being committed."[126] American officials managed to break up the meeting, but over the next few months, Mormons houses were stoned in the night and haystacks set on fire. Truman Brace was accosted and threatened with death for believing in the Book of Mormon.[127]

Even so, Mormons held out hope. "Though often persecuted and vilified for the difference in religious opinions . . . they fondly looked forward to a future big with hope," wrote Elias Higbee. He had arrived in Jackson County in 1833, and believed that "the prejudice existing against" Mormons would eventually fade.[128] Another Mormon "lived in peace" with his Gentile neighbors before the summer of 1833.[129] On April 6, 1833, the Missouri Mormons held a public celebration of the anniversary of their church's founding. That same month, anti-Mormons held another mass meeting to discuss a response to the Mormons, but it again broke up with no resolution.[130]

The third time was the charm: Jackson County anti-Mormons met in early July 1833 and formed a "secret constitution" among themselves to revoke, on their own authority, the Mormons' right to live in the county. On July 20, they wrote their demands for Mormons to leave peaceably if they could and forcibly if they must. Hundreds of citizens signed it, then sent it on to Mormon leaders. No officials dispersed the meeting; indeed, several elected officials joined it.[131]

The Saints came to call the petition the "Mob Manifesto," and the anti-Mormons intended it for a wide readership: "to lay before the public," they wrote, "an exposé of our peculiar situation, in regard to this singular sect of pretended Christians, and a solemn declaration of our unalterable determination to amend it." The petition aimed to be a statement of public opinion, a primer on true Christianity, and a threat, all at the same time. It was here they aped the Declaration of Independence in pledging "lives, fortunes, and sacred honors" to the task of removing the Mormons, and like the Declaration, the petition listed the purported crimes of their enemies. Mormons were "the very dregs" of Ohio and New York, "lazy, Idle, & Vicious"; they "have been taught to believe that our lands are to be taken from us by the sword." They "swear that they have wrought miracles and supernatural cures," give "pretended revelations from Heaven," and speak "contemptible gibberish with which they habitually profane the Sabbath and which they dignify" as "unknown tongues." Worst of all, however, Mormon "numbers are increasing beyond every rational calculation," and therefore "the day is not far distant, when the government of the county shall be in their hands. When the Sheriff, the Justices, and the county Judges will be Mormons," such officials would destroy the rights of non-Mormons, and a "stench both physical and moral . . . would attend the civil rule of these fanatics."[132]

The Mob Manifesto also made a series of demands. The Mormons in Jackson County must leave. No new Mormons were to arrive. The *Evening and Morning Star* must cease publication. If Missouri's Mormons failed to meet these demands, the Manifesto claimed, they could consult "those of their brethren who have the gift of divination, and of unknown tongues to inform them of the lot that awaits them." The anti-Mormons were threatening violence, and possibly death, without saying so directly.

It is a haunting document. Historians have spent many pages discussing the motives behind it. Often, historians held the Mormons "partly responsible for causing . . . the suspicions and prejudice against them" through claims that God had brought them to Independence and that they would eventually own all the land there.[133] Other historians pointed to the Manifesto's references to slavery, and slave owners' fears that Saints intended to advocate for abolitionism within Missouri. The July 1833 edition of the *Evening and Morning Star* had included a vague message intended to "prevent any misunderstanding among the churches abroad, respecting Free people of color, who may think of coming to the western boundaries of Missouri." Phelps then quoted from Missouri's draconian legal code regarding free Blacks, specifically the laws that made it virtually impossible for free African Americans to settle in the state. Phelps emphasized to Mormon readers that "slaves are real estate." Therefore, "so long as we have no special rule in the church, as to people of color," Phelps wrote, "let prudence guide."[134] It was less an invitation than a warning against Black Mormons ever coming to Zion.

The notion that Saints were abolitionists usually requires historians to assume that, because most Mormons were northerners, they were therefore abolitionists. That is not the case, and indeed, there appears to be little evidence that any abolitionist activity took place among the Independence Saints. Indeed, Phelps's article in the *Star* had essentially said that Black Mormons should not come to Missouri.

The Mob Manifesto made much of this article. The Gentiles accused the *Star* of encouraging both slave revolt and interracial sex—raising the specter of Nat Turner and of the great taboo in antebellum white society (which was nevertheless not uncommon). "We are not prepared," the document insisted, "to receive into the bosom of our families, as fit companions for our wives and daughters, the degraded and corrupted free negroes and mulattoes that are now invited to settle among us." The Manifesto's claim that the *Star* had explicitly invited free African Americans from Illinois into Jackson County was patently untrue.

Indeed, Phelps rushed out an "extra" to the *Star* shortly after publication of the July issue; the extra used language nearly as racist as the Manifesto itself. Phelps wrote that Mormons *feared* that "blacks should rise and spill innocent blood." African Americans were "ignorant, and a little may lead them to disturb the peace of society." Based on this assumption, Phelps promised that Mormons "are opposed to have free people of color admitted to the state; and we say, that none will be admitted into the church." Here, Phelps was winging it; African Americans like Peter and Elijah Abel had been admitted to the church and even risen to prominence. Phelps either did not know or did not care about the actual approach to race within the developing church—an approach that in any case had not solidified in 1833.

William Phelps also called for solidarity between white Mormons and white Gentiles: "Amid a dense population of blacks . . . the life of every white is in danger." He claimed that all white Mormons feared an insurrection of "jealous and ignorant slaves." Phelps then promoted his own rumors about interracial rape, claiming to have heard from a friend that the mob had sent slaves to attack Mormon women: "There would be one or more negroes sent to molest his daughters," he wrote. (Again, Phelps's story implied that the slaves had been *ordered* by white owners to attack white Mormon women at a specific time.)[135] John Corrill blamed some of the Gentiles for accepting the testimony of an enslaved man in crafting their rumor.[136]

Mormonism's relationship with African Americans, as it existed in the print and rhetorical wars of 1833, was mostly about rumor, prejudice, and fearmongering. The Mob Manifesto mentioned slaveholding as a reason to fear

Mormons, interracial sex as a reason to fear Mormons, and slave revolts as reason to fear Mormons—each of these reasons once in the document. These were less coherent arguments than they were repetitions of rumors designed to stoke fear.[137] Newel Knight summarized the July 1833 meeting by noting that "all kinds of strange stories were set afloat."[138]

The Manifesto contained another central argument that anti-Mormons mentioned repeatedly and that drove all the other rumors and hints: Mormon religion was wrong and Mormons were deluded, and therefore they could not be trusted with the government. "What would be the fate of our lives and property, in the hands of jurors and witnesses who do not blush to declare . . . that they have wrought miracles and supernatural cures?"[139] Mormons were weaklings led by "the arts of a few designing leaders." They "blaspheme the Most High God"; they were "fanatics," "knaves," and "members of a pretended religious sect." Josiah Gregg repeated the Manifesto's main point: "At the rate the intruders were increasing, they would soon be able to command a majority . . . the entire control of affairs would fall into their hands."[140] In November 1833, Pixley again listed Mormon crimes as desiring to possess land, inviting free Blacks to join their church, and "their pretended power to work miracles and speak with tongues."[141] Approximately five hundred Gentiles were telling approximately twelve hundred Saints that they could not both believe in miracles and live in Jackson County.

The Mob Manifesto crawled out from the tension between democracy and power. In a democracy, the majority is supposed to rule. But can the majority, once in power, make rules and provisions that maintain its rule at the expense of the minority? Rumors about race and violence obviously fed the fire in 1833 Jackson County; it's also clear that the anti-Mormons of Jackson County had to try several times to get a manifesto signed—likely a sign that their support was not truly that deep. But anti-Mormons kept returning to a point echoed throughout anti-Mormon literature from across the country: certain beliefs were dangerous to a democracy. To believe in tongues, prophecy, or modern miracles was to be inherently untrustworthy and, therefore, a threat to a republic. The Manifesto repeatedly distinguished between "citizens" and "Mormons." Mormons simply did not count, and if the Mormons were so brash as to try to defend their rights, they would suffer for it. Mormon Chapman Duncan wrote that the trouble came in July because "a few brethren voted at the election."[142] If so, then the attempt by Mormons to act as citizens (which they were) proved to be the tipping point that allowed the anti-Mormons to publicize their resolution undaunted. The Jackson County mob instituted a tactic common among enemies of democracy: they redefined citizenship to exclude those with whom they disagreed. In modern times, these attacks usually come through spurious legal changes and loopholes. In 1833, it was an open threat of a massacre. Democracy had to be scuttled in the name of the people.

The Mob Manifesto was delivered to Partridge, Phelps, and others on July 20. They "declined giving any direct answers" and asked instead for three months to consult with the Mormons in Independence and Kirtland. The mob told them they could have fifteen minutes. At that point, Phelps remembered drily, "the conversation broke up."[143] The mob then took a vote and decided to act. They "proceeded at once to raze the obnoxious printing establishment to the ground," Gregg later wrote, chuckling as Partridge and some others "were treated to a clean suit of 'tar and feathers.'"[144] (Gregg's father, Harmon, was one of the Gentile "negotiators."[145]) As with many American lynchings, this one took place in front of the courthouse; as the mobbers applied the tar, they asked the men to renounce their faith.[146] Phelps recalled an old Protestant declaring, "The people of Jackson can stand any thing but men who profess to see angels, and to believe the Book of Mormon."[147] Two Saints were tarred and feathered but did not renounce their faith. The printing office of the *Star* was torn down and its type strewn in the street. An effort was made to sack Sidney Gilbert's store, but he managed to convince the Gentiles "to let it stand until Tuesday next," when he would pack his goods and go.[148]

"Tuesday arrived," Whitmer wrote, "and death and destruction stared us in the face." It seemed as if the "whole County turned out," armed with firearms, clubs, and a red flag. They rode through the town screaming and declared their intention to whip the Mormons, destroy their houses, and ruin their crops.[149] The mob "determined to massacre us unless we agreed to leave the County immediately." Led by Moses Wilson, a veteran of the Black Hawk War, the mob surrounded Partridge and other Mormon leaders, who somehow kept cool under pressure. Phelps reported that the mob meant to "gratify their wantonness upon innocent mothers and virgins! For this was their last threat."[150] According to Cowdery, this demand broke the Saint leadership's will to resist. Mormon leaders, under threat of death, signed a statement promising that most of the leadership would leave the county before the year's end and would "use all their influence" to convince the other Mormons to leave:

"One half, say, by the first of January next, and all by the first day of April next."[151] The contract satisfied the Gentiles. It also gave the Mormons time to mount some kind of response.

Saints desperately called for aid from what they considered the most likely source of help: heaven. "Marvelous to tell in the midst of all the rage . . . God is pouring out his Spirit upon his people," the Kirtland Saints wrote to Cowdery. On July 25, a surfeit of Saints in Independence "received the gift of tongues & spake & prophesied," while at Kaw township, "everyone who is a saint or nearly so . . . speaks in tongues." Divine signs of the true church in the wake of the mob likely reinforced the faith of most of the Missouri Mormons. In some ways it could be seen as an act of defiance; if Americans would not trust them because they were "so deluded as to speak in tongues," the Mormons would continue to speak in tongues.[152]

Of course not all of the Saints stood firm; the Mormon problem with apostasy continued. Whitmer explained to Smith that "very few . . . have denied the faith in consequence" of the mob attacks—which of course meant that some *did* leave as a result. On the whole, however, the mob activity did little to dissuade the Mormons. Indeed, some seemed to want more than just signs from God. "Our daily cry to God," Whitmer wrote, "is deliver thy people from the hand of our enemies, send thy destroying angels."[153] (It was not the first time Mormons discussed destroying angels marching on Zion; in May 1833, Phelps reminded Saints to "walk perfectly, so that when the destroying angel goes through, he may pass over them and not slay them.")[154]

In Kirtland, Smith took a more conciliatory tone. Writing to the Independence Mormons on August 10, he instructed them to find somewhere else to go. Another "place of beginning will be no injury to Zion in the end," he wrote. As for "the compromise to remove . . . there was no other way to save the lives of all the church in Zion." God was "well pleased with that act." Smith initially saw the trouble in Zion as an outgrowth of the problem of dissent: "This great tribulation would not have come upon Zion had it not been for rebellion." As for dissenters, let the "brethren purge them out. . . . It was necessary that these things should come upon us," for "there was no other way to cleanse the church."[155]

Eight days later, Smith discovered that mob mentality was contagious. News of the riot in Independence reached Ohio newspapers by August 9, and local anti-Mormons caught the bug and began to harass the Saints. "Since the intelligence of the Calamity of Zion has reached the ears of the wicked there is no safety for us here," Smith wrote to Partridge; "every man has to watch their houses every night to keep off the Mobbers." Smith felt as though all of Pharaoh's armies had massed against him; "we are no safer here in Kirtland then you are in Zion."[156] Indeed, "we know not how soon they may be permitted to follow the example of the Missourians."[157]

Yet another apostate was leading the Ohio charge. Doctor Hurlbut ("Doctor" was his first name) had spent only a few months as a Mormon before his expulsion. Like Ezra Booth, he led a crusade against his former faith. Unlike Booth, Hurlbut used more than just words. "People are running after him and giving him money to break down Mormonism," Smith wrote, "which much endangers our lives at present." Smith ultimately took Hurlbut to court when the ex-Saint publicly threatened to kill him. In the meantime, Smith had to post guards in Kirtland.[158] With danger in both Mormon strongholds, Smith advised the Missouri Saints to stay put, relaunch the *Star*, and avoid violence: "If our kingdom were of this world then we would fight but our weapons are not carnal." If any Saints did leave, he told them, "make a show" of it—possibly hoping to convince Gentiles their threats had worked and Mormons were leaving. Then, while the Gentiles were pacified, Mormons would have time to get help.[159]

This approach had mixed success. The mobs stayed away for two months, but constant reminders and threats pockmarked Mormon lives. Mormon houses were broken into and Mormon residents threatened. When a contingent of Saints actually made plans to move south to Van Buren County, Gentiles there threatened to shoot their livestock.[160] A neighbor encountering David Pettigrew working his farm said, "Mr. Pettigrew, you are at work as though you intended to remain here." Pettigrew acknowledged he planned to stay, and his neighbor told him, "We are determined to drive you away."[161]

By October the charade was over. Some Mormons never accepted the July agreement, given that it had essentially been signed at gunpoint. The Saints hired lawyers and wrote to the governor, Daniel Dunklin, asking for help from the state militia to defend Mormon "rights, privileges, immunities, and religion."[162] Dunklin dithered. He advised the Mormons to seek redress through the courts, but word that the Mormons did not plan to leave had already gotten out, and in the words of Chapman Duncan, "soon the people of the county gathered in a mob, and anarchy reigned."[163]

Isaac McCoy related that rumors abounded in Independence that fall; Mormons "became strongly suspected of secretly tampering with the neighboring Indians" to form a military alliance. McCoy himself "could not resist the belief," though he had no "legal evidence of that fact." He also heard of a conspiracy "formed by several Mormons to kill one of the citizens." Again, he had no proof. He did know, however, that Gentiles had increased their threats "to throw down houses, to whip their leaders, and to apply tar and feathers." Then, without irony, he condemned the Mormons for arming themselves and threatening violent retaliation.[164] Pixley also wrote in the papers that Mormon efforts to defend themselves were a sign of tyranny and bad faith; he was mostly silent on the Gentile efforts that provoked such behavior, blaming the riots on "the more wild and ungovernable among us." Pixley, the author of numerous anti-Mormon sermons and letters, took no personal responsibility.[165]

The Mormons *had* armed themselves and, on October 20, declared their intent to defend their homes. As Gentile threats and brickbatting continued, the fragile peace collapsed. "From the 31st of October until the 4th of November, there was one continual scene of outrages," Knight wrote. Gentiles ransacked houses, collapsed roofs, and threw stones. A host of Gentiles descended on Mormons in their fields. Gunfire began to accompany the mobs and militias, though each side claimed the other fired first.[166] Emily Austin's family were held at gunpoint while their home was wrecked around them. Lydia English watched her husband die slowly; "being wounded by the Mob in Jackson Co the exposures & hardships were too much for his feeble constitution . . . he died in Oct following the pain & distress of his body as well as mind."[167] Mormons detained Richard McCarty for hurling stones at Gilbert's store; when released, McCarty got the local judge to arrest the Mormons for wrongful imprisonment. Thus, John Corrill wrote, "we could not obtain a warrant against him for breaching open the store, yet he had gotten one for us by catching him at it."[168]

Somehow, no one was killed until November 4. On that day, rumors swirled among Gentiles that Mormons were seeking to have a battle; another rumor circulating that day was that "the Mormons have riz and have killed six men."[169] These "floating stories" may have brought the mob to the Mormon settlement at Blue River, where they commenced another attack on Mormon homes. This time, about thirty Mormons responded, with eleven firearms among them and the rest wielding "pitch forks &c." By the time the Mormons arrived, however, the Gentile mob had left. Mormons turned back. Then news reached the mob that the Mormons had shown up at Blue River, and the ad hoc militia immediately returned to look for them.[170]

The two forces ran into each other in one of the Whitmers' cornfields, flanked by single-story long houses and the woods.[171] "A firing of guns commenced," wrote Corrill, "they say, by our men, but our men say, by them upon us." Philo Judd remembered being fired on "with out Cause." One Mormon died, and Philo Dibble "was shot in the bowels with a ball and two buck shots." He recovered, but another Mormon and two Gentiles died from their wounds. Among the Gentile dead was Hugh Brazil, who had pledged to "expel them [Mormons] if he had to wade up to his neck in blood."[172]

This skirmish has gone down in history as the "Battle of Blue River," and it has little to offer in the way of constructive military or historical value. But it played into the hands of the Gentile rumor mill. No matter that Mormons had been provoked or that the violence against them had been going on for days; the death of Brazil seemed to justify fear of the Saints. The deaths "raised as it were the whole country in arms," wrote John Greene, "and nothing would satisfy them but an immediate surrender of the arms of our people, and they forthwith to leave the county."[173] The story of the battle joined with other rumors blazing across western Missouri. "Runners were dispatched in every direction, under pretence of calling out the militia: spreading as they went, every rumor calculated to excite the unwary; such as, that the Mormons had taken Independence, and the Indians had surrounded it, being allied together, &c," wrote Parley Pratt.[174] Other rumors rushed about. One claimed the

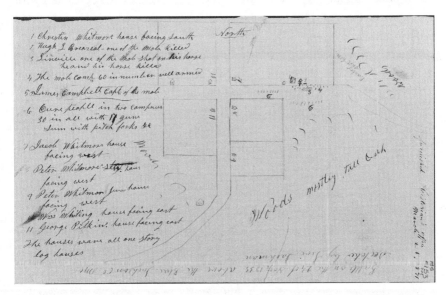

Battle of Blue River, November 4, 1833. Levi Jackson drew this diagram of the battle based on his recollection of the conflict. Church History Library, Salt Lake City

Mormons had attacked and killed the son of the mob's ersatz general, Moses Wilson. That was untrue, but it brought Gentiles into the field.[175] Alexander Majors recalled that "every [Gentile] citizen, as soon as he could run bullets and fill his powder horn with powder, gathered his gun . . . in a few hours men enough had gathered to exterminate them."[176]

At the same time, Corrill, Morley, Gilbert, and others were at the court-house, charged with illegally imprisoning McCarty, whom they had caught smashing a Mormon store. The news of Blue River arrived during the trial; Wilson appeared with a team of men threatening to "kill every Mormon present."[177] A scuffle broke out. Chapman Duncan, armed with a knife, pledged to "sell my life as dearly as possible," but instead found himself thrown out of the door.[178] It was "with difficulty they escaped massacre," Orson Hyde wrote.[179] The local jailor—despite having signed the Mob Manifesto—managed to hide the accused Mormons for the evening.[180] In prison, Corrill sent word to the rest of the Saints "that they might not expect any thing the next day but a general slaughter of our people."[181]

As Corrill, Morley, and Gilbert sat in prison, they decided to surrender: "It would be wisdom to leave the county immediately, rather than to have so many lives lost as probably would be." The jailer and the sheriff smuggled the men out of prison under cover of darkness, and the Saints' leaders consulted with the rank and file. "Our brethren agreed to it," Corrill wrote, and they hurried back to jail while mobbers shot at them.[182]

The following morning, a state militia positioned itself between the Mormon settlements and the county seat, but "it would have been difficult for one to have distinguished between the militia and the mob, for all the most conspicuous characters engaged in the riot were found" among the militia.[183] At the head of that militia was Lilburn Boggs, the lieutenant governor, and Thomas Pitcher, an active member of the anti-Mormon movement. Boggs later claimed he called out the militia "for the purpose of suppressing the insurrection." In December, he published a refutation of swirling rumors "taking the rounds in the public papers" that he had brought out the militia to attack and persecute the Mormons.[184] Events as they transpired did not bear out this refutation.

Corrill, Morley, and Gilbert presented their plan to the militia; the Mormons would leave Jackson County immediately. Boggs and Pitcher agreed, but insisted that the Saints surrender their weapons. The militia under Pitcher and Boggs confiscated Mormon firearms, and then all hell broke loose. "Companies of ruffians were ranging the county in every direction, bursting into houses without fear," recalled Parley Pratt. Charles Hulet marched to Independence to surrender his gun, and found "the next day came and the mob with it." The mobbers bore down on Mormon families: "A scene of sorrow and confusion I never saw before," wrote Mormon Lemuel Herrick. Women and children were "crying aloud some scared almost into fits others who were sick." Herrick found Isaac McCoy leading a mob, threatening the Mormons by saying, "If we was not out of the Co within three days, they would massacre men, women, and children and leave none alive to carry the news: for they wouldn't have the d—d Mormons in their county."[185]

It had essentially become open season on the Mormons; "we were obliged to skulk in every direction," wrote Hulet. Numerous families fled to the open prairies nearby, some for days and others for weeks. Calvin Beebe put his family up in a stable, "or rather a hovel," he wrote, where the wind brought freezing temperatures and all of them became ill. While anti-Mormons burned Saints' houses, many of the faithful lined up to take the ferry to Clay County, hoping for some solace there.[186] Independence was in "great confusion," wrote a correspondent to the *Intelligencer*. Gentiles were being drafted into the militia on the spot and were razing Mormon houses.[187]

Those Saints who fled to the prairies were woefully unprepared. More than one hundred of them, mostly women and children, hid in the grasslands for over a week, "hourly expecting to be massacred" before crossing the river to Clay County. The prairie had recently been fired, and the stubble cut the feet of shoeless children. Then the rivers flooded and the refugees waded through water and mud. At least one women gave birth under these conditions.[188] An exhausted Pratt was ready to surrender: "The struggle was now over, our liberties were gone, our homes to be deserted."[189]

A few Mormons remained in the county, settling fifteen miles from Independence and believing the mob would not care about them. Two weeks later, "a mob made their appearance among them, pistols cocked & presented to their breasts commanding them to leave the county."[190] They left. A Saint named David Frampton went to Boggs and Pitcher to ask if he could remain for an extra two weeks; as Frampton recalled, the answer was swift: "By God, the Mormons should go Except 2 families that had denied the faith." When Ira Willes returned to Independence a few months later to retrieve his cow, locals seized him and gave him "6 to 8 blows with a hickory whip."[191] Lewis Abbott later got lost and accidentally put himself back in Jackson County; he too was savagely beaten.[192] When Pettigrew returned to collect supplies, he was accosted by a local who threatened to burn the house of anyone who gave him shelter. When Pettigrew explained to another local that his house and goods had been taken from him, the Gentile insisted, "The Mormons robbed your house, sir."[193] By December 1833, Jackson County had not a single Mormon left, the result of a nineteenth-century religious cleansing. Still, the Saints did not believe God had left them. Whitmer recorded the defeat—and a subsequent sign from God—in his official church history: "The Church was driven by the Mob of Jackson County on the 4. of November 1833 [and] on the night of the 13th of the same month the stars fell."[194]

This military and political exodus threatened to bring on a Mormon crisis of faith. As Oliver Cowdery asked, how could the Mormons preach that people "flee to Zion for refuge, when there is no Zion"?[195] Kirtland Saints had to ask themselves that question when news arrived of the fall of Independence. John Corrill published a letter in the January 1834 *Evening and Morning Star*, now relocated to Kirtland. If the Saints were to arm themselves, he wrote, "and become organized in independent companies . . . to stand in our own defense, it would be much better for us." Yet, Corrill also wrote, they would be outnumbered, and even to arm themselves might invite "another scene of murder and bloodshed."[196]

The Mormons seemed to be nursing personal fears for family and loved ones, along with a sense of democratic indignity that Americans had been expelled from their homes by Americans—that democracy and freedom of religion had meant nothing and, as one Saint wrote, "every officer of the peace had abandoned us to our fate."[197] "I think that the state of Missouri is brought to the test," Corrill wrote, "whether it can and will protect the persons and rights of its own citizens or not." This mix of faith, fear, and anger radicalized the Ohio Mormons, and they resolved to do something never before done in America: their church would form a militia, not under the control or consent of any governmental authority. It would march out to secure those political rights that Missouri had failed to defend. The name of this force was Zion's Camp. It was the army of a church preparing to make war against an American state.[198]

# 5

## A War for Zion

ZION'S CAMP WAS ALMOST CERTAINLY a tactical blunder. Given that tensions in Ohio and Missouri centered on Mormon claims to supernatural powers and the politics thereof, sending an army across four states to defend belief in supernatural visitations seems like a bad idea. The Mormons had actually gained some sympathy in the wake of their expulsion; all but the most virulent anti-Mormon papers condemned the mobbing in Missouri. "Although we have always viewed the Mormons with abhorrence," wrote the *Missouri Intelligencer*, "we are not prepared to justify such outrageous proceedings on the part of the citizens. The former have *rights* guaranteed by the constitution and the laws of the land."[1] The *Missouri Republican*, which had always taken a dim view of Mormonism, declared: "The Mormons are as much protected in their religion, their property, and persons, as any other denomination or class of men. We think that they acted perfectly right in offering the resistance which they did." Another newspaper cried, "Were the worshippers of the moon to settle in this State, no one would have a right to molest them, on account of those tenets."[2]

In Erie, Pennsylvania (across the border from Kirtland), the local paper asked, "What will avail our toleration principles, if no sect is to be endured but such as are free from extravagance and fanaticism?" Mormons were "a nuisance," but "such a mode of breaking it up is illegal & riotous, however respectable may have been the individuals concerned."[3] The *Allegheny Democrat* had a different angle: "We trust that the good people of Missouri will take care of these fanatics, and see that they do not violate the laws with impunity."[4]

The Mormon press built on this sympathy, stressing constitutional and American themes rather than religious language. The *Evening and Morning Star* was resurrected in Kirtland in December 1833. Its first Kirtland issue declared, "The freedom of speech, the liberty of conscience, and the liberty of the press, are three main principles in the Constitution of a free government; take from it these, and adieu to the blessings of civil society." The *Star* missed no opportunity to mention that the mobs had violated "patriotism and liberal principles . . . to rise up in open violation of the Constitution of our country, and persecute, even unto death a fellow being for his religion." It also emphasized the common threat to all Americans implicit in the anti-Mormon mobs by citing persecution of Quakers and Baptists "in time gone by."[5]

Threats to the Constitution were a common theme of political discourse in the 1830s. The crisis of nullification—brought on by South Carolina's 1832–33 refusal to abide by federal tariffs—was also seen as a threat to union and order. President Jackson opposed nullification; Missouri's governor was a Jackson man. In their long letter to Governor Daniel Dunklin requesting aid in December 1833, the Missouri Mormons pleaded that the "law of the land may not be defied, nor nullified." If South Carolina threatened the Union to sidestep the law, then the Union was also at stake when mobs ran rampant. "Whenever that fatal hour shall arrive," the Mormons' petition continued, "that the poorest citizen's person, property, or rights and privileges, shall be trampled upon by a lawless mob with impunity, that moment a dagger is plunged into the heart of the Constitution, and the Union must tremble!"[6] The Mormons wrote to Jacksonians in Jacksonian language. They stressed religion and union, and presumably believed the government would send help, as the Jacksonian government too believed in union.

Kirtland's Mormons also embraced this stalwart approach, appealing to US authorities to do the right thing. Smith insisted that Missouri's Saints hold their lands and fight back in the courts. They were planning to play by the rules even though the game was rigged. He wrote to Partridge that "it is not the will of the Lord for you to sell your lands in Zion . . . use every lawful means in your power to seek redress for grievances of your enemies." A revelation in December told the Missouri Saints to "importune for redress, and redemption, by the hands of those who are placed as rulers, and are in authority over you." In fact, "let them importune at the feet of the President, and if the President heed them not, then will the Lord arise and come forth from his hiding place, and in his fury vex the nation." Smith was sufficiently sanguine about the Missouri situation to set off on a personal missionary tour to Canada in the months after the expulsion. He made a few dozen converts in Canada, got locked out of several churches, and howled at by ministers.[7]

Missouri Mormons, however, were not all in for passive resistance: "We supposed that if we prepared ourselves as well as we could for self-defense, that this would have a tendency to stop the enemy from coming on us."[8] They petitioned repeatedly to have their firearms returned. They formed into small units to watch their neighborhoods, even without weapons; Parley Pratt received a blow to the head when he went unarmed to stop two ruffians.[9] As late as December 1833, however, Smith was still writing that the Missouri Saints needed to remember that God sometimes required his followers to suffer for the gospel.[10] Phelps, in Clay County, echoed that sentiment: "I am sensible that we shall not be able to live again in Zion, till God, or the president rules out the mob."[11]

The attitude in Kirtland changed in February 1834, when Parley Pratt and Lyman Wight arrived and described their expulsion to the whole Mormon community. These personal accounts, delivered before their fellow Saints at a Sunday service, stimulated demands for a show of strength. "The church in Kirtland concluded with one accord to die with you or redeem you," Smith told the Independence branch.[12] Nor did the decision come only from this world; a February 17 revelation declared that "the redemption of Zion must needs come by power" and ordered the Saints to form companies to march to Missouri. The revelation went further: if Saints hearkened to the commands of God, "they shall never cease to prevail until the kingdoms of the world are subdued under my feet, and the earth is given unto the saints." But if "they keep not my commandments," their enemies would prevail.[13]

It was settled. Eight Mormon recruiters, including Smith himself, visited church branches in New York and Ohio, seeking volunteers for an impromptu militia. Smith pressed the urgency of the moment, informing recruiters to beseech their brethren, "by the Son of God, to lend us a helping hand." If they would not help fellow Saints in Missouri "stand against that wicked mob," they would never obtain "so goodly a land (which now can be obtained for one dollar and a quarter per acre)." Unless they performed "the will of God, God will not help them, and if God does not help them, all is in vain." The message convinced John Murdock, who wrote that he had "never shed the blood of any man, nor with firearms, any animal, save one dog." Nevertheless, to redeem Zion, "I took my rifle over my shoulder, my pistol in my pocket, my Dirk by my side" to serve in "a camp of Israel by the order of God."[14] More than one hundred Mormons joined Murdock in the initial call, short of the five hundred to a thousand Smith hoped for.[15] As often happened, Saints also told one another of supernatural encouragements for their actions. Nathaniel Baldwin, on a missionary trip across Massachusetts, heard the Holy Spirit command him to "Go West!" Baldwin hurried back to Kirtland and signed up for the muster to Independence.[16]

The Saints called their force the "Camp of Israel" or "Zion's Camp." They embarked for Missouri in early May. As usual for the Saints in the 1830s, organization was multiform and overlapping. Smith was named Supreme-General-of-the-Camp, but Lyman Wight would eventually also become a General-of-the-Camp. One participant remembered Smith imposing an organizational scheme straight out of Deuteronomy, but Smith himself recalled splitting the group into companies of twelve men and giving each company a captain. Intriguingly, the captains Smith picked included both his staunch allies (including Brigham Young) and some of his most vocal critics (Sylvester Smith, for example). As often in the hodgepodge organization of early Mormonism, maintaining peace and unity among a diverse church took top priority. In the same spirit, the whole camp joined in communal prayer each evening and morning to the sounds of a "common brass French horn" they called "our trumpet."[17]

Mormon leaders in Ohio invested a good deal of preparation in the march to Missouri, but outsiders might have scoffed. The Saints did not have the number of soldiers they had planned for initially, and they raised less than 10 percent of the $2,000 they sought to fund the march.[18] Provisions were thin, with one soldier documenting the lack of milk and bread—except in his dreams. The land offered little sustenance; part of the woods en route were decimated by grasshoppers and caterpillars, making the summer woods "look like winter." At one point the Camp filled empty powder kegs with water from a slough, only to find the water "filled with red living animals."[19] There was little training. While on the march, Zion's Camp engaged in a "sham fight," a faux battle that likely provided the only military training most of the men ever had. Perhaps that was just as well, given that Levi Hancock painted a white cloth with red tips and the word "PEACE" to be used as a Mormon flag.[20]

The journey was an armed pilgrimage; the religious nature of the quest shaped the Mormon march across the Midwest. Hyrum Smith gave new sacred names to locations they passed, as when he "called this place Ezengeber for in it were blest of the Lord" or "called the place Manhikel because it is a place of many waters." Traveling through Illinois, the Mormons unearthed an Indian mound and discovered a skeleton, which Joseph Smith identified as that of Zelph, a righteous Lamanite. Amasa Lyman called Missouri "the land of captivity." Hosea Stout was so swayed by Mormon preaching about Zion's Camp that he almost joined the effort—even though he was a Gentile! Nancy Lampson Holbrook—one of numerous women who served as camp followers on the expedition—endured "the Missouri troubles" with a faith "firm and unshaken in the cause of the Lord . . . without a murmur or a reflection." (Unfortunately, none of over a dozen women who served with Zion's Camp left a record in her own hand.)[21]

The Mormons made little effort to retain the element of surprise; by the end of April, a local postmaster in Ohio had sent warnings back to Missouri that "the *Mormons* are organizing an army" armed with weapons "from scalping knife to double-barreled rifle." A Mormon dissenter apparently told the Ohio official that the Mormons "have emissaries among the neighboring Indians . . . to join them in their 'holy war.'"[22] The Saints did not have emissaries among Native Americans, and the Mormon dissenter was never identified, but this information appeared in Gentile newspapers in Missouri and joined the swirl of rumor in Independence. Missouri militias began drilling to prepare for the Mormon army even before Zion's Camp left Ohio.[23]

Saints occasionally concealed themselves on the march, at one point even feigning to be ministers from competing denominations—not a difficult feat, given that Campbellite, Baptist, and Methodist ex-ministers were all in Zion's Camp. When they preached to one gathering of Gentiles, an undercover Saint stressed "the importance of a union of all the different sects & denominations."[24] Still, Joseph Smith wrote, the people "suspected we were 'Mormons.'" Nathan Tanner avoided the question when strangers in Indiana asked them where they were from; when the men sarcastically asked if they were the "New York company," Tanner assumed it was a reference to Mormon origins and that the strangers were up to no good.[25]

Smith's 1837 *History of the Church* refers to numerous spies seeking knowledge about the movements of Zion's Camp. Smith recalled hearing threats of violence promised around Indianapolis or the Illinois River that never materialized.[26] It is unclear whether any of the visitors were spies—almost anyone could enter the camp, perhaps "professing to be drunk" and swearing "we never shd. reach Jackson Co. alive," as happened on June 25—but even if these visitors were just curious (if bad-mannered) onlookers, the anxiety in Zion's Camp steadily mounted as they approached Missouri.[27]

Perhaps it was nerves that spread dissension and conflict in the ranks. "Roger Orton made an attempt to get my gun from me by approaching me in a familiar manner," remembered George A. Smith. Orton failed, but another member of the company filched the gun and pawned it for whiskey. A foraging party argued with Smith over whether the eggs they had found on the Mississippi River were turtle or snake eggs; Smith advised against eating them, and the argument became heated. Some members ate the eggs anyway and became ill.[28] Martin Harris proclaimed he had the power to hold serpents without being bitten; he picked up a serpent and was proven incorrect. Smith rebuked him. Rations went short; fears of "milk sickness" came from a rumor that tainted milk "might be sold to us by our enemies for the purpose of doing us injury." Sylvester Smith blamed the Prophet and let everyone know it. (Sylvester also found time to complain vocally about Joseph's dog.) Six rotten hams, procured for meals, were thrown in front of Joseph Smith's tent.[29]

In the first week of June, the camp frayed. Sylvester Smith and Joseph Smith got into a shouting match. Joseph said Sylvester was possessed by an evil spirit, while Sylvester accused the prophet of teaching lies in the name of God. Each man retreated to an opposite end of camp, taking his partisans with him. The two men were at each other's throats for the rest of the expedition. On June 17, as they approached Independence, Wight and Smith disagreed on where to establish camp. The argument escalated and the camp split, with each general establishing his own bivouac with his own supporters. Yet neither man quit; each had confidence that what he was doing was a divine activity undertaken in the name of the restored church. Once again, early Mormonism was not simply a vehicle for Joseph Smith's wishes; it was a multiform, diverse group trying to stake out a new religious path.[30]

Meanwhile, the former Jackson County Saints—by 1834, living in Clay County—continued searching for a political solution, desperately hoping someone in authority would recognize the crisis of freedom that was at hand: "Those sacred rights guaranteed to every religious sect have been publicly invaded, in open hostility to the spirit and genius of free government." What Mormon housing and property had not been destroyed was now occupied by "a band of outlaws" in Jackson County. At least that was how the Saints explained it to President Andrew Jackson in a letter begging him to acknowledge this "unprecedented emergency in the history of these United States." Worse still, they told the president, the crisis was unfolding among "almost wholly native born citizens," a characterization used perhaps to set themselves apart from the violence against Irish Catholic immigrants (whom Jackson usually supported) and the Native Americans (whom Jackson loathed).[31] The Mormons eventually received a response from Secretary of War Lewis Cass, who informed them that the "offenses, of which you complain, are violations of the laws . . . of Missouri"—and so they fell under state, not federal, jurisdiction.[32]

This adherence to a states' rights philosophy was bad news for Mormons who had already spent five months trying to get justice from Missouri officials. They had some initial success with Judge John Ryland, who described the Mormon expulsion as "a disgrace to the state." Ryland informed the Saints that Missouri must "insure the punishment of such offenders." In a late November 1833 letter, he requested that the Saints provide him with all the information they could as they began the legal process of reclaiming their land.[33]

The Saints at last had some kind of ally. Ryland recommended making another request to Governor Dunklin. The Saints had had little luck thus far with Dunklin, but they wrote anyway. Their letter asked for a court of inquiry into "the whole matter of the mob against the Mormons" and requested protection during the trial. The Mormons suggested that a detachment of US Rangers might come down from Fort Leavenworth in Indian Territory to protect them from "the unhallowed power of the mob," at least until "our friends in the east" could arrive to protect them.[34] The local militia, they explained, was under the influence of "certain religious sects," and its commitment to the free exercise of religion was highly suspect. Gilbert told Dunklin that only one in four Mormon witnesses to the violence would be willing to return through Jackson County for a trial unless federal protection could be arranged.[35]

Dunklin's reply likely gave some hope; he knew "the injuries your people complain of" and suggested he would "do every thing in my power" to afford them the "redress to which they seem entitled." He affirmed the Saints should have their property back, but rejected their call for state militia to protect them or to "*prevent* the commission of crime." Such action would "transcend the powers" of his office, since he could only command state forces in the case of emergencies "of a public nature."[36]

Dunklin's reasoning—like that of the Mormons and the mobbers—depended very much on the definition of "the public." For Mormons, the public was every "free born citizen of the United States," as David Pettigrew phrased it, entitled to "protection by the law of the land." For the Jackson County Gentile extremists, "the public" consisted of people like them. That was why they had distinguished between "citizen" and "Mormon" in the Mob Manifesto. Pettigrew recalled the words of a mob member who demanded the Mormons forsake their religion and said, if they did so, "the mob would be our brothers and would fight for us but if not we are ready and will drive you from the country." Virtually all anti-Mormon communications after 1832 defined the public as the community of the like-minded; the "true" settlers were brothers and devoted to one another. Mormons—not being of the same faith or ideology—were invaders and, hence, not subject to the laws or privileges Americans possessed. Virtually all Gentile documents differentiated between "citizens" and Mormons. Pettigrew's interrogator even went so far as to describe Pettigrew's view of American citizenship as "the old law," declaring that the "Constitution is wornout and we are about to make a new one."[37]

Dunklin made an odd dance around the issue. Clearly, he understood what was at stake, for he wrote, "The case of the *Mormons* to-day, may be the case of the *Catholics* to-morrow, and after them any other sect that may become obnoxious to a majority of the people of any section of the state." It was, therefore, "as if the war had been waged against the whole state." Yet Dunklin took no action, because "the *public* has no other interest in it, than that the laws be faithfully executed." What happened was wrong, it could happen to any other citizen, and the community should care, but "the public" could do nothing, because the public was a set of institutions, operations, and laws. The public was the government and had to abide by the letter of the law; "the laws are sufficient," he wrote, "to afford a remedy to every injury." Dunklin sympathized with the Saints, but because no specific law required the state governor to protect religion, the "public" had no interest in the case. (Recall that

First Amendment protections did not apply to state governments in 1834; only the Fourteenth Amendment, ratified in 1868, required that.) The law indicated that Mormons should take their persecutors to court, so that was what they should do. If Mormons were threatened, it was the duty of judges "to have the offenders apprehended." Dunklin seemed oblivious to the fact that a county judge and jailer had signed the pledge to expel all Mormons.[38]

Of course, the law also allowed Dunklin to declare Jackson County in a state of insurrection, which *would* have permitted him to call out the militia to enforce Mormon property rights. Dunklin said he might take further action if the laws could not be "peaceably executed." This was a veiled way of declining to intervene—essentially telling the Saints that they could trust the judges and militia officers kicking them off their land to enforce laws that prevented people from kicking them off their land. His actions seem less a principled philosophical stand than a pragmatic reluctance to interfere in any kind of removal in a state rapidly filling with white Protestants. His only concession was to send the "Liberty Blues"—a militia led by David Atchison, the Saints' own lawyer—to escort the Saints from Clay to Jackson County.[39]

Dunklin continued to equivocate even as Zion's Camp marched closer and Gentiles dug in to defend their land seizure. It is not clear whether the governor's actions were a political cover or reflected a genuine feeling of legal helplessness. Even as he refused to ask the president to help the Saints, he reminded Mormons that "*public sentiment* is a powerful corrective of error" and urged them to make their case there, essentially telling the Mormons they needed rebranding before they could expect justice.[40] In June, Dunklin wrote "I consider it the duty of every good citizen of Jackson County and the adjoining counties to exert themselves to effect a compromise." The citizens of Jackson County felt otherwise; they encouraged the governor "not to interfere neither one way, nor the other, in the Case of the citizens of Jackson, and the poor deluded Mormons."[41] Anti-Mormons understood that Dunklin's official neutrality provided sideways support for Gentile seizures in Jackson County; Mormons had no way to counter an armed mob without state support. Jackson County was now under the authority of anti-Mormon militias.

William Phelps, the editor of the *Evening and Morning Star*, also tried to play the political game, though with less subtlety. Writing to Missouri's US senator Thomas Hart Benton—another Jacksonian—Phelps requested federal help for the Mormons—and also explained that he could easily "publish a weekly paper in favor of the present administration, in Jackson County, as soon as our society is restored to its legal rights." He added that his old press, "wrested from me, is now printing a mean opposition paper."[42] Phelps was offering political support in exchange for federal assistance.

Sidney Gilbert, once he was made the manager of Zion's storehouse, continued his efforts as a negotiator with diminishing results. He kept lobbying Dunklin, but by late April, sarcasm began seeping into his letters; he requested a return of Mormon firearms from Jackson County officials, so they could "defend our persons & property from a lawless mob, when[ever] it shall please the Executive, at some future day, to put us in possession of our Homes." Gilbert also informed the governor that two hundred to three hundred men from Kirtland were on their way "to defend ourselves and our possessions, inasmuch as the Executive of this State cannot keep up a military force 'to protect our people in that county without transcending his power.' We want therefore the privilege of defending ourselves."[43]

In making this dramatic announcement—of a fact Dunklin might already have known—Gilbert added a warning against rumor: "When the Jackson mob get the intelligence that a large number of our people are about to remove into that county, they will raise a great hue & cry, and circulate many bug bears through the medium of their favorite press." Rumors would fly, and Gilbert hoped Dunklin would not listen to them. Yet Gilbert could not help adding a bit of snark; Mormons wanted only "legal possession of our homes . . . without further wearying the patience of our worthy Chief Magistrate."[44]

Perhaps Gilbert recognized that Dunklin's patience with anti-Mormons never seemed to wear thin. The governor did issue a terse request for Jackson County to restore the Mormons' firearms. Since there had been "*no insurrection*" to prompt the initial seizure, Dunklin wrote to Jackson County, the militia "was *not authorized* to call out troops" to evict the Mormons. By extension, it had also been illegal to seize Mormon firearms, and the county needed to return them. These orders went unheeded. Dunklin waited a month, then repeated his order. Again, nothing.[45]

In correspondence with non-Mormons, Dunklin passionately defended freedom of religion, even if he missed some major parts of the Mormon faith: "The religious opinion and practices of the Mormons, is at the bottom of the outrages committed against them. They have the right constitutionally guaranteed to them . . . to believe and worship JOE SMITH as a man, an angel, or even as the only true and living God." Yet Dunklin refused to broker a compromise or resolve the issue; if he were to attempt that, he feared "it might be said that I was partial to one side or another." This stance might have been political cover or have reflected shortsightedness or even ideology—as the incarnation of "the public," Dunklin believed he could not act for one or the other side, even as he wrote about rumors that both Mormons and Gentiles had acquired cannon to use against each other. Dunklin believed in religious freedom, but he had little sense of urgency.[46]

Then Zion's Camp crossed into Missouri. "We are in the midst of war and rumors of war," wrote Clay County's John Chauncey. Smith's "holy crusade" had armed itself and camped nearby, while the "citizens of Jackson hearing of this movement imbodied themselves for the conflict."[47] On July 3, 1834, three Presbyterian ministers were detained by locals on suspicion of being Saints: "I don't know but you are Mormons, don't care if you are," a local farmer told them, but "I will shoot every Mormon I find in the County." The Presbyterians were searched for copies of the Book of Mormon and then sent on their way.[48]

A host of compromise plans suddenly emerged. Most involved having the Gentiles pay Mormons for the lands seized (an approach Gentiles more often suggested). A more radical idea was to cut the county in half and ensure that Mormons and Gentiles "confine their numbers within their respective limits." Eventually, the state of Missouri tried something like this, carving out Caldwell County for the Mormons in 1836 in the northwest portion of the state. But in 1834, the notion went nowhere.[49]

As Dunklin dithered, the Gentile mobbers sought to consolidate their gains. In the last week of April, when news reached them of Zion's Camp, they set fire to seized Mormon homes in Independence and then distributed seized Mormon weapons to allies in Jackson County.[50] In June, Samuel Campbell and other anti-Mormons headed to adjoining counties "to harangue the people . . . on the subject of mobocracy." Campbell got only twenty signatures for an anti-Mormon petition in Clay County, where most of the Missouri Saints had fled.[51]

The efforts of anti-Mormons seemed to steel Mormon resolve in Missouri. As early as May 10, John Whitmer noted that "the Saints are and were preparing to go back to Jackson Co. as soon as the way should open." Whitmer did not know how that could work—for "the mob rages, and the peoples hearts are hardened"—but his fellow Saints, "despised, mocked at and laughed to scorn," with no money or homes for six months, had had enough.[52] With news of the runners in their ears, Mormons decided, Whitmer wrote, "to arm themselves and otherwise prepare to go to Jackson Co. when the Camp arrives."[53]

In this poisonous atmosphere—and with Hyrum Smith adding several dozen militiamen to Zion's Camp as they crossed the Mississippi into Missouri—a last attempt at serious negotiations began. Absent gubernatorial leadership, Judge Ryland made arrangements for a kind of Mormon-Gentile summit. He asked the Mormons in Clay County to send representatives to meet with "some of the most respectable *citizens* of Jackson County" in the town of Liberty, ten miles north and across the Missouri River from Independence. The Mormon reply pointedly referred instead to "the *inhabitants* of Jackson County," but they agreed to meet, with one precondition: as for "the sale of our lands in Jackson county . . . no such proposition could possibly be acceded to by our society." The Mormon leadership specifically cited rumors, printed in Liberty's *Upper Missouri Enquirer*, claiming that Dunklin planned to force Mormons to sell their land, while Dunklin had told the Mormons he had withdrawn that idea.[54]

The meeting went forward on June 16. The Jackson County representatives named Samuel Owens, a prominent merchant, as their chief negotiator (and commander in chief); the Mormons sent Isaac Morley, John Corrill, and others.[55] Hundreds were in attendance at Liberty, and Clay County judge Joel Turnham was named moderator. As the debate escalated, Turnham urged participants to remember who they were: "Let us be republicans; let us honor our country, and not disgrace it like Jackson County."[56]

The initial positions of each side, however, made compromise unlikely. Mormons refused to accept that public opinion and organized violence could invalidate their rights: "We want possession of our homes . . . and those rights which belong to us as native free born citizens of the United States."[57] Owens gave "a flaming war-speech" against the Mormons. The rest of the Jackson County delegation forwarded a proposition that stuck by the suggestion to have the mobbers purchase the property from the Saints and retain possession.

The Jackson County delegation had other demands, as well. Although their proposal would pay the Saints for the land at twice the going rate, it explicitly forbade Mormons from entering the county except to appraise the value of their property. Mormons would have to promise "not to make any effort, ever after, to settle, either collectively or individually, within the limits of Jackson County."[58] Here was both an offer to pay Mormons for what rioters had already stolen and a threat to shoot them if they ever returned. John Whitmer thought the whole thing was for show: to "buy our possessions in a manner that they knew that we could not comply with . . . which served to blind the mind of those who had heretofore said nothing, but now advised us to comply because they thought we had better have something than nothing."[59] The proposition had less to do with buying the land—an idea Dunklin had already suggested—than with making the Saints who had lost their lands seem unreasonable in the public eye for wanting it back.

The meeting grew heated, and Turnham ruled that inflammatory speeches would not be tolerated. Few followed that ruling, for Owens and company "were not in a very good frame of feeling to do justice to the Mormon citizens," remembered one participant.[60] A Baptist minister gave a "hot speech" insisting the Mormons "must either clear out, or be cleared out" of Clay as well as Jackson County.[61] Alexander Doniphan—now the nominal military commander in the region—also "gave vent to his feelings," but he argued on the Saints' behalf.[62] Owens blasted back that the non-Mormon residents were prepared to "dispute every inch of ground, burn every blade of grass, and suffer their bones to bleach on the hills, rather than the Mormons should return to Jackson County."[63] In the midst of the shouting, a fight broke out. Apparently two Gentiles stabbed each other for unrelated reasons, but the meeting broke up. Gentiles and Mormons retreated to separate quarters.

The break was fortuitous for the Mormon negotiators, who had a moment to catch their breath and prepare a measured response that actually opened the door to a negotiated settlement. The Mormons asked for a week to bring the matter before the church. In the meantime, they pledged not to "commence hostilities against the aforesaid citizens of Jackson county or any other people." Moreover, noting the imminent arrival of Zion's Camp, "we agree to use our influence . . . to prevent said company from entering into Jackson County." A twenty-first-century observer might call this strategy triangulation—an effort by Missouri Mormons to situate themselves as a reasonable alternative to armed Ohio Mormons and violent Gentile mobs. Perhaps just as important, the Missouri Saints were talking about a nonviolent resolution, even one in which they might accept injustice to procure peace. Significantly, the letter mentioned nothing about having Saints get their land or property back. The negotiators wrote only "that peace is what we desire and what we are disposed to cultivate with all men: and to effect peace, we feel disposed to use all our influence."[64]

By June 16, therefore, the Mormon insistence on restoration of their stolen lands had begun to crack. Mormons back in Ohio had started to feel the same. "You won't be able to live in Independence any more in peace," Nathaniel

Judd wrote to his daughter Sally. "The old breach can't be healed." Judd wanted Sally back in Ohio but also wondered if his letter would even reach her in the upheaval.[65] Perhaps the heat of the meeting suggested the stiff resistance that military actions would bring; perhaps the Mormons were simply playing for more time to let things cool off. Even before Zion's Camp reached Independence, Mormons who had been arming themselves in May were now ready for further negotiations.

But by the next morning, several of the Gentile negotiators were dead. While crossing back to Jackson County that evening, Owens and seven other members of his committee overloaded a ferry by traveling together with three horses. In the middle of the river, the ferry sank. Three of Owens's men drowned, and Owens himself escaped only with his skin. "It was owing perhaps to the craziness of the boat," wrote one of the mobbers of 1833, "yet some persons suspected the Mormons of having scuttled it by secretly boring auger-holes in the bottom just before they had left it." How the Mormons had managed to do that when they were threatened with death not to cross the river—or how they did it only for the last ferry trip of the day—were not questions rumor answered. Owens was more direct: "Something had been done to the boat to sink her." Alexander Majors, another non-Mormon, later wrote that the sinking "caused in the whole population the most intense feeling against" the Mormons and likely ended any further efforts at remuneration, let alone a return to the county.[66] Any Mormon efforts at détente were over.

Zion's Camp edged closer to Independence; on June 19 they reached the Fishing River on the eastern edge of Clay County, perhaps thirty miles from Independence. The *Missouri Intelligencer* went ahead and reported that they had probably crossed the river ("we presume [they] are now in Jackson county"). They had not, but the newspaper continued to report that the situation "with the Mormons appears to be getting into a worse state than ever."[67] Clay County Mormons began trickling into Zion's Camp, bringing food or volunteering services.[68]

Then five armed men rode into the camp "and told us we should see hell before morning," Heber Kimball wrote. They informed the Saints they had a force of more than 300 men "and the whole country was in a rage against us."[69] George A. Smith heard that 370 Gentiles were prepared to attack during the night.[70] It looked as if the long-awaited battle was to commence.

Instead, something happened that has gone down in Latter-day Saint history as a preeminent divine intervention—not as remarkable as the golden plates, but a sign that God was with the Mormons. Twenty minutes after the men left, a storm blew up, lobbing hailstones "as big as hen eggs." The hail sliced through tree boughs as "big as your finger." Tents toppled over in the wind, trees blew down, the sky "liteniged and thunderd to exceed all," and the Mormons fled to the safety of a nearby Baptist meetinghouse. "Red lightnings flashed," Kimball recalled, "making it so light that I could see to pick up a pin." The river rose rapidly.[71] Reuben McBride found himself up to his sides in water as he tried to sleep; it was "terrible in the extreme." At the door of the meetinghouse, Smith told Wilford Woodruff, "God is in the storm." Kimball and others agreed: "We felt calm all night and the Lord was with us."[72]

The storm likely prevented open warfare from coming to Clay County; whatever anti-Mormon forces were there had retreated. In the morning, the Saints found relatively little damage to their supplies; they immediately fired their rifles to check for wet powder and found that there was hardly a misfire (though making these tests cost the Saints six hundred rounds of powder.) The rising rivers forced Zion's Camp to head north instead of west, possibly taking them out of the path of angry Gentiles. The Saints saw divine providence. "I have ever after felt thankful to my Heavenly Father that he by this storm & sudden rise of the streams prevented our having a bloody battle with our enemies," wrote George Smith.[73]

But at least one enemy was still in the camp: cholera. The first case appeared on June 20. On June 24, several others fell victim even as the army camped less than three miles from Liberty. They got no farther. That night, "many of the Brethren" fell victim to the disease, their moans "truly terrific." The suddenness of the onset made it all the more terrible; Reuben McBride felt the initial pangs while foraging and found "it was all we could do to get back to camp."[74] Men fell with the disease while on guard duty, their guns clattering to the ground.[75]

The cholera epidemic also seemed resistant to prayer and divine healing, and for Saints who had just seen God in a thunderstorm, the effect must have been chilling. Even as John Carter attempted to rebuke the cholera, he was struck down with the disease. He perished from his condition shortly after. The camp prayed and covenanted for deliverance from the disease, but in the middle of the prayer meeting, Eber Wilcox died.[76] Joseph and Hyrum Smith tried to "rebuke the disease" and were struck with cramps "like the talons of a hawk."[77] Some Mormons held weapons to stand guard while others dug graves. A. S. Gilbert, who had done much work as an impromptu Mormon diplomat, succumbed to the disease. All in all, sixty-eight men contracted cholera and fourteen perished.[78]

Simultaneous with the outbreak were further warnings about negotiations with the Gentiles. Joseph Smith himself listed the rumors he had heard: "One report is that we intend to demolish the printing office in Liberty. . . . Another is, that our men were employed to perform this expedition"—that they were out-of-work eastern laborers paid to carry arms. "Another report is, that we intend crossing the Missouri River on Sunday next and falling upon women and children."[79] In fact, the *Upper Missouri Enquirer* suggested that "an exterminating war" would come on Saturday, June 22 (barring an unlikely compromise); sure enough, a Lafayette County volunteer wrote to his father that he planned to join volunteers to fight Mormons on that Saturday: "Should they [Mormons] cross the river, there will be a battle, and probably much blood shed."[80] A Catholic missionary in Kansas wrote that Jackson County had "armed themselves to the teeth with the most determined resolution to sustain the bloodiest fight. Everywhere in Jackson County resound these words 'War to the Mormons.'" The priest was simply waiting "for the bomb to explode." He added: "Combat ideas replace religious ideas and religion does not hold the first place in the Jacksonian hearts."[81]

Rumor had been busy. A June rumor that the Mormons had crossed into Jackson County mustered out the militia and sent other citizens fleeing. A local newspaper gravely informed readers "that this matter is about to involve the whole upper country in civil war and bloodshed."[82] Another Gentile wrote that "we thought it was all a hoax . . . until they actually arrived." The Mormons had come, he was informed, "to butcher a portion of our citizens" and, therefore, he explained, the county rose up against them.[83]

Dunklin's hopes of a sensible, self-regulating citizenry working out its prejudices had vanished; local officials were now simply trying to avoid a bloodbath. On June 21—a day after the first cholera case and a day before the rumored Mormon invasion—Ryland sent a delegation headed by Clay County sheriff Cornelius Gilliam. Their instructions were to figure out what was true or false—to meet the Mormons and "obtain from the leaders thereof the Correctness of the various reports in Circulation & the true intent and meaning of their present movement."[84]

Gilliam and the other delegates "seemed very much agitated" and had heard "many inflammatory stories," but they had a long conversation with Smith "which resulted in making them our friends." Smith showed the men the Mormon flag, since rumor had it that it bore the words "peace" on one side and "war" on the other. Gilliam must have been relieved to see only "peace," and more relieved when Smith, Wight, and other Mormon commanders agreed to sign a declaration that "it is not our intentions to commence hostilities against any man or boddy [sic] of men." Mormon arms, they affirmed, were "for the purpose of self-defense . . . considering the abuse that we have suffered in Jackson County."[85]

The Mormon leaders who met with Gilliam went further, expressing a desire for compromise not yet seen among the Ohio Saints. The Saints offered to purchase lands from any Gentile who refused to live in Jackson County with them, "or they may all live in the county if they choose and we will never molest them if they will let us alone and let us enjoy equal rights." Again, the Mormons set the precondition that their rights to property and religion were nonnegotiable. "The shedding of blood we will not be guilty of," they further declared, "until all just and honorable principles among men prove ineffectual to restore peace."[86]

And so Gilliam returned to Clay County with a peace offer, albeit one the Gentiles were not likely to accept. Before they could respond, however, supernatural events changed matters once again. On June 22, Smith received the "Fishing River Revelation," which revealed that the war was over: "Sue for peace, not only to the people that have smitten you, but also to all people; and lift up an ensign of peace, and make a proclamation of peace unto the ends of the earth." The redemption of Zion would be delayed "for a little season," as a consequence of the Mormons' failure to contribute personnel and materiel to the war effort: "I have commanded my servant Joseph Smith, Jun., to say unto the strength of my house, even my warriors . . . throw down the towers of my enemies, and scatter their watchmen. But the strength of my house have not hearkened unto my words." That was the lesson Reuben McBride took: "The Strength of the Lord's House had not listened to the call but it was necessary to bring us thus far for a trial of our faith and our offering was excepted."[87]

The revelation had a predictable effect on a divided camp. "Several of the brethren apostatized [sic] because they were not going to have the privilege of fighting," wrote George Smith. Others said "they had rether die than to return without a fite." Several of them instead attacked and destroyed a pawpaw bush. The revelation was also likely the final straw for Sylvester Smith, who would return to Kirtland and levy charges against Smith for "criminal conduct during his journey to and from Missouri" and for "prophecying lies in the name of the Lord."[88]

The Fishing River Revelation was not entirely pacific; it hinted that there were still towers to throw down, but "first let my army become very great." In the meantime, Saints were to buy land in Jackson County and the surrounding areas, which God would redeem when "the kingdoms of this world may be constrained to acknowledge that the kingdom of Zion is in very deed the kingdom of our God and his Christ." It also reminded Mormons to "reveal not the things which I have revealed unto them," at least for now.[89] (That may explain why this revelation, advocating a future home in Jackson County, was not included in the 1835 publication of the Doctrine and Covenants.)

Nor did the revelation require Zion's Camp to disband; Smith marched them toward Liberty on June 23. The army had promised not to enter Jackson County, but Liberty was in Clay. Five miles from the town, Doniphan, Atchison, and others met the band and "informed us that the people of Liberty were very much excited."[90] Perhaps they had seen a copy of that day's *Upper Missouri Enquirer*, which contained Samuel Owens's official response to the Mormon peace plan. It was an emphatic "no," and likely aimed at aggravating fears in Clay County. Owens lambasted the Ohio Saints and suggested that all Mormon promises to reclaim their land were "done with a view to deceive." Owens launched into a roundabout argument that, since Ohio Mormons owned no land in Missouri, they could not possibly be serious about taking "possession of their lands, when in fact they have no lands to take possession of." Owens thereby conveniently sidestepped the question of whether the Gentile mob had done wrong to seize and burn Mormon property in the first place. Instead, he concentrated on whipping locals into a frenzy: "They are determined . . . to shake and convulse not only Jackson, but the surrounding counties, to their very center, and imbrue the whole upper Missouri in blood and carnage." Owens's tactic seemed to have worked; Gentiles in nearby Lafayette County wrote to Smith days later that they would rise to defend Jackson County if Zion's Camp crossed the river.[91]

Smith turned what remained of his army away from Liberty and made camp at Gilbert's house that night. The next day, cholera struck with full force. The fact that Mormons stood guard as they dug graves suggests that tensions had not been reduced; indeed, Gilbert approached the camp "taking a bye way for fear for ambush in the tall hazle [sic] bush."[92] The Mormons fought the epidemic for a week, not very successfully.

Whatever military or organizational discipline had been in place began to break down. Small groups began to drift away and pursue independent objectives, and most of "the camp dispersed to different parts of the county." A logic might have been at work; smaller groups would isolate the sick and possibly allay the governor's fears. Smith wrote that the division was meant "to quiet the prejudices and fears of some part of the citizens of this county" until "every effort for an adjustment of differences between us and the people of Jackson has been made."[93] Still, organization was lacking. George Smith had to ride through Clay County to find Joseph Smith one evening, since the prophet had neglected to tell his guards where he was headed. George found him but then remained bedridden until he "passed from my bowels several large worms."[94] Luke Johnson and a few others decided to cross the Missouri River—despite military and divine orders not to—just so they could say they had set foot in Jackson County. When they did, they were met with a hail of gunfire. They retreated.[95]

Thus by the time Joseph Smith formally disbanded Zion's Camp on June 25, the effort had already foundered. A third of the camp had sickened and nearly 10 percent had died from cholera. Every effort to convince Jackson County mobbers that Americans had rights to property regardless of religious belief had been met with stonewalling. The governor would not help, and rumors said Mormons intended to kill women and children and had assassinated rival negotiators by sinking the ferry. Even God had said that the redemption need not take place right then. It is possible Smith believed on June 22 that the "little season" of waiting promised in the Fishing River Revelation meant a months-long bivouac in Clay County; on June 26 the elders told Governor Dunklin that "we intend to make another effort" to obtain "our right to our soil in Jackson County."[96] By June 30, there was no stomach for more. Smith ordered Wight to issue an "honorable discharge" to each soldier and told them to head home, though "some who had not families were counciled to stay."[97]

The Gentiles, however, remained eager for battle. The week the cholera struck, Jackson County militiamen patrolled the river. "If they had crossed the river," wrote a participant, "I very much question if one would have been left to tell the tale. No quarter would have been given. We could have killed most of them before they got across."[98] Anti-Mormons, however, had no qualms about crossing county lines. Men from Jackson County entered Clay County to raid Mormon homes, taking firearms while "loaded guns were presented to the females."[99] Owens hardened his stance, promising that Jackson County "would do nothing like according to their [Mormons'] last proposition." On

June 26, he suggested the Mormons retreat to Clinton County, north of Clay.[100] In mid-July, the *Missouri Intelligencer* gleefully reported that "excitement in this county about the time the Mormons from Ohio arrived, has entirely subsided. . . . We rather think that the WAR is over!"[101]

There was little doubt who had won. Over the course of two weeks, the Jackson County mobbers had doubled down on their demands, engaged in fairly spurious negotiation, and kept up a front of sporadic violence even as Zion's Camp closed in on their county. Owens and the other Gentile leaders had confidence that the governor would not intervene, and were betting the Mormons would blink. They certainly succeeded in ratcheting fear up in Jackson County; one volunteer acknowledged that he "knew we had neither law nor gospel on our side," but "self-preservation" made him walk the pickets to stop Mormons.[102]

In this way, the Jackson County mob rioted and intimidated their way into free land, houses, and goods, and reserved to themselves the right to dictate what did and did not count as legal religion within the limits of their county. There should be no illusions about what they fought for. "The cause of all this trouble," wrote mob member Alexander Majors, "was solely from the claim that they had a new revelation direct from the Almighty, making them the chosen instruments . . . to build the New Jerusalem."[103]

Battered and sickened, with no political support, the Mormons walked away rather than risk death. Even as they trudged home, rumor threw in a few more notices. Roger Orton had left Zion's Camp when the cholera broke out and had headed back to Kirtland, where he "spread the news that the cholera was killing all of us." George Smith returned home to a family who had thought him dead. Some Ohio newspapers reported in July that Joseph Smith had been killed. The *Ohio Atlas* wrote that fighting had commenced between Mormons and Gentiles and "Joe Smith was wounded in the leg—the Mormons were driven back. Smith had his leg amputated, and died three days after."[104] Smith actually met with one of the editors on the way home to Kirtland, but had difficulty convincing the editor that he was still alive.[105] Between mid-June and mid-July, the Mormons in Kirtland continually heard reports that Zion's Camp had not merely failed but been destroyed.

Later generations of historians and Mormons have drawn lessons from the imbroglio. B. H. Roberts, writing in an official church capacity, blamed the failure on the Saints' lack of unity within Zion's Camp but expressed no doubt that Zion would eventually be redeemed.[106] Secular historians have seen the event as a chance for Mormon leaders to have their "backs stiffened," and have noted especially that the next generation of church ecclesiarchs came predominantly from the ranks of Zion's Camp.[107] It was certainly true that Smith almost immediately began another round of restructuring the church and that, once back in Kirtland, he presided over several more quiet years of growth and harmony for the church. The Fishing River Revelation had stipulated that the Saints who *had* made sacrifices and joined Zion's Camp would receive "an endowment of power." This action likely referred to the efforts to build and complete the Latter-day Saint temple in Kirtland; almost immediately, two of the three presidents of the Missouri High Council were ordered to head to Kirtland to receive endowments. In 1835, Smith would establish the Quorum of the Twelve Apostles and the Quorum of the Seventy in Kirtland to govern "the church abroad."[108] These organizational signals indicated that while Missouri Saints would remain, the center of church life had decisively shifted to Ohio.

But two curious incidents in the wake of Zion's Camp suggest just how little had changed. The church was still struggling with organization, revelation, and competing internal arguments about how to know and interpret the will of God. Days after Smith decamped, the newly created Missouri High Council of the Saints encountered an apostate branch performing supernatural acts. The council likely wanted to focus on its stated intention to instruct Clay County Saints "how to escape the indignation of their enemies, and keep in favor with those who feel well disposed towards us." (As part of that effort, David Whitmer told the Saints "it was not the will of the Lord that our brethren should vote at this approaching Election.") But first the council had to deal with the rebellion of Samuel Brown, Sally Crandall, and Sylvester Hulet. Brown, an ordained Mormon, began encouraging Missouri Mormons to speak in tongues, "insisting that he had obtained a witness of the Lord" to do so, and sought to ordain Hulet in a clandestine manner. Brown confessed his error.[109]

Not so Hulet and Crandall. They announced to their followers (the "Hulet branch") that they would proceed with no temporal business "without receiving the word of the Lord" through tongues. Hulet would speak, and Crandall interpret, and "they would not receive the teachings of ordained members, even br. Joseph Smith Jr. unless it agreed with their gifts." They had received divine notice that "they were to be persecuted by their brethren in Clay County" as well.[110] Hiram Page, who had once offered his own seer stone visions as an independent source of supernatural knowledge, now testified against Crandall, who apparently could "see men's hearts." Nathan West said that Crandall had told him his heart was "full of eyes"; another person had a heart with "three young women in it," and a third heart had "two books in it" and a Nephite standing behind it. The Hulet branch had apparently snuck back into Jackson County, for its members were there in the spring of 1834 and "said in tongues that they would be safe during the night from any interruption by the mob," but the Gentiles found them and whipped them.[111] The Missouri High Council ruled that "the devil deceived" the Hulet branch, particularly in the use of tongues.

In Kirtland, it was Joseph Smith himself who was on trial. He returned to find Kirtland up in arms about him: "The cry was Tyrant! Pope!! King!!! Usurper!!!!"[112] Sylvester Smith had preceded the prophet to Ohio and had circulated his complaints about abuse of authority and misuse of consecrated funds. It was not Sylvester Smith alone who had such concerns, for apparently some branches in Ohio were "in the same transgression." A formal council convened, and determined the prophet was innocent, apparently by a large margin. And yet still—*still*—they did not remove Sylvester Smith from fellowship. He apologized in a Mormon publication and remained a faithful Saint.[113]

Mormonism had not fundamentally changed with the advent of Zion's Camp; it was still a diverse group of religious truth seekers, embracing a variety of different approaches, opinions, and claims about how God worked in this strange new age. It still argued with itself, and it still teetered with internal divisions. The experience of Jackson County by 1834 does not appear to have militarized or changed Mormon faith. Nor had it changed Mormon objectives; on August 16, Smith wrote to Lyman Wight about plans to continue to petition Andrew Jackson for a restoration of their Missouri claims. If the entreaty was unsuccessful, Wight should plan a "little army" for protection. These plans never came to anything.[114]

The Mormons had been successfully exiled. Religious violence had won. "Our fond hopes of being redeemed," wrote Whitmer, "were blasted."[115] The *Painesville Telegraph* mocked Zion's Camp as "the veriest wild goose chase," and Eber Howe wondered how it had not loosened "the scales from the eyes of most of the dupes to the imposition."[116] Isaac McCoy denied any religious justification for his role in kicking them out; the Mormons were, he insisted, "ignorant of the laws" and "obnoxious to the citizens." In the end, the inaction of the government meant that McCoy and his allies got their way and were allowed the privilege to choose who their neighbors would be at the point of a gun. That was Jacksonian democracy.

# Faith and Citizenship

HATE AND VIOLENCE ARE NOT the same thing, but they are near allies. How does the former turn into the latter? How did jokes about the Book of Mormon turn into anti-Mormon vigilante mobs in just four years? How did the criticism of Smith as a juggler or necromancer become an armed conflict between his followers and other Christians? Does the way we talk about religion influence the politics of religion? Is democracy particularly susceptible to this kind of talk? And, if so, when does legitimate criticism of a religious viewpoint morph into a screaming match backed by firearms?

These are not pleasant questions to ask. Most Americans prefer to think of the United States as a haven of religious liberty, a place for the persecuted to be free and to worship God in their own way. Facing up to the fact that America does have a history of religious violence can be difficult. Looking back to the Latter-day Saint experience in the nineteenth century can provide some historical distance and give us a chance to consider these difficult problems.

Then and now, when a religion gets criticized, one of the first questions that gets asked is, "Did they bring it on themselves?" Historians of the Mormons have asked that question, and so did Isaac McCoy in 1833. McCoy denied any religious motivation in the expulsion of the Saints. "I never heard that they had once been interrupted in the performance of their religious services," he wrote. Instead, the problem was that they were "shiftless and ignorant," were "obnoxious to the citizens," and would "at no distant day . . . control all county business." McCoy also criticized them for having the audacity to arm themselves when their houses were attacked. He concluded that the expulsion of the Mormons was a good thing because they might have sought retribution for the violence against them: "What an awful catastrophe have we escaped!"[1]

McCoy was deploying an old canard: because the Mormons were legally allowed to worship, the case against them was not about religion. Mormons thought otherwise. Eli Chase described himself as having received "threatenings & persecutions . . . [o]n account of our religion." Stephen Chase requested legal redress for "damages which I consider sustained in consequence of my religion." John Patten directly asked his persecutors why they attacked him, and they replied "that our faith on the subject of religion was disgusting."[2] Multiple times, Mormons were told that if they denied the faith, the attacks would end. When Partridge, Morley, Corrill, and others met with mob representatives on July 23, they were informed "that their lives would be spared" if "they should deny the faith which they professed, which if they would, all should be peace and friendship on the part of the mob toward them." Gates Gipson was told the same thing on a Missouri street.[3] As the Mormons were forcibly removed in November, Boggs and Pitcher allowed two Mormon families to stay; both of those families had "denied the faith."[4] Alexander Majors later wrote that the trouble really came when "the citizens, and particularly the religious portion of them, made up their minds that it was wrong to allow them to be printing their literature and preaching."[5]

McCoy was flat wrong: religious objections to Mormon sermons, Mormon printing, and Mormon preaching seem to have been a major reason behind the expulsion of the Saints. There is another, deeper problem with McCoy's explanation. McCoy—who was described in multiple reports as a participant in the mob rather than a neutral observer—claimed that Mormons were removed because they were lazy and arrogant. But, of course, it was not *lazy* Americans or *arrogant* Americans who were removed from Jackson County— it was *Mormon* Americans. Indeed, McCoy's letter, written in the immediate wake of the expulsion, performed a neat logical trick. By defining the Mormons as lazy or arrogant or capable of defending themselves, McCoy implicitly justified the removal of Mormons on nonreligious grounds—it was the lazy who were being exiled and, therefore, no discrimination had occurred. In so doing, McCoy conveniently passed over the way in which he had defined everyone of a particular background as lazy or arrogant. This trick happens often in our own media discussions; voices for religious restrictions or denials of rights often justify those claims by saying that certain religions are by their very nature lazy or arrogant or foreign or violent or dangerous or sneaky or whatever. In this way, the argument stops being about religion and rights and starts to be about whether laziness or arrogance or sneakiness is good or bad.

But it is—and it was—a case about rights and religion. The Mormons were targeted and noticed in the first place because of their religious beliefs; "all of this," wrote a group of Mormons, because "of our belief in direct revelation of God to the children of men."[6] Between 1783 and 1834, Catholics, Jews, Shakers, Baptists, and the followers of Native American prophets would face religious restrictions and physical attacks based on the same logic that such religions were dangerous for democracy and therefore had to be put down.

At its heart, the struggle was over the question of citizenship. McCoy, after all, called the Mormons "obnoxious *to the citizens.*" Most anti-Mormon diatribes in Missouri insisted that Mormons were not citizens. Legally, of course, there was no basis for this claim. With the exception of a few Canadian converts, all the Mormons in 1833 were US citizens. Nor did anti-Mormons bother to explain *why* Mormons were different than "citizens." But by writing this difference into rhetoric and rumor, the anti-Mormons won a huge victory even before the mob rose or a gun was fired. By defining the struggle as "citizens" against "Mormons," anti-Mormons gave themselves a huge advantage: citizens have rights; by extension, Mormons had none. And if people without rights—noncitizens—began making laws by winning elections, then a crisis of democracy was at hand. In this way, anti-Mormon language turned the struggle over Mormonism from a discussion of religious beliefs and practices into a crisis in which "Mormons" might make laws for "citizens." They framed the fight as one over democracy rather than over theology.

The afflicted Mormons understood the stakes perfectly; they knew that their battle was over citizenship, and they said so. A group of Mormon elders wrote to President Jackson that "those sacred rights . . . guaranteed to every religious sect, have been publicly invaded in open hostility to the spirit and genius of our free government."[7] Other Mormons did not have such erudition, but they said much the same thing. Charles Patten claimed he was denied his "Writes of sitisenship" in being permitted to worship as he saw fit. George Washington Voorhees similarly wrote about "being driven from Jackson County and not aloud miy Privileges as other Citizens." Truman Brace was surrounded while in the woods and beaten for being a Mormon. He responded by writing,

"In the revalutionary war my father Was ingaged fiting for liberty which is all that I clame according to the constituticion."[8] Mormons knew that, as citizens, they had a right to choose not only how to worship but also how to believe and live by their beliefs. And they knew the challenge was couched not as an argument over scripture but as a challenge to their rights as citizens.

This is perhaps where Mormonism in the 1830s sheds light on the challenging questions about religious freedom and democracy in the twenty-first century. Conflicts over Mormon doctrine and practice had emerged with the movement itself; many early critiques focused on denouncing Mormon claims to modern miracles, or the golden plates, or seer stones and magic. Denying the truth of Mormon religious claims, however, did not usually breed violence. An undercurrent, however, claimed that Mormon beliefs threatened democracy itself. And when those ideas became the main case against Mormonism— when it was defined not as a theological error but as a group of non-Americans threatening the state—violence broke out. In a democracy, the first step in lending credence to violence against any religion is to define it as *not* a religion—to instead claim it is a conspiracy, a delusion, a secret plot, or a threat to the state.[9]

Rumor promotes this volatile combination of politics and anger because rumor relies more on preconceived ideas than on actual facts; rumor spreads because it *sounds* right rather than because it necessarily *is* right. Newel Knight noted that the July 1833 meeting of the mob was immediately followed by a blast of rumor: "All kinds of strange stories were set afloat."[10] Once someone believes a particular religion is out to destroy America, it is easy to find rumor to support that conclusion. McCoy certainly did. He openly acknowledged in his November letter that Mormons in Jackson County became "strongly suspected of tampering with the neighboring Indians. . . . I could not resist the belief that they had sought aid from the Indians though I have not ascertained that legal evidence of the fact could be obtained." Nor was that all. "Reports believed to be true, for the correctness of which I cannot vouch, says that they repeatedly declared that if the Almighty should not give it to them by any other miracle, it would be done by their sword."[11] One of McCoy's central claims against Mormons was that they *might* have risen up to harm their Gentile neighbors. He had no evidence for the claim, and he knew he had no evidence for the claim, and he helped force them from their homes anyway. That was how jokes and stories about ghosts and angels and warnings about false prophets in Palmyra turned into bodies and refugees in Independence.

# NOTES

## ABBREVIATIONS

| | |
|---|---|
| CHL | Church History Library, Salt Lake City |
| D&C | *Doctrine and Covenants of the Church of Jesus Christ of Latter-day Saints* (Salt Lake City: Church of Jesus Christ of Latter-day Saints, 1981) |
| EM&GA | *Evangelical Magazine & Gospel Advocate* |
| EMD | Dan Vogel, ed., *Early Mormon Documents* (Salt Lake City: Signature, 2002) |
| EMS | *Evening and Morning Star* |
| FWR | Donald Q. Cannon and Lyndon W. Cook, eds. *Far West Record: Minutes of the Church of Jesus Christ of Latter-day Saints* (Salt Lake City: Deseret, 1983) |
| GAS | George A. Smith, "History of George A. Smith," George A. Smith Papers, 1834–77, CHL |
| HBLL | Harold B. Lee Library, Brigham Young University |
| HC | Joseph Smith Jr., *History of the Church of Jesus Christ of Latter-day Saints, 1830–1844*, ed. B. H. Roberts. 7 vols (Salt Lake City: Deseret, 1971) |
| JS | Joseph Smith Jr. |
| JSP-D | Dean C. Jessee et al., eds. *The Joseph Smith Papers.* Documents Series, 11 vols. to date (Salt Lake City: Church Historian's Press, 2013–) |
| JSP-H | Dean C. Jessee et al., eds. *The Joseph Smith Papers.* Histories Series, 2 vols. (Salt Lake City: Church Historian's Press, 2012) |
| MoU | Eber Howe, *Mormonism Unvailed* (Painesville, OH: privately printed, 1834) |
| MRP | Clark V. Johnson, ed., *Mormon Redress Petitions: Documents of the 1833–1838 Missouri Conflict* (Provo, UT: Religious Studies Center, Brigham Young University, 1992) |
| MWV | D. Michael Quinn, *Early Mormonism and the Magic World View* (Salt Lake City: Signature, 1998) |

| RSR | Richard Bushman, *Joseph Smith: Rough Stone Rolling* (New York: Vintage, 2007) |
| T&S | *Times and Seasons* |
| Temple lot suit | *The Reorganized Church of Jesus Christ of Latter Day Saints, complainant, v. The Church of Christ at Independence, Missouri* (Lamoni, IA: Herald Publishing House, 1893) |
| WWP | W. W. Phelps Collection, CHL |

### PROLOGUE

1. *(Columbia) Missouri Intelligencer*, Aug. 10, 1833.

2. Marvin S. Hill, *Quest for Refuge: The Mormon Flight from American Pluralism* (Salt Lake City: Signature, 1989), 41; *(Columbia) Missouri Intelligencer*, Aug. 10, 1833.

3. John P. Greene, "Facts Relative to the Expulsion of Mormons or Latter-day Saints, from the State of Missouri, under the 'Exterminating Order,'" in MRP, 22.

4. Greene, "Facts Relative to the Expulsion of Mormons," 15, 22.

5. Parley Pratt, "History of the Late Persecution," in MRP, 65; John Corrill to Oliver Cowdery, Dec. 1833, reprinted in EMS, Jan. 1834.

6. Citizenship is defined by law, but also by custom. The Fourteenth Amendment recodified citizenship in the 1860s, but before then, a raft of state laws defined the term. Contested legal definitions made citizenship slippery and therefore malleable. As Martha Jones has written, sometimes people claimed citizenship by exercising rights, and sometimes claimed rights by proving citizenship. See Martha Jones, *Birthright Citizens: A History of Race and Rights in Antebellum America* (New York: Cambridge University Press, 2018), 10. See also Douglas Bradburn, *The Citizenship Revolution* (Charlottesville: University of Virginia Press, 2009).

7. MoU, 83; *Painesville (OH) Telegraph*, Jan. 3, 1834.

8. *Palmyra (NY) Reflector*, June 12, 1830.

9. See J. Spencer Fluhman, *"A Peculiar People": Anti-Mormonism and the Making of Religion in Nineteenth-Century America* (Chapel Hill: University of North Carolina Press, 2012), 4–5, 13; Patrick Q. Mason, *Mormonism and Violence: The Battles of Zion* (Cambridge: Cambridge University Press, 2019), ch. 2. The 1835 "mention" of polygamy by the Latter-day Saints was a condemnation of the practice.

10. Statement of Isaac McCoy, Nov. 28, 1833, printed in *Missouri Republican*, Dec. 20, 1833.

11. *(Columbia) Missouri Intelligencer*, April 18, 1833.

12. My two notes follow the general approach of Laurel Thatcher Ulrich in *A House Full of Females* (New York: Vintage, 2017), xx, xxiv; RSR, 17, xxi; quote from Ramsey MacMullen, *Christianizing the Roman Empire* (New Haven, CT: Yale University Press, 1984), 19–20.

CHAPTER ONE:  **The Sectarian Dilemma**

1. HC, 1:18.

2. Diedrich Willers to Reverend Brethren, June 18, 1830, Vanessa Whiteley trans., in Whiteley, "The Diedrich Willers Letter—Revisited," *Journal of Mormon History* 46:3 (July 2020): 149; Origin Bachelor, "Mormonism Exposed," and James M'Chesney, "Antidote to Mormonism," in *A New Witness for Christ in America*, ed. Francis Kirkham (Independence, MO: Zion's, 1951), 2:159, 162.

3. Barnes Frisbie, *History of Middletown, Vermont* (Rutland, VT: Tuttle, 1867), 51 (emphasis original), 45–46, 55.

4. Frisbie's history is borne out by what little primary-source evidence is available. See Robert Parks, *History of Wells, Vermont* (Rutland, VT: Tuttle, 1869), 80–81, for Nancy Glass's oral history.

5. Frisbie, *History of Middletown, Vermont*, 60, 64.

6. See MWV, 35–36, 121–30; John L. Brooke, *The Refiner's Fire: The Making of Mormon Cosmology, 1644–1844* (New York: Cambridge University Press, 1994); Daniel Walker Howe, "Emergent Mormonism in Context," in *The Oxford Handbook of Mormonism*, ed. Terryl Givens and Philip Barlow (New York: Oxford University Press, 2015), 31. On Handsome Lake and Smith, see Brooke, *Refiner's Fire*, 164, and Peter Manseau, *One Nation Under Gods: A New American History* (New York: Little, Brown, 2015); on Noah and Smith, see Richard Bushman, *Joseph Smith and the Beginnings of Mormonism* (Urbana: University of Illinois Press, 1984), 138; Eran Shalev, *American Zion* (New Haven, CT: Yale University Press, 2013), 149.

7. Frances Trollope, *Domestic Manners of the Americans* (1832; reprint, New York: Vintage, 1960), 108.

8. Peter Cartwright, *The Autobiography of Peter Cartwright*, ed. Charles L. Wallis (Nashville, TN: Abingdon, 1956), 43–47.

9. Barton Warren Stone, *Biography of Elder Barton Warren Stone*, ed. John Rogers (Cincinnati: J. A. and U. P. James., 1847), 62.

10. "A Narrative of the Elder Caleb Rich," *Candid Examiner* 2 (1826): 186.

11. Jefferson quoted Steven Waldman, *Founding Faith: Providence, Politics, and the Birth of Religious Freedom in America* (New York: Random House, 2008), 77.

12. Edward Augustus Kendall, *Travels through the Northern Parts of the United States in the Years 1807 and 1808* (New York: I. Riley, 1809), 3:84.

13. David Young, *The Wonderful History of the Morristown Ghost: Thoroughly and Carefully Revised* (Newark, NJ: Benjamin Olds, 1826), 13.

14. Johannes Dillinger, *Magical Treasure Hunting in Europe and North America* (New York: Palgrave, 2012), 61–66.

15. Caleb Butler, *History of the Town of Groton* (Boston: T. R. Marvin, 1848), 256.

16. Nathaniel Stacy, *Memoirs of the Life of Nathaniel Stacy* (Columbus, PA: Abner Vedder, 1850), 171–72.

17. Philanthropist, *An Account of the Beginnings, Transactions, and Discovery, of Ransford Rogers Who Seduced Many by Pretended Hobgoblins and Apparitions* (Newark, NJ: n.p., 1792), 19.

18. William Bentley, *The Diary of William Bentley* (Salem, MA: Essex Institute, 1914), 3:358.

19. "History of the Divining Rod: With the Adventures of an Old Rodsman," *United States Magazine and Democratic Review* 26 (1850): 223–24.

20. Clark Jillson, ed., *Green Leaves from Whittingham, Vermont* (Worcester, MA: privately printed, 1894), 122; Merchant of Boston, *Nahant, and Other Places on the North-Shore* (Boston: William Chadwick, 1848), 26; *Boston Herald of Freedom*, Dec. 1, 1788; Charles Skinner, *Myths and Legends of Our Own Land* (Philadelphia: J. B. Lippincott, 1896), 2:282–83.

21. John George Hohman, *The Long Lost Friend: A 19th Century Grimoire*, ed. Daniel Harms (Woodbury, MN: Llewellyn, 2012); Adam Jortner, *Blood from the Sky: Miracles and Politics in the Early American Republic* (Charlottesville: University of Virginia Press, 2017), 58, 48.

22. Jortner, *Blood from the Sky*, 108–9, 16; Edmund S. Morgan, "The Witch and We, the People," *American Heritage* 34:5 (Aug.–Sept. 1983): 6–12; Thomas Kidd, *God of Liberty: A Religious History of the American Revolution* (New York: Basic Books, 2010), 172.

23. John L. Brooke, "'The True Spiritual Seed': Sectarian Religion and the Persistence of the Occult in Eighteenth-Century New England," in *Wonders of the Invisible World: 1600–1900*, ed. Peter Benes (Boston: Boston University Press, 1995).

24. William Pencak, *Jews and Gentiles in Early America* (Ann Arbor: University of Michigan Press, 2005), 85–87.

25. Constitution of Delaware, 1776, Avalon Project, accessed April 19, 2020, https://avalon.law.yale.edu/18th_century/de02.asp; Constitution of Massachusetts, 1780, in *Massachusetts: Colony to Commonwealth*, ed. Robert J. Taylor (Chapel Hill: University of North Carolina Press, 1961), 127–46. See also Stanley F. Chyet, "The Political Rights of the Jews in the United States, 1776–1840," *American Jewish Archives Journal* 10:1 (1958): 14–75.

26. Waldman, *Founding Faith*, 119–20.

27. Waldman, *Founding Faith*, 123.

28. Madison to Thomas Jefferson, Oct. 24, 1787, *Founders Online* (National Archives), accessed Oct. 18, 2020, https://founders.archives.gov/?q=inefficacy%20 Author%3A%22Madison%2C%20James%22&s=1111311111&r=7&sr=.

29. "Act for Establishing Religious Freedom, [31 October] 1785," *Founders Online* (National Archives), accessed Dec. 4, 2020, https://founders.archives.gov/documents /Madison/01-08-02-0206.

30. Waldman, *Founding Faith*, 119. Madison was referring specifically to Anglicans and Presbyterians.

31. Jortner, *Blood from the Sky*, 164.

32. Jortner, *Blood from the Sky*, 43.

33. Elhanan Winchester, *The Seed of the Woman Bruising the Serpent's Head* (Philadelphia: n.p., 1781), 18.

34. RSR, 17.

35. MWV, 106–8.

36. Fawn Brodie, *No Man Knows My History: The Life of Joseph Smith the Mormon Prophet*, 2nd ed. (New York: Knopf, 1971; reprint, New York: Vintage, 1995), 85.

37. Christopher Baldwin, *Diary of Christopher Columbus Baldwin* (Worcester, MA: American Antiquarian Society, 1901), 177–79.

38. Robert McAfee Journal, entry for July 31, 1804, Filson Historical Society, Louisville, KY; Susan Arrington Madsen, "Mary Fielding Smith," in *Encyclopedia of Mormonism*, ed. Daniel H. Ludlow (New York: Macmillan, 1992), 3:1358.

39. "A Narrative of the Elder Caleb Rich," 179.

40. "Abridged Record of the Life of John Murdock," John Murdock Journal and Autobiographies, L. Tom Perry Special Collections Library, Harold B. Lee Library, Brigham Young University, Provo, UT; Joseph Smith Jr., "Church History," *Times and Seasons* 3:9 (March 1, 1842): 706–10.

41. Richard McNemar, *Abstract of an Apology for Renouncing the Jurisdiction of the Synod of Kentucky* (N.p. [Lexington, KY?]: privately printed, 1804), 147–57.

42. Stone quoted in John Boles, *The Great Revival: The Beginnings of the Bible Belt* (Lexington: University Press of Kentucky, 1972), 151.

43. James Bradley Finley, *Pioneer Life in the West* (New York: Hunt and Eaton, 1853), 257–58.

44. Alexander Campbell, *Delusions* (Boston: Benjamin H. Green, 1832). For the historians of the Burned-Over District, see ch. 3, note 5.

45. HC, 1:4.

46. Joseph Smith Jr., "Draft 2," History of the Church, in JSP-H, 1:208.

47. RSR, 37–38.

48. There are several versions of the First Vision; for discussion of sources, see JSP-H, 1:212–14.

49. JSP-H, 1:54.

50. JSP-H, 1:217–21.

51. David Rice, *A Sermon on the Present Revival of Religion* (Washington, GA: Monitor Press, 1804), 10–11; Trollope, *Domestic Manners*, 110.

52. James D. Bratt, "Anti-revivalism in Antebellum America," *Journal of the Early Republic* 24:1 (Spring 2004): 65–106. Work that credits revivalism for its social more than its religious implications includes William G. McLoughlin, *Revivals, Awakenings, and Reform: An Essay on Religion and Social Change in America, 1607–1977* (Chicago: University of Chicago Press, 1978), and Kidd, *God of Liberty*.

53. Rice, *Sermon on the Present Revival*, 23.

54. Asahel Nettleton, Lyman Beecher, and James Walker, quoted in Bratt, "Anti-revivalism in Antebellum America," 80–81.

55. Booth quoted in MoU, 202.

56. Lucy Mack Smith's version is well summarized in RSR, 43.

57. Willers to Reverend Brethren, June 18, 1830, 149.

58. Baldwin, *Diary*, 177–79; Joshua Gordon Witchcraft Book, 1784, South Caroliniana Manuscripts, University of South Carolina Library; "History of the Divining Rod," 223–24.

59. John Sherer to Absalom Peters, Nov. 18, 1830, in EMD, 4:92.

60. Abram W. Benton reminiscence, March 1831, in EMD 4:95.

61. J. T. Crane, "Mystic Arts in Our Own Day," *Methodist Quarterly Review*, 3rd ser., 8:1 (April 1848): 211; MWV 27; Lucy Crawford, *History of the White Mountains* (White Hills, NH: Gerrish, 1846), 106; *Washington* (DC) *National Intelligencer*, Nov. 24, 1851; J. W. Hanson, *History of Gardiner, Pittston, and West Gardiner* (Gardiner, ME: William Palmer, 1852), 169; *Methodist Quarterly Review, 1848*, ed. George Peck (New York: Lane and Scott, 1848), 210.

62. Dillinger, *Magical Treasure Hunting*, 58. See also Alan Taylor, "The Early Republic's Supernatural Economy: Treasure Seeking in the Northeast, 1780–1830," *American Quarterly* 38:1 (Spring 1986): 6–34.

63. Jillson, *Green Leaves*, 117–18.

64. Chloe Russel, *The Complete Fortune Teller and Dream Book*, in Eric Gardner, "'The Complete Fortune Teller and Dream Book': An Antebellum Text 'By Chloe Russel, a Woman of Colour,'" *New England Quarterly* 78:2 (June 2005): 259–88, quote on 272. We should not assume that Russel's autobiographical notes in this text were her own; Gardner points out how unlikely that is, given that the text claims that she saw "Tygers" while living in Africa. Tigers are native to Asia. If we are considering what people understood about magic rather than evaluating any particular claim about magic, however, the referent to this remarkable story of treasure digging yielding freedom is irrelevant. The language of magic in the early republic was the language of freedom—literally, in Russel's case.

65. *Methodist Quarterly Review, 1848*, 211.

66. Frisbie, *History of Middletown, Vermont*, 48–49.

67. Kendall, *Travels through the Northern Parts of the United States*, 3:85.

68. Kendall, *Travels through the Northern Parts of the United States*, 3:85–87.

69. Quoted in MWV, 40.

70. Stacy, *Memoirs of the Life of Nathaniel Stacy*, 171–72.

71. Stacy, *Memoirs of the Life of Nathaniel Stacy*, 171–72; MWV, 41, 247.

72. I quote here from William Purple's account, in EMD 4:134. Purple was the copyist for the 1826 Bainbridge trial and then wrote a more descriptive version many years later. The details in the later text, however, are largely confirmed in Brigham Young's account. (See MWV, 42; and EMD, 4:128.) The contemporary court record from Bainbridge (EMD, 4:239–56) does not discuss the "neighboring girl," but it does describe extensive seer stone work by Smith. Most scholars accept that the woman (usually identified as Sally Chase) provided Smith with his first stone.

73. EMD, 4:134, 253; RSR, 49. See also "Seer Stone," *The Joseph Smith Papers*, accessed Dec. 4, 2020, https://www.josephsmithpapers.org/topic/seer-stone.

74. EMD, 4:255.

75. MoU, 237–38.

76. EMD, 4:252.

77. MoU, 239.

78. JSP-D, 1:351n21. Note also that while the "Articles of Agreement" from 1825 are widely accepted as legitimate, the originals have not been found. Ibid., 1:349.

79. JSP-D, 1:347.

80. RSR, 48; "Joseph Smith Answers to Questions," May 8, 1838, in EMD, 1:53 & n2; EMD, 4:251.

81. Jortner, *Blood from the Sky*, 71; *Laws of the State of New York* (Albany, NY: H. C. Southwick, 1813), 1:114.

82. Jortner, *Blood From the Sky*, 71; Owen Davies, *America Bewitched: The Story of Witchcraft after Salem* (New York: Oxford University Press, 2013), 56.

83. Brian P. Levack, "The Decline and End of Witchcraft Prosecutions," in *Witchcraft and Magic: The Eighteenth and Nineteenth Centuries*, ed. Bengt Ankarloo and Stuart Clark (Philadelphia: University of Pennsylvania Press, 1999), 1–89.

84. Jortner, *Blood from the Sky*, 38.

85. Roy Porter, "Witchcraft and Magic in Enlightenment, Romantic, and Liberal Thought," in Ankarloo and Clark, *Witchcraft and Magic*, 191–282, quote on 195–96.

86. Joseph Lathrop, *Illustrations . . . Witch of Endor* (Springfield, MA: Henry Brewer, 1806), 14.

87. *Laws of the State of Maryland*, ed. Virgil Maxcy (Baltimore: Nicklin and Co., 1811), 3:211.

88. *Laws of the State of New Jersey* (Trenton, NJ: Joseph Justice, 1821), 248.

89. Alan Taylor, *The Civil War of 1812: American Citizens, British Subjects, Irish Rebels, and Indian Allies* (New York: Knopf, 2012), 90.

90. Q. K. Philander Doesticks, *The Witches of New York* (New York: Rudd and Carleton, 1854), 18.

91. Purple reminiscence, in EMD, 4:133.

92. Gordon A. Marsden, "Joseph Smith's 1826 Trial: The Legal Setting," *BYU Studies Quarterly* 30:2 (1990): 91–108, quote on 92.

93. On the veracity of documents surrounding the Stowells' agreement and the Bainbridge trial, see EMD, 4:239–41; and JSP-D, 1:345–50.

94. EMD, 4:250, 135.

95. EMD, 4:251, 254.

96. EMD, 4:253.

97. Joel K. Noble to Jonathan B. Turner, March 8, 1842, in EMD, 4:108. The exact result of the trial is in some dispute (see EMD, 4:243–48), but by any account, any punishment handed down to Smith was not significant.

98. EMD, 1:597.

99. Orasmus Turner, 1851, in EMD, 3:48.

100. Joseph Williamson, "Castine, and the Old Coins Found There," in *Collections of the Maine Historical Society*, 1st ser., 6 (1859): 107–26, 115; Caleb Atwater,

"Description of the Antiquities Discovered in the State of Ohio," *Archaeologia Americana: Transactions & Collections of the American Antiquarian Society* 1 (1820): 119–20.

101. Jortner, *Blood from the Sky*, 184; Nancy Lusignan Schultz, "Introduction," in *Veil of Fear: Nineteenth-Century Convent Tales* (West Lafayette, IN: NotaBell, 1999), vii–ix.

102. Washington to George Mason, Oct. 3, 1785, in *The Papers of George Washington*, Confederation Series, ed. W. W. Abbot (Charlottesville: University of Virginia Press, 1994), 292–93.

103. Dillinger, *Magical Treasure Hunting*, 177.

104. MWV, 64.

105. Lucy Mack Smith, *Lucy's Book: A Critical Edition of Lucy Mack Smith's Family Memoir*, ed. Lavina Fielding Anderson et al. (Salt Lake City: Signature, 2001), 323.

CHAPTER TWO:  **The Bible Quarry**

1. Joseph Knight Sr., "Joseph Knight's Recollection of Early Mormon History," ed. Dean C. Jessee, *BYU Studies* 17: 1 (1976): 3, https://byustudies.byu.edu/content /joseph-knights-recollection-early-mormon-history; "Martin Harris interview with Joel Tiffany," 1859, EMD, 2:300–310; "Willard Chase Statement," in EMD, 2:243.

2. Knight, "Joseph Knight's Recollection," 3.

3. Eli Bruce Diary, entry for Nov. 5, 1830, in EMD, 3:4.

4. Knight, "Joseph Knight's Recollection," 3. On Beman, see MWV, 39. On the early responses to the Book of Mormon, see Grant Underwood, *The Millenarian World of Early Mormonism* (Urbana: University of Illinois Press, 1993); Terryl Givens, *By the Hand of Mormon: The American Scripture That Launched a New World Religion* (New York: Oxford University Press, 2002); Nathan Hatch, *The Democratization of American Christianity* (New Haven, CT: Yale University Press, 1989), 113–22; and Fluhman, *"A Peculiar People,"* chs. 1–2.

5. HC, 1:18.

6. Harris interview, in EMD, 2:308.

7. Jesse Smith to Hyrum Smith, June 17, 1829, in EMD, 1:552–53.

8. JS, "History, 1839," in EMD, 1:67.

9. JS, "History, 1832," in EMD, 1:29.

10. JS, "History, 1839," in EMD, 1:67.

11. Truman Coe account, 1836, in EMD, 1:47. On the chronology of Smith's histories, see "The Histories of Joseph Smith, 1832–1844," in JSP-H, 1:xxxiv–xxxv.

12. Knight, "Joseph Knight's Recollection," 2.

13. Interview with Fayette Lapham, in EMD, 1:461.

14. "Last Testimony of Sister Emma," *Saints' Herald*, Jan. 10, 1879, 290; Henry Caswall, *The City of Mormons* (London: Rivington, 1842), 27; "William Smith Testimony, 1884," in EMD, 1:505; John Whitmer, quoted in Theodore Turley memoranda, ca. 1845, CHL.

15. On differing interpretations of the materiality of the Book of Mormon, see Givens, *By the Hand of Mormon*, ch. 1; Dan Vogel, introduction, in *Joseph Smith: The Making of a Prophet* (Salt Lake City: Signature, 2004); and Ann Taves, *Revelatory Events: Three Case Studies of the Emergence of New Spiritual Paths* (Princeton, NJ: Princeton University Press, 2016), 17–81. Thanks to Michael MacKay for his insights into material culture and the plates.

16. Givens, *By the Hand of Mormon*, 39–41.

17. JS to Noah C. Saxton, Jan. 4, 1833, in JSP-D, 2:354.

18. Lucy Mack Smith, "Biographical Sketches of Joseph Smith the Prophet," EMD, 1:328–29.

19. MoU, 243.

20. Knight, "Joseph Knight's Recollection," 4.

21. David Whitmer, *An Address to All Believers in Christ* (Richmond, MO: privately printed, 1887), 12.

22. JSP-D, 1:353–55.

23. For background on this process, see RSR, ch. 4, and Michael Hubbard MacKay and Gerrit Dirkmaat, *From Darkness unto Light: Joseph Smith's Translation of the Book of Mormon* (Provo, UT: Deseret Book, 2015).

24. Harris interview, in EMD, 2:376.

25. John A. Clark, *Episcopal Recorder*, Aug. 24, 1840, in EMD, 2:266.

26. Poe, "The Literati," in *The Works of the Late Edgar Allan Poe* (New York: Redfield, 1858), 3:45.

27. HC, 1:20.

28. Anthon to Howe, Feb. 17, 1834, in MoU, 271–72.

29. JSP-D, 1:357–66. Terryl Givens has suggested that Smith himself possibly wanted to procure a simplified lexicon for his task and so sent Harris for expert opinion. *By the Hand of Mormon*, 28.

30. D&C 3:1. A summary of Harris's odyssey with the pages can be found in Paul Gutjahr, *The Book of Mormon: A Biography* (Princeton, NJ: Princeton University Press, 2012), 19–24.

31. MoU, 22–23.

32. Thurlow Weed, *Life of Thurlow Weed* (Boston: Houghton and Mifflin, 1884), 7.

33. Grandin quoted in Gerrit J. Dirkmaat and Michael Hubbard MacKay, "Joseph Smith's Negotiations to Publish the Book of Mormon," in *The Coming Forth of the Book of Mormon: A Marvelous Work and a Wonder*, ed. Dennis L. Largey, Andrew H. Hedges, John Hilton III, and Kerry Hull (Salt Lake City: Deseret, 2015), 156–71; Gutjahr, *Book of Mormon*, 31.

34. Parley P. Pratt, *Autobiography of Parley P. Pratt* (New York: Russell Brothers, 1874), 38.

35. "Testimony of Brother E. Thayre [Thayer] Concerning the Latter Day Work," *True Latter Day Saints Herald* 3:4 (Oct. 1862): 80.

36. David Patten Journal, 1832–34, CHL.

37. Edward W. Tullidge, *The Women of Mormondom* (New York: Widener, Tullidge, and Crandall, 1877), 162–64.

38. Benjamin Brown, *Testimonies of the Truth* (Liverpool: S. W. Richards, 1853), 8. The Three Nephites are referenced in 3 Nephi 28.

39. Sarah Pea Rich, Autobiography and Journal, CHL.

40. Noah Packard, "A Synopsis of the Life and Travels of Noah Packard, Written by Himself," HBLL.

41. Ashbel Kitchell, "A Shaker View of a Mormon Mission," ed. Lawrence Flake, *BYU Studies* 20:1 (1979): 2.

42. Grant Hardy, *Understanding the Book of Mormon* (New York: Oxford University Press, 2010), xii–xiii.

43. Brodie, *No Man Knows My History*, 62; Jesse J. Smith to Elias Smith, March 7, 1834, Elias Smith Papers, Folder 1, CHL. Jesse was a distant relative of Joseph Smith Jr., but did not convert until 1833. Gutjahr, *Book of Mormon*, 96, 34. In 1879 and 1920, the metatext of the official LDS editions of the Book of Mormon were revised with new numbering and presentation methods that more closely resembled the Protestant Bible. 1 Nephi, for example, had seven chapter divisions in the 1830 edition, but has twenty-two in the current version. This numbering has not affected the text itself. Biblical numbering, of course, is also a later addition to the canon; the author of Matthew, for example, did not stop to write chapter and verse numbers into the text.

44. 1 Nephi 9:2, 22:7–8.

45. Brandon S. Plewe, ed., *Mapping Mormonism* (Provo, UT: Brigham Young University Press, 2012), 190–91.

46. 2 Nephi 5:34.

47. JSP-D, 2:354.

48. JS to the Elders of the Church, in *Messenger & Advocate* 2:3 (December 1835): 227.

49. Randel quoted in Thomas Kidd and Benjamin Hawkins, *Baptists in America* (New York: Oxford University Press, 2015), 55.

50. John Jea, *The Life, History, and Unparalleled Sufferings of John Jea* (Portsea, UK: privately printed, 1811), 35.

51. Rebecca Jackson, *Gifts of Power: The Writings of Rebecca Jackson, Black Visionary, Shaker Eldress*, ed. Jean McMahon Humez (Amherst: University of Massachusetts Press, 1981), 114, 164.

52. Holland was quoting a sermon, recalled by United Church of Christ minister Anne Gordon, describing the differences in Christian approaches to the canon. See Holland, *Sacred Borders: Continuing Revelation and Canonical Restraint in Early America* (New York: Oxford University Press, 2011), 6.

53. *Testimony of Christ's Second Appearing* (Albany, NY: Horsford, 1810), xii (emphasis original).

54. Byrd to Williamson, October 28, 1827, in William S. Byrd, *Letters from a Young Shaker: William S. Byrd at Pleasant Hill*, ed. Stephen Stein (Lexington: University Press of Kentucky, 1985), 110–11.

55. Alfred A. Cave, *Prophets of the Great Spirit* (Lincoln: University of Nebraska Press, 2006), 199–201.

56. John H. Wigger, *Taking Heaven by Storm: Methodism and the Rise of Popular Christianity in America* (Urbana: University of Illinois Press, 1998), 110; Kidd and Hawkins, *Baptists in America*, 46.

57. Nathan Hatch, *The Democratization of American Christianity* (New Haven, CT: Yale University Press, 1989), 10.

58. Campbell, *Delusions*; Willers to Reverend Brethren, June 18, 1830, 150.

59. MoU, 61, 78, 84.

60. MoU, 93.

61. Russell R. Rich, "The Dogberry Papers and the Book of Mormon," *BYU Studies Quarterly* 10:3 (1970): 315–17.

62. *Rochester Gem*, May 15, 1830, in *New Witness for Christ in America*, 2:46–47. See also Donald Q. Cannon, "In the Press: Early Newspaper Reports on the Initial Publication of the Book of Mormon," *Journal of the Book of Mormon Studies* 16:2 (2007): 4–15, 92–93.

63. *Palmyra (NY) Reflector*, Aug. 4, 1830; *Geneva Gazette*, Nov. 1, 1830; *Palmyra (NY) Reflector*, Aug. 14, 1830.

64. *New York Telescope*, Feb. 20, 1830, in Cannon, "In the Press," 7.

65. *Painesville (OH) Telegraph*, Nov. 30, 1830.

66. HC, 1:18.

67. *New York Morning Courier*, Sept. 1, 1831.

68. EM&GA, April 9, 1831.

69. EM&GA, Feb. 5, 1831.

70. Campbell, *Delusions*, 94.

71. EM&GA, April 9, 1831.

72. HC, 1:86, 10.

73. John Whitmer, *From Historian to Dissident: The Book of John Whitmer*, ed. Bruse Westergren (Salt Lake City: Signature, 1995), 13.

CHAPTER THREE: **Kirtland**

1. Mark Lyman Staker, *Hearken, O Ye People: The Historical Setting for Joseph Smith's Ohio Revelations* (Salt Lake City: Greg Kofford Books, 2009), xxi.

2. Lucy Mack Smith, "Biographical Sketches," in EMD, 1:419–20.

3. Knight, "Manuscript of the Early History of Joseph Smith," 12; RSR, 116–17.

4. Knight, "Manuscript of the Early History of Joseph Smith," 11–12; JS to Newel Knight and the Church at Colesville, August 28, 1830, JSP-D 1:172–77.

5. Whitney Cross, in *The Burned-Over District* (Ithaca, NY: Cornell University Press, 1950), 3, coined the term Burned-Over District, referring to New York topography altered by the coming of the Erie Canal. Cross argued that economic disruption along the Canal bred religious change. By extension, religious change develops from economic and social stress. As noted here and elsewhere, however,

the content of ideas matters. According to Judith Wellman, Cross borrowed the term from Charles Grandison Finney's reference to the place as a "burnt district"; Cross's dissertation advisor, Arthur Schlesinger, thought "burned-over" sounded better. See Wellman, "Crossing Over Cross: Whitney Cross's Burned-Over District as Social History," *Reviews in American History* 17:1 (March 1989): 164. See also Marianne Perciaccante, *Calling Down Fire: Charles Grandison Finney and Revivalism in Jefferson County, New York, 1800–1840* (Albany: State University of New York Press, 2003); and Paul Johnson, *A Shopkeeper's Millennium: Society and Revivals in Rochester, New York, 1815–1837* (New York: Hill and Wang, 1978).

6. Roger D. Launius, *Zion's Camp: Expedition to Missouri, 1834* (Independence, MO: Herald, 1984), 32.

7. MoU, 215.

8. Newel Knight, "Newel Knight's Journal," in *Scraps of Autobiography* (Salt Lake City: Juvenile Instructor's Office, 1883), 64.

9. JSP-D, 1:183; MoU, 216.

10. HC, 1:109–10.

11. Terryl Givens has referred to this phenomena as "dialogic revelation." Givens, *By the Hand of Mormon*, 226, 218–39. For the names of individuals requesting and receiving revelations in early June 1831, see HC, 1:179–82.

12. Joseph Smith, "History of the Church 1839" draft, in EMD, 1:134. The reference to "a few of us got together" was removed in the printed edition; see EMD, 1:134n175.

13. Histories of the Saints often debate the extent to which Smith sought the ecclesiastical (and temporal) power he achieved. The experiences of early Saints seem not to emphasize this aspect of his career, while early anti-Mormon writings stress Smith's "tyranny." See Brodie, *No Man Knows My History*, 284–85; Klaus J. Hansen, *Mormonism and the American Experience* (Chicago: University of Chicago Press, 1981), 113–27. Steven Harper analyzes this approach in "'Dictated by Christ': Joseph Smith and the Politics of Revelation," *Journal of the Early Republic* 26:2 (Summer 2006): 275–304.

14. Richard McClellan, "Sidney Rigdon's 1820 Ministry: Preparing the Way for Mormonism in Ohio," *Dialogue* 36:4 (Winter 2003): 151–59.

15. Mary Fielding Smith to Mercy F. Thompson, July 8, 1837, Mary Fielding Smith Letters to Mercy F. Thompson, Mary Fielding Smith Collection, CHL.

16. *Painesville (OH) Telegraph*, Feb. 15, 1831.

17. Staker, *Hearken, O Ye People*, 43.

18. Staker, *Hearken, O Ye People*, 44; Josiah Jones, "History of the Mormonites," in Milton V. Backman, ed., "A Non-Mormon View of the Birth of Mormonism in Ohio," *BYU Studies* 12:3 (Summer 1972), 306–11; quote at 308.

19. Terryl Givens and Matthew Grow, *Parley P. Pratt: The Apostle Paul of Mormonism* (New York: Oxford University Press, 2011), 23–25.

20. Pratt, *Autobiography*, 63.

21. Jones, "History of the Mormonites," 309.

22. Tamma D. Curtis autobiography, CHL.

23. Philo Dibble, "Early Scenes in Church History," in *Four Faith-Promoting Classics* (Salt Lake City: Bookcraft, 1968), 75–76.

24. Corrill, "Brief History of the Church," in JSP-H, 2:133. Bushman carefully reconstructs Corrill's conversion in RSR, 150–52.

25. Dibble, "Early Scenes in Church History," 76.

26. D&C 37:3.

27. Pratt, *Autobiography*, 27.

28. *History of Geauga and Lake Counties, Ohio* (Philadelphia: Williams Brothers, 1878), 248.

29. Oliver Huntington diary and autobiography, HBLL.

30. D&C 57:1

31. Warren Foote autobiography, HBLL.

32. Thomas B. Marsh, autobiography (1857), in Historian's Office Histories of the Twelve, CHL.

33. Staker, *Hearken, O Ye People*, 94.

34. Whitmer, *Historian to Dissident*, 37–38.

35. Whitmer, *Historian to Dissident*, 37.

36. Staker, *Hearken, O Ye People*, 111–12.

37. Catherine A. Brekus, *Strangers and Pilgrims: Female Preaching in America, 1740–1845* (Chapel Hill: University of North Carolina Press, 1998), 1–2.

38. Ann Braude, *Radical Spirits: Spiritualism and Women's Rights in Nineteenth-Century America* (Bloomington: Indiana University Press, 2001), 11–12.

39. On Wilkinson and genderlessness, see Jortner, *Blood from the Sky*, 172; Brekus, *Strangers and Pilgrims*, 95; and Scott Larson, "'Indescribable Being': Theological Performances of Genderlessness in the Society of the Publick Universal Friend, 1776–1819," *Early American Studies* 12:3 (Fall 2014), 576–600.

40. Ann Braude, "Women's History Is American Religious History," in *Retelling U.S. Religious History*, ed. Thomas Tweed (Berkeley: University of California Press, 1997), 87.

41. Quoted in Nancy Cott, *The Bonds of Womanhood: "Woman's Sphere" in New England, 1780–1835* (New Haven, CT: Yale University Press, 1977), 23.

42. Braude, "Women's History," 90.

43. Laurel Thatcher Ulrich, *A House Full of Females: Plural Marriage and Women's Rights in Early Mormonism, 1835–1870* (New York: Vintage, 2017), 63; Sarah Studevant Leavitt, "History of Sarah S. Leavitt," typescript made from the original journal by Juanita Leavitt Pulsipher (1919), CHL.

44. Matilda Davidson, *The Folly and Falsehood of the Golden Book of Mormon* (Paisley, Scotland: A. Gardner, 1839), 3–4.

45. Nancy Towle, *Vicissitudes Illustrated* (Portsmouth, NH: John Caldwell, 1833), 157.

46. Quoted in Tullidge, *The Women of Mormondom*, 208.

47. Sarah Studevant Leavitt, "History of Sarah S. Leavitt"; *Painesville (OH) Telegraph*, Feb. 15, 1831.

48. D&C 43:3, 12.

49. Richard Bushman, for example, writes that Smith "laid down a line between Mormonism and the visionary culture." RSR, 151–52. See also Hill, *Quest for Refuge*, 35.

50. *Painesville (OH) Telegraph*, Feb. 15, 1831.

51. Christopher C. Smith, "Playing Lamanite: Ecstatic Performance of American Indian Roles in Early Mormon Ohio," *Journal of Mormon History* 41:3 (July 2015): 131–66.

52. Staker, *Hearken, O Ye People*, 5–7.

53. W. Paul Reeve, *Religion of a Different Color: Race and the Mormon Struggle for Whiteness* (New York: Oxford University Press, 2015), 117; W. Kesler Jackson, *Elijah Abel: The Incredible True Story of a Black Pioneer* (Springville, UT: Cedar Point, 2013), 27–28; Ulrich, *House Full of Females*, 21.

54. Albert Raboteau, *Slave Religion: The "Invisible Institution" in the Antebellum South* (New York: Oxford University Press, 1978), 215; Woods quoted in John B. Cade, "Out of the Mouths of Ex-Slaves," *Journal of Negro History* 20:3 (1935): 330–31.

55. Peter Kalm, *Travels into North America* (London: Lowndes, 1772), 1:311.

56. Richard S. Newman, *Freedom's Prophet: Bishop Richard Allen, the AME Church, and the Black Founding Fathers* (New York: New York University Press, 2008), 105.

57. Henry Bibb, *Narrative of the Life and Adventures of Henry Bibb* (New York: privately printed, 1849), 30.

58. Raboteau, *Slave Religion*, 281–84.

59. William Wells Brown, *My Southern Home* (Boston: A. G. Brown, 1880), 70–71.

60. Brown, *My Southern Home*, 75.

61. Charles C. Jones, *Religious Instruction of the Negroes* (Savannah, GA: Purse, 1842), 128.

62. *Cleveland Advertiser*, Feb, 8, 1831; Staker, *Hearken, O Ye People*, 77. Kirtland is now in Lake County, which split from Geauga later in the century.

63. Jones, "History of the Mormonites," 310.

64. MoU, 105.

65. *Cleveland Advertiser*, Feb. 8, 1831; Jones, "History of the Mormonites," 309.

66. EM&GA, Feb. 5, 1831; Underhill quoted in Staker, *Hearken, O Ye People*, 62.

67. Staker, *Hearken, O Ye People*, 78. Staker dates this experience to December 1830—the same period when the Lamanite pantomime and physical worship began.

68. Jared Carter journal, typescript, 3, CHL; MoU, 107.

69. Stephen Stein, *The Shaker Experience in America* (New Haven, CT: Yale University Press, 1992), 177–81.

70. Julia Foote, *A Brand Plucked from the Fire* (Cleveland, OH: Schneider, 1879), 66–68; Whitmer, *Historian to Dissident*, 14.

71. *Philadelphia Saturday Courier*, April 19, 1834.

72. Stanley Thayne, "Walking on Water: Nineteenth-Century Prophets and a Legend of Religious Imposture," *Journal of Mormon History* 36:2 (Spring 2010): 160–204; Terryl Givens, "Fraud, Philandery, and Football: Negotiating the Mormon Image," *International Journal of Mormon Studies* 4 (2011): 1–13.

73. MoU, 105 (emphasis original).

74. Jones, "History of the Mormonites," 309.

75. Smith, "Playing Lamanite," 142–43, 147.

76. See Staker, *Hearken, O Ye People*, 101; RSR, 151–56; Brooke, *Refiner's Fire*, 191. Brooke suggested that the prophet wanted to lead his church on absolutist terms but couldn't until 1840. *Refiner's Fire*, 209.

77. Whitmer, *Historian to Dissident*, 69.

78. William Shepard and H. Michael Marquardt, *Lost Apostles: Forgotten Members of Mormonism's Original Quorum of Twelve* (Salt Lake City: Signature, 2014), 20–21. For an extended discussion of the changing roles and designations for Mormon leadership in this period, see JSP-D, 2:xxiv*ff.*

79. Staker, *Hearken, O Ye People*, 95.

80. Earl E. Olson, "Chronology of Ohio Revelations," *BYU Studies* 11:4 (Summer 1971): 339–40. See also JSP-D, 1:257.

81. Staker, *Hearken, O Ye People*, 96.

82. Caroline Barnes Crosby diary, in *Women's Voices: An Untold History of the Latter-day Saints*, ed. Kenneth W. Godfrey, Audrey M. Godfrey, and Jill Mulvay Derr (Salt Lake City: Deseret, 1982), 49.

83. Pratt, *Autobiography*, 76.

84. Whitmer, *Historian to Dissident*, 81–82; D&C 52:42, 57:3, 28:9; JSP-D, 1:340.

85. Olson, "Chronology of Ohio Revelations," 338; "Laws of the Church of Christ," in JSP-D, 1:249–50; see also the editors' notes in "Historical Introduction," 1:249 and 250n66.

86. JSP-D, 1:250.

87. JSP-D, 1:251–52.

88. A brief account of Mormon priesthood can be found in Richard L. Bushman, *Mormonism: A Very Short Introduction* (New York: Oxford University Press, 2008), ch. 4; and in Brooke, *Refiner's Fire*, 191–95.

89. Autobiography of Levi Hancock, quoted in "Historical Introduction," JSP-D, 2:79.

90. JSP-D, 1:255.

91. JSP-D 1:266n142, 266, 281, 287. For the names of individuals requesting and receiving revelations in early June 1831, see HC, 1:179–82.

92. William McLellin, *The Journals of William McLellin*, ed. Jan Shipps and John Welch (Provo, UT: Brigham Young University Press, 1994), 57n52; D&C 47 (Whitmer); D&C 66 (McLellin).

93. "Minutes, circa 3–4 June 1831," in JSP-D, 1:324; Hill, *Quest for Refuge*, 35. Eleven men are marked as having left the church; Corrill is not so marked but was expelled in 1839.

94. Smith to Martin Harris, Feb. 22, 1831, in JSP-D, 1:263.

95. MoU, 189; Corrill, "Brief History of the Church," in JSP-H, 2:145; Whitmer, *Historian to Dissident*, 71.

96. Adam Rankin, *Review of the Noted Revival in Kentucky* (Washington, DC: John Israel, 1802), 25–27, 32.

97. Lorenzo Dow, *The Life, Travels, and Labors of Lorenzo Dow* (New York: C. M. Saxton, 1859), 37; Harvey Rice, *Pioneers of the Western Reserve* (Boston: Lee and Shepard, 1883), 109.

98. Hohman, *The Long Lost Friend*, 88.

99. Jortner, *Blood from the Sky*, 45–48; MWV, 106–8.

100. Demons, as historian Stuart Clark writes, can serve as "perfect antagonists of those who claimed power by divine right, since their defeat could result only from supernatural, not physical, authority." Clark, *Thinking with Demons: The Idea of Witchcraft in Early Modern Europe* (Oxford: Clarendon Press, 2005), 549. Clark refers to witch trials in the 1500s, but the idea applies as well to the chaotic religious reorganization of the early American republic.

101. Joshua V. Himes, introduction, in Campbell, *Delusions*, 4.

102. Bernard Whitman, *A Lecture on Popular Superstitions* (Boston: Bowles and Dearborn, 1829), 63.

103. HC, 1:82.

104. McLellin, *Journals*, 106–12; "Journal of Orson Hyde," entry for March 20, 1832, journal bound with "Miscellaneous Mormon Diaries," vol. 11, HBLL.

105. Jared Carter journal, typescript, 5, CHL.

106. Smoot to Joseph Fielding Smith, 1894, reprinted in Lycurgus Wilson, *The Life of David W. Patten, the First Apostolic Martyr* (1900; reprinted, Peoria, AZ: Eborn Books, 1992). An undated reminiscence about Nauvoo in 1847 reports another sighting of Cain and refers as well to Patten's having told the story of meeting Cain. See Horace Strong Rawson reminiscence, n.d., microfilm, CHL. See also Matthew Bowman, "A Mormon Bigfoot: David Patten's Cain and the Concept of Evil in LDS Folklore," *Journal of Mormon History* 33:3 (2007): 62–82.

107. Whitmer to Cowdery and Smith, July 29, 1833, in FWR 63n2.

108. Evan M. Green journal, January 1833–April 1835, entry for Oct. 4, 1833, CHL.

109. Fred C. Collier and William S. Hartwell, eds., *Kirtland Council Minute Book* (Salt Lake City: Collier's, 1996), 6.

110. Joseph Smith, "Church History," in *Times and Seasons*, March 1, 1842. This essay is commonly referred to as the "Wentworth Letter" among Saints, as it was written in response to a question from John Wentworth.

111. Carter journal, 21.

112. John Murdock Papers, entry for April 12, 1833, HBLL.

113. David Patten journals, undated entry, CHL.

114. Corrill, "Brief History of the Church," in JSP-H, 2:145.

115. MoU, 190.

116. See JSP-H, 2:40n114.

117. MoU, 22–23.

118. McLellin, *Journals*, 37; Levi Jackman, "A Short Sketch of the Life of Levi Jackman," entry for June 7, 1835, CHL.

119. Whitmer, *Historian to Dissident*, 57. Whitmer's original wording of "shaker-quaker" is found in another, edited version of his "History," JSP-H, 2:37.

120. D&C 49:1–2.

121. Robert F. W. Meader, "The Shakers and the Mormons," *Shaker Quarterly* 2 (Fall 1962): 92.

122. D&C 49:4.

123. Kitchell, "Shaker View of a Mormon Mission," 1–2 (emphasis original).

124. Kitchell, "Shaker View of a Mormon Mission," 1; McNemar quoted in Givens and Grow, *Parley P. Pratt*, 49.

125. Kitchell, "Shaker View of a Mormon Mission," 2, 6n6.

126. Kitchell, "Shaker View of a Mormon Mission," 2, 4.

127. D&C 49:22.

128. Meader, "The Shakers and the Mormons," 94; Kitchell, "Shaker View of a Mormon Mission," 3.

129. Kitchell, "Shaker View of a Mormon Mission," 3.

130. Whitmer, *Historian to Dissident*, 81.

131. Knight, "Manuscript of the Early History of Joseph Smith," 13.

132. See, for example, Dale B. Light, *Rome and the New Republic* (Notre Dame, IN: Notre Dame University Press, 1996); and Margaret Wilson Gillikin, "Competing Loyalties: Nationality, Church Governance, and the Development of an American Catholic Identity," *Early American Studies* 11:1 (Winter 2013): 146–60.

133. MoU 182; see also JSP-D, 2:95–96.

134. Mark R. Grandstaff, "Having More Learning than Sense: William E. McLellin and the Book of Commandments Revisited," *Dialogue* 26:4 (Winter 1993): 23–48.

135. D&C 67:6–7.

136. Grandstaff, "Having More Learning than Sense," 28–34.

137. McLellin, *Journals*, 237.

138. Grandstaff, "Having More Learning than Sense," 43.

139. Conference Minutes, Nov. 2, 1831, in FWR, 28.

140. Conference Minutes, Nov. 8, 1831, in FWR, 28–29.

141. William McLellin to Samuel McLellin, Aug. 4, 1832, quoted in Grandstaff, "Having More Learning than Sense," 36.

142. RSR, 170.

143. Shepard and Marquardt, *Lost Apostles*, 30; D. Michael Quinn, "Jesse Gause: Joseph Smith's Little Known Counselor," *BYU Studies* 23:4 (Fall 1983): 487–93.

144. Staker, *Hearken, O Ye People*, 188.

145. Staker, *Hearken, O Ye People*, 294–95.

146. *Painesville (OH) Telegraph*, Sept. 13, 1831.

147. *Painesville (OH) Telegraph*, Nov. 18, 1831.

148. Whitman, *Popular Superstitions*, 33.

149. James Thacher, *An Essay on Demonology, Ghosts, and Apparitions* (Boston: Carter and Hendee, 1831), 1.

150. Ames quoted in Shepard and Marquardt, *Lost Apostles*, 48–49.

151. McLellin, *Journals*, 61.

152. Whitmer, *Historian to Dissident*, 47.

153. David Bitton, "Kirtland as a Center of Missionary Activity," *BYU Studies* 11.4 (Summer 1971): 506–7.

154. Staker, *Hearken, O Ye People*, 300–302.

155. Staker, *Hearken, O Ye People*, 301, 348.

156. Holger Hoock, *Scars of Independence: America's Violent Birth* (New York: Crown, 2017), 40–41.

157. Paul Gilje, *Rioting in America* (Bloomington: Indiana University Press, 1996), 48, 137.

158. HC, 1:263; RSR, 178–79.

159. Staker, *Hearken, O Ye People*, 354.

160. McLellin, *Journals*, 81.

161. HC, 1:264.

162. HC, 1:265.


CHAPTER FOUR: **"Their God Is the Devil"**

1. On settlement of the Missouri and Arkansas river valleys, see Kathleen DuVal, *The Native Ground: Indians and Colonists in the Heart of the Continent* (Philadelphia: University of Pennsylvania Press, 2006); and Stephen Aron, *American Confluence: The Missouri Frontier from Borderland to Border State* (Bloomington: Indiana University Press, 2009).

2. Aron, *American Confluence*, 73, 91–93.

3. Warren Jennings, "Zion Is Fled: The Expulsion of Mormons from Jackson County, Missouri" (PhD dissertation, University of Florida, 1962), 12–13; Kenneth Winn, "The Missouri Context of Antebellum Mormonism," in *The Missouri Mormon Experience*, ed. Thomas M. Spencer (Columbia: University of Missouri Press, 2010), 23; Colin G. Calloway, *The Shawnees and the War for America* (New York: Penguin, 2007), 160–61.

4. John P. Bowes, in *Land Too Good for Indians: Northern Indian Removal* (Norman: University of Oklahoma Press, 2016), describes this phenomenon by writing that "Indian Removal was a societal condition" as much as a political choice (11).

5. R. David Edmunds, *The Shawnee Prophet* (Lincoln: University of Nebraska Press, 1983), 179–81; Black Hawk, *Life of Black Hawk, or Ma-ka-tai-me-she-kia-kiak: Dictated by Himself*, ed. J. Gerald Kennedy (New York: Penguin, 2008), 57; Aron, *American Confluence*, 208–17.

6. MRP, 62.

7. Pratt, *Autobiography*, 103.

8. David Pettigrew, "History," typescript, sec. 16, David Pettegrew Family Collection, CHL. Pettigrew's name is also spelled "Pettegrew" in the document and archival files.

9. Alexander Majors, *Seventy Years on the Frontier*, ed. Prentiss Ingraham (New York: Rand McNally, 1893), 46.

10. Gilje, *Rioting in America*, 67–68, 74. For a wealth of examples of anti-temperance and anti-abolitionist violence that began, like anti-Mormonism, with jokes in the newspapers, see Maartje Janse, "'Anti-societies Are Now All the Rage': Jokes, Criticism, and Violence in Response to the Transformation of American Reform, 1825–1835," *Journal of the Early Republic* 36:2 (Jan. 2016): 247–82.

11. Adam Jortner, *The Gods of Prophetstown* (New York: Oxford University Press, 2012), 179.

12. Edmunds, *The Shawnee Prophet*, 184–85. The Argentine district is in Kansas City, Kansas, not the larger Kansas City, Missouri.

13. Warren Jennings, "First Mormon Mission to the Indians," *Kansas Historical Quarterly* 37:3 (Autumn 1971): 293; Pratt, *Autobiography*, 56–61.

14. Cowdery to Smith, April 8, 1831, JSP-D, 1:292; Cowdery to Smith, May 7, 1831, JSP-D, 1:296.

15. Oliver Cowdery to William Clark, Feb. 14, 1831; Richards Cummins to William Clark, Feb. 15, 1831, both in Leland H. Gentry, "Light on the 'Mission to the Lamanites,'" *BYU Studies* 36:2 (1996): 233–34.

16. Charles Murray, *Travels in North America* (London: Richard Bentley, 1854), 2:108.

17. Cowdery and the Saints did request official documentation to continue their mission to Native Americans, but none was forthcoming. See Oliver Cowdery, Independence, Mo., to William Clark, [St. Louis], Feb. 14, 1831, U.S. Office of Indian Affairs, Central Superintendency, Records, vol. 6, p. 103; Pratt, *Autobiography*, 61. Thanks to Brent Rogers for this insight and reference.

18. Timothy Flint, *Recollections of the Last Ten Years* (Boston: Cummings, Hilliard, and Co., 1826), 238–39.

19. Stephen C. LeSueur, *The 1838 Mormon War in Missouri* (Columbia: University of Missouri Press, 1990), 21.

20. Majors, *Seventy Years on the Frontier*, 44.

21. Cowdery to Smith, May 7, 1831, JSP-D, 1:296.

22. *(Columbia) Missouri Intelligencer*, March 8, 1834, Aug. 13, 1834.

23. *(Columbia) Missouri Intelligencer*, June 23, 1832.

24. Jennings, "Zion Is Fled," 70–71; *(Columbia) Missouri Intelligencer*, April 13, 1833; EMS, April 1833.

25. *(Columbia) Missouri Intelligencer*, July 28, 1831; Harry Watson, *Liberty and Power: The Politics of Jacksonian America* (New York: Noonday, 1990), 10. On this approach in the Jacksonian period, see Watson, *Liberty and Power*; Michael Holt, *The Rise and Fall of the American Whig Party* (New York: Oxford University Press,

1999); and Amy S. Greenberg, *A Wicked War: Polk, Clay, Lincoln, and the 1846 Invasion of Mexico* (New York: Vintage, 2013).

26. HC, 1:189

27. See, for example, RSR, 162; LeSueur, *The 1838 Mormon War in Missouri*, 22–23.

28. Josiah Gregg, *Commerce of the Prairies* (New York: Langley, 1845), 1:314; Knight, "Joseph Knight's Recollection," 13.

29. *The Unitarian*, May 1834, collected in Bernard Whitman, ed., *The Unitarian* (Boston: James Munroe, 1834), 252.

30. McLellin, *Journals*, 33.

31. Memorial of Titus Billings, MRP, 139.

32. Joseph Thorp, *Early Days in the West* (Liberty, MO: Liberty Tribune, 1824), 76–77.

33. Greene, "Facts Relative to the Expulsion of Mormons," 15.

34. Majors, *Seventy Years on the Frontier*, 45.

35. Carroll and England, quoted in James T. Fisher, *Communion of Immigrants: A History of Catholics in America* (New York: Oxford University Press, 2002), 23, 39–41.

36. Hugh Nolan, ed., *Pastoral Letters of United States Catholic Bishops* (Washington, DC: National Council of Catholic Bishops, 1983–2005), 1:80.

37. Lyman Beecher, *A Plea for the West* (Bedford, MA: Applewood, 1835), 113–14; Committee of Vigilance and Protection Records, 1834–35, Massachusetts Historical Society, Boston.

38. Charles Augustus Murray, *Travels in North America* (London: Richard Bentley, 1854), 114.

39. Lincoln quoted in Michael Feldberg, *The Turbulent Era: Riot and Disorder in Jacksonian America* (New York: Oxford University Press, 1980), 4.

40. *(Columbia) Missouri Intelligencer*, June 30, 1832; Amy S. Greenberg, "'The Way of the Transgressor Is Hard': The Black Hawk and Mormon Wars in the Construction of Illinois Political Culture, 1832–1846," in *Contingent Citizens: Shifting Perceptions of Latter-day Saints in American Political Culture*, ed. Spencer McBride, Brent Rogers, and Keith Erekson (Ithaca, NY: Cornell University Press, 2020), 80.

41. *(Columbia) Missouri Intelligencer*, June 16, 1832.

42. *St. Louis Beacon*, April 7, 1832.

43. *(Columbia) Missouri Intelligencer*, June 23, 1832; Claudio Saunt, *Unworthy Republic: The Dispossession of Native Americans and the Road to Indian Territory* (New York: Norton, 2020), 146–47.

44. LeSueur, *The 1838 Mormon War in Missouri*, 21.

45. MoU, 197.

46. MoU, 130; *New York Commercial Advertiser*, quoted in Greenberg, "'The Way of the Transgressor Is Hard,'" 80–82. Greenberg provides a full analysis of the relationship between Indian hating and Mormon hating along the Mississippi, arguing that both became vectors for white Gentile men to prove their

masculinity—and, therefore, that anti-Mormonism was far more than merely anti-abolitionist sentiment.

47. Diane Mutti Burke, *On Slavery's Border: Missouri's Small-Slaveholding Households, 1815–1865* (Athens: University of Georgia Press, 2010), 181–82, 189.

48. Timothy Flint, *Letters*, vol. 9 of Reuben Gold Thwaites, ed., *Early Western Travels* (Cleveland, OH: Arthur H. Clark, 1904), 193.

49. *The Confessions of Nat Turner . . . as Fully and Voluntarily Made to Thomas R. Gray* (Richmond, VA: Thomas R. Gray, 1832), 9.

50. *(Columbia) Missouri Intelligencer*, Sept. 17, 1831.

51. The view of a previous generation of historians was that slavery and the slave question turned Gentiles against Mormons in Jackson County. While slavery was certainly an issue in 1833, I contend that a more general recourse to violence and the legitimation of violence as a weapon of popular democracy probably had greater significance in the expulsion. See Newell G. Bringhurst, "The 'Missouri Thesis' Revisited," in *Black and Mormon*, ed. Newell G. Bringhurst and Darron T. Smith (Urbana: University of Illinois Press, 2004), 13–33; Reeve, *Religion of a Different Color*, esp. 114–23; and Matthew Lund, "The Vox Populi Is the Vox Dei: American Localism and the Mormon Expulsion from Jackson County, Missouri" (master's thesis, Utah State University, 2012). For examples of the northern-southern split as the primary source of the Jackson County expulsion, see RSR, 223–25, 326–27; LeSueur, *The 1838 Mormon War in Missouri*, 17–23; and Givens and Grow, *Parley P. Pratt*, 60.

52. Ezra Booth said the temple was a half mile from Independence. Modern Kaw township is in Kansas City; the "center place" is still in Independence. MoU, 199.

53. *(Columbia) Missouri Intelligencer*, April 13, 1833.

54. Rigdon to "Beloved Brethren," Aug. 31, 1831, reprinted in Whitmer, *Historian to Dissident*, 90.

55. Pratt, *Autobiography*, 61.

56. Thomas M. Spencer, "Persecution in the Most Odious Sense of the Word," in *Missouri Mormon Experience*, 1; MoU, 196; Gregg, *Commerce of the Prairies*, 1:34.

57. Benjamin Latrobe, *Rambler in North America* (London: Seeley and Burnside, 1835), 1:128.

58. Jennings, "Zion Is Fled," 15, 17 n19.

59. Launius, *Zion's Camp*, 12; Whitmer, *Historian to Dissident*, 85.

60. Reynolds Cahoon diaries, 1831–32, 11, CHL.

61. MRP, 172.

62. Phoebe C. Lott to Anna Pratt, Aug. 10, 1832, CHL.

63. Jennings, "Zion Is Fled," 56; MoU, 139.

64. Temple lot suit, 215–16.

65. Affidavit of L. Corkins, in MRP, 432.

66. "Plat of the City of Zion," JSP-D, 3:121–31; "Revised Plat of the City of Zion," JSP-D, 3:243–58.

67. MoU, 194, 177, 198–99. There were a few local converts, including the Lewis family, but in general, Mormons found western Missouri rocky soil. See JSP-D, 2:22.

68. Whitmer, *Historian to Dissident*, 87.

69. MoU, 207. Later historians assumed that Booth joined in order to witness miracles, and left when they were not forthcoming. Booth's letters suggest a slight revision: he left when he ceased to believe in miracles. Max Parkin, *Conflict in Kirtland* (Salt Lake City: Brigham Young University Press, 1966), 101; RSR, 151.

70. MoU, 205, 176.

71. JSP-D, 2:60–61.

72. RSR, 151.

73. MoU, 202.

74. D&C 64.

75. Whitmer, *Historian to Dissident*, 85.

76. FWR, 11. On Fuller's family relations, see "Fuller, Edson," and "Minute Book 2," *The Joseph Smith Papers*, accessed Aug. 15, 2019, https://www.josephsmithpapers .org/person/edson-fuller, https://www.josephsmithpapers.org/paper-summary/minute -book-2/5.

77. FWR, 11–12. Being "silenced" referred to a revocation of the right to preach in the name of the Latter-day Saints; see JSP-D, 2:58.

78. Cahoon diaries, 30–31, 36

79. McLellin, *Journals*, 73.

80. JSP-D, 2:83.

81. MoU, 216.

82. Fred C. Collier and William S. Hartwell, eds., *Kirtland Council Minute Book* (Salt Lake City: Collier's, 1996), 9.

83. FWR, 59.

84. Parkin, *Conflict in Kirtland*, 101; HC, 1:215–16.

85. MoU, 178.

86. MoU, 181, 190.

87. Cahoon diaries, 18, 30; Dennis Rowley, "The Ezra Booth Letters," *Dialogue* 16:3 (1983): 135–36.

88. Wesley Perkins to Jacob Perkins, Feb. 11, 1832, reprinted in Rowley, "Ezra Booth Letters," 133–37.

89. *St. Louis Beacon*, Dec. 29, 1832.

90. Journal of Lorenzo Barnes, entry for April 29, 1836, CHL.

91. Pratt, *Shameful Outrage Committed by a Part of the Inhabitants of the Town of Mentor* . . . (Mentor, OH: n.p., 1835), 10.

92. Joseph Antrim to Elisha and Bethiab Hancock, June 5, 1832, Joseph Antrim Papers, Ohio History Connection, Columbus.

93. EMS, June 1833.

94. Evan Green journal, entry for Oct. 25, 1833, CHL.

95. Jennings, "Zion Is Fled," 128; Stephen C. Taysom, *Shakers, Mormons, and Religious Worlds: Conflicting Visions, Contested Boundaries* (Bloomington: Indiana University Press, 2011), 59–61.

96. *(Columbia) Missouri Intelligencer*, April 13, 1833.

97. Pixley quoted in William Mulder and A. Russell Mortensen, eds., *Among the Mormons: Historic Accounts by Contemporary Observers* (New York: Knopf, 1958), 72–75; *Christian Watchman*, Dec. 23, 1833.

98. Launius, *Zion's Camp*, 19; JSP-D, 2:167.

99. JSP-D, 2:176–77.

100. Phoebe C. Lott to Anna Pratt, Aug. 10, 1832, CHL.

101. EMS, July 1832.

102. RSR, 180.

103. FWR, 33, 38.

104. Jennings, "Zion Is Fled," 93; *(St. Louis) Missouri Republican*, May 3, 1833.

105. FWR, 41.

106. JSP-D, 2:174n168.

107. *Painesville (OH) Telegraph*, May 23, 1834.

108. *Christian Watchman*, reprinted in *Cincinnati Journal*, March 22, 1833.

109. MoU, 201.

110. Temple lot suit, 189*ff.*

111. Quoted in Quinn, "Jesse Gause," 491.

112. JSP-D, 2:175.

113. JSP-D, 2:232; RSR, 187.

114. Phoebe C. Lott to Anna Pratt, Aug. 10, 1832, CHL.

115. JS to Phelps, July 31, 1832, JSP-D, 2:262–63.

116. Givens and Grow, *Parley P. Pratt*, 60; JSP-D, 2:264.

117. FWR, 49; JS to Edward Partridge and others, Jan. 14, 1833, JPS-D, 2:373; responses to Gilbert and Phelps from Orson Hyde and Hyrum Smith, quoted in JPS-D, 2:364.

118. RSR, 186.

119. JS to Phelps, Jan. 11, 1833, JSP-D, 2:367; D&C 88:119. See also Givens and Grow, *Parley P. Pratt*, 60.

120. Jortner, *Blood from the Sky*, 174–76.

121. Gregg, *Commerce of the Prairies*, 1:314–15.

122. Majors, *Seventy Years on the Frontier*, 44.

123. Emily Austin, *Life among the Mormons* (Madison, WI: Cantwell, 1882), 68.

124. McCoy statement, Nov. 28, 1833, printed in *(St. Louis) Missouri Republican*, Dec. 20, 1833.

125. Givens and Grow, *Parley P. Pratt*, 56–60.

126. Corrill to Cowdery, December 1833, reprinted in EMS, January 1834.

127. Jennings, "Zion Is Fled," 124–25; MRP, 423.

128. Elias Higbee, John Taylor, and Elias Smith, "The Second Memorial," January 10, 1842, in MRP, 395.

129. MRP, 315.

130. Newel Knight, "Newel Knight's Journal," in *Scraps of Autobiography* (Salt Lake City: Juvenile Instructor's Office, 1883), 75.

131. Hill, *Quest for Refuge*, 41, 212n98; Givens and Grow, *Parley P. Pratt*, 60–61.

132. *(Columbia) Missouri Intelligencer*, Aug. 10, 1833.

133. LeSueur, *The 1838 Mormon War in Missouri*, 17–18.

134. EMS, July 1833.

135. EMS, Feb. 1834.

136. Corrill to Cowdery, December 1833, reprinted in EMS, January 1834.

137. For some scattered references to Mormons preaching before interracial crowds, see HC, 1:191; and Reeve, *Religion of a Different Color*, 120–21.

138. Knight, "Newel Knight's Journal," 92.

139. Mulder and Mortensen, *Among the Mormons*, 78.

140. Gregg, *Commerce of the Prairies*, 1:315.

141. Pixley, in Mulder and Mortensen, *Among the Mormons*, 82.

142. "Chapman Duncan Reminiscences about Experiences in Missouri," typescript, 3, CHL.

143. Knight, "Newel Knight's Journal," 77–78; EMS, Dec. 1833.

144. Gregg, *Commerce of the Prairies*, 1:316.

145. *Niles Weekly Register*, Sept. 14, 1833.

146. Knight, "Newel Knight's Journal," 78; EMS, Dec. 1833.

147. EMS, Jan. 1834.

148. Whitmer, *Historian to Dissident*, 106.

149. EMS, Dec. 1833.

150. EMS, Feb. 1834.

151. EMS, Dec. 1833.

152. John Whitmer to JS (and Cowdery), July 29, 1833, JSP-D, 3:188–98.

153. JSP-D, 3:190.

154. EMS, May 1833.

155. JS to Church Leaders in Jackson County, Aug. 10, 1833, JSP-D, 3:238–43.

156. JS to Partridge et al., Aug. 18, 1833, JSP-D, 3:263–64.

157. JS quoted in David W. Grua, "Joseph Smith and the 1834 Hurlbut Case," *BYU Studies Quarterly* 44:1 (2005): 36.

158. JSP-D, 3:268; Grua, "Joseph Smith and the 1834 Hurlbut Case," 33; GAS, 11.

159. JSP-D, 3:266.

160. EMS, Dec. 1833.

161. Pettigrew, "History," typescript, sec. 18.

162. EMS, Dec. 1833.

163. "Chapman Duncan Reminiscences," 9.

164. McCoy statement, *(St. Louis) Missouri Republican*, Dec. 20, 1833.

165. *Christian Watchman*, Dec. 21, 1833.

166. Knight, "Newel Knight's Journal," 80; Mulder and Mortensen, *Among the Mormons*, 82; McCoy statement, *(St. Louis) Missouri Republican*, Dec. 20, 1833.

167. Austin, *Life among the Mormons*, 70; MRP, 197.

168. Brandon G. Kinney, *The Mormon War* (Yardley, PA: Westholme, 2011), 40.

169. MRP, 67.

170. EMS, Jan. 1834; James H. Hunt, *Mormonism* (St. Louis: G. W. Westbrook, 1844), 163–64. Hunt's claim that the Whitmers ambushed the Gentiles is certainly untrue, and Hunt himself describes it as a "floating story."

171. Levi Jackman, drawing of the battle on the Big Blue River, CHL.

172. Judd petition, in MRP, 254; Dibble petition, ibid., 187; Greene, "Facts Relative to the Expulsion of Mormons," 22; Pettigrew, "History," typescript, sec. 18.

173. Greene, "Facts Relative to the Expulsion of Mormons," MRP, 16.

174. MRP, 68.

175. Corrill to Cowdery, December 1833, EMS, Jan. 1834.

176. Majors, *Seventy Years on the Frontier*, 47.

177. "Chapman Duncan Reminiscences," 7; Knight, "Newel Knight's Journal," 82–83.

178. "Chapman Duncan Reminiscences," 4.

179. EMS, Dec. 1833.

180. MRP, 500.

181. Corrill to Cowdery, December 1833.

182. Corrill to Cowdery, December 1833.

183. Launius, *Zion's Camp*, 30–32; Corrill to Cowdery, December 1833.

184. *(Columbia) Missouri Intelligencer*, Dec. 14, 1833.

185. Pratt, *Autobiography*, 108; MRP, 460, 469.

186. MRP, 23, 469, 70, 69, 134.

187. *(Columbia) Missouri Intelligencer*, Nov. 16, 1833.

188. Greene, "Facts Relative to the Expulsion of Mormons," 23; Jennings, "Zion Is Fled," 192, 196.

189. Pratt, *Autobiography*, 108.

190. Gilbert to Dunklin, Nov. 29, 1833, W. W. Phelps Collection, CHL.

191. Willes Family Papers, "Journal entries and poems," 15, CHL.

192. MRP, 209, 411.

193. Pettigrew, "History," secs. 22, 23.

194. Whitmer, *Historian to Dissident*, 108.

195. Quoted in Hill, *Quest for Refuge*, 42.

196. Corrill to Cowdery, Dec. 1833.

197. Pratt, MRP, 67.

198. Corrill to Cowdery, Dec. 1833.

CHAPTER FIVE:  **A War for Zion**

1. *(Columbia) Missouri Intelligencer*, Nov. 16, 1833.
2. *(St. Louis) Missouri Republican*, Nov. 15, 1833; *(Bowling Green, MO) Salt River Journal*, quoted in *(Columbia) Missouri Intelligencer*, Nov. 30, 1833.
3. *Erie (PA) Gazette*, Sept. 5, 1833.
4. *(Pittsburgh) Allegheny Democrat*, May 27, 1834.
5. EMS, Dec. 1833.
6. Saints to Dunklin, EMS, Dec. 1833.
7. Smith to Partridge, Dec. 5, 1833, JSP-D, 3:371–73; D&C 101.
8. "Extract of a Letter," EMS, Dec. 1833.
9. Pratt, *Autobiography*, 104.
10. JS to Partridge, Dec. 5, 1833, JSP-D, 3:371.
11. Phelps to JS, Dec. 15, 1833, JSP-D, 3:384.
12. JS to Church Leaders in Jackson County, Missouri, Aug. 18, 1833, JSP-D, 3:263.
13. D&C 103:15, 7–8.
14. John Murdock journal, 17, 77, CHL.
15. JS, Williams, and Cowdery to Orson Hyde, April 7, 1834, reprinted in T&S, Dec. 1, 1845.
16. Launius, *Zion's Camp*, 43–45.
17. Launius, *Zion's Camp*, 53, 55, 61. The "trumpet" is mentioned in "History of George A. Smith," 24, GAS. Major works on Zion's Camp include Launius, *Zion's Camp*; Matthew Godfrey, "'The Redemption of Zion Must Needs Come by Power': Insights into the Camp of Israel Expedition, 1834," *BYU Studies Quarterly* 53:4 (2014): 125–46; Andrea G. Radke, "We Also Marched: The Women and Children of Zion's Camp, 1834," *BYU Studies* 39:1 (2000): 147–65; Craig K. Manscill, "'Journal of the Branch of the Church of Christ in Pontiac, . . . 1834': Hyrum Smith's Division of Zion's Camp," *BYU Studies* 39:1 (2000): 167–88.
18. Launius, *Zion's Camp*, 43–47.
19. "Journal of the Branch of the Church of Christ in Pontiac" (manuscript), CHL, 8; GAS, 12 (verso), 27.
20. Moses Martin journals, 1834, 9, CHL; Launius, *Zion's Camp*, 103.
21. "Journal of the Branch of the Church of Christ in Pontiac," 5; Manscill, "'Journal of the Branch,'" 174; Amasa Lyman, "Journal, 1834 January 1–December 21," in Amasa M. Lyman Collection, CHL; Joseph Holbrook quoted in Radke, "We Also Marched," 154. Hosea Stout eventually became a Saint in 1838.
22. J. M. Henderson report, April 29, 1834, reprinted in *(Columbia) Missouri Intelligencer*, June 7, 1834.
23. Launius, *Zion's Camp*, 49–50.
24. GAS, 19.
25. Tanner quoted in Launius, *Zion's Camp*, 76.
26. See HC, 2:7 (preaching), 70, 79 (threats), 68, 70, 76–77 (spies).
27. GAS, 15.

28. GAS, 23.

29. GAS, 12–14, 23, 26; Moses Martin journals, 6; HC, 2:81.

30. Launius, *Zion's Camp*, 97–99; GAS, 27.

31. Missouri Saints to Jackson, April 10, 1834, reprinted in T&S, Dec. 1, 1845; also reprinted in Whitmer, *Historian to Dissident*, 113–18.

32. Cass to Gilbert et al., May 2, 1834, CHL.

33. Ryland to Rees, Nov. 24, 1833, WWP.

34. Petition to Daniel Dunklin, Dec. 1833, WWP.

35. Petition to Daniel Dunklin, Jan. 9, 1834, WWP. See also Gilbert to Dunklin, Nov. 29, 1833, ibid.

36. Dunklin to Phelps, Feb. 4, 1834, WWP (emphasis original).

37. MRP, 316.

38. Dunklin to the Mormons, Oct. 19, 1833, reprinted in *(Columbia) Missouri Intelligencer*, Nov. 30, 1833.

39. Dunklin to Phelps, Feb. 4, 1834, WWP (emphasis original). See also Ryland to Atchison, reprinted in *(Columbia) Missouri Intelligencer*, March 8, 1834.

40. Dunklin to Phelps, April 20, 1834, WWP (emphasis original).

41. Joel Haden to Dunklin, Aug. 8, 1834, quoted in Launius, *Zion's Camp*, 112.

42. Phelps to Benton, April 10, 1834, WWP. Phelps was likely wasting his time; Jackson County was already heavily Jacksonian.

43. Gilbert to Dunklin, April 24, 1834, WWP.

44. Gilbert to Dunklin, April 24, 1834, WWP.

45. Dunklin to Lucas, May 2, 1834, WWP.

46. Dunklin to Thornton, June 6, 1834, reprinted in T&S, Jan. 1, 1846; Launius, *Zion's Camp*, 127.

47. John Chauncey to Francis Dallam, June 27, 1834, reprinted in William Hoyt, ed., "A Clay Countian's Letters of 1834," *Missouri Historical Review* 45:4 (July 1951): 352–53.

48. Launius, *Zion's Camp*, 118–20.

49. Dunklin to Thornton, June 6, 1834, in T&S, June 1, 1846.

50. Gilbert and Phelps to Dunklin, May 7, 1834, in Whitmer, *Historian to Dissident*, 128–29.

51. Jennings, *Zion Is Fled*, 259–60.

52. Whitmer, *Historian to Dissident*, 125.

53. Whitmer, *Historian to Dissident*, 131–32.

54. Ryland to Gilbert et al., June 10, 1834; Elders to Ryland, June 14, 1834, both reprinted in T&S, Jan. 15, 1846; *Upper Missouri Enquirer*, June 11, 1834, reprinted in *Painesville (OH) Telegraph*, July 11, 1834 (emphasis added).

55. Launius, *Zion's Camp*, 131.

56. T&S, Jan. 15, 1846.

57. Elders to Ryland, June 14, 1834.

58. "Propositions of the People of Jackson County to the Mormons," T&S, Jan. 15, 1846.

59. Whitmer, *Historian to Dissident*, 132.

60. Joseph Thorp, *Early Days in the West* (Liberty, MO: Irving Gilmer, 1924), 79.

61. T&S, Jan. 15, 1846.

62. Thorp, *Early Days in the West*, 80.

63. Owens quoted in *Upper Missouri Enquirer*, June 18, 1834.

64. T&S, Jan. 15, 1846.

65. Nathaniel Judd to Sally Judd Herrick, June 24, 1834, Lemuel Herrick Papers, CHL.

66. Launius, *Zion's Camp*, 134; Majors, *Seventy Years on the Frontier*, 54.

67. *(Columbia) Missouri Intelligencer*, June 21, 1834.

68. Kimball, "Extracts," T&S, Feb. 4, 1845; Launius, *Zion's Camp*, 116, 122.

69. Kimball, "Extracts," T&S, Feb. 4, 1845; GAS, 28.

70. GAS, 28.

71. Reuben McBride, "Reminiscence," 5, CHL; Kimball, "Extracts," T&S, Feb. 4, 1845; Charles Rich, "Original Manuscript Diary," 5–6, CHL.

72. Kimball, "Extracts," T&S, March 15, 1845.

73. GAS, 29.

74. McBride, "Reminiscence," 7.

75. Kimball, "Extracts", T&S, March 15, 1845.

76. Kimball, "Extracts", T&S, March 15, 1845.

77. GAS, 30.

78. RSR, 245–46.

79. JS, "Declaration," June 21, 1834, JSP-D, 4:65–66.

80. Quote from *Maysville (KY) Eagle*, republished in *Washington* (DC) *Daily National Intelligencer*, July 23, 1834; *Upper Missouri Enquirer* (Liberty, MO), June 18, 1834, reprinted in *Niles Weekly Register*, July 12, 1834.

81. Benedict Roux to Bishop Rosati, June 27, 1834, in Stanley Kimball, "Missouri Mormon Manuscripts," *BYU Studies* 14:4 (1974): 487.

82. *(Columbia) Missouri Intelligencer*, June 28, 1834.

83. *Richmond (VA) Enquirer*, Aug. 1, 1834.

84. Gilliam(?), opening paragraph of "Declaration, 21 June 1834," in JSP-D, 4:65. See also clarification on handwriting in JSP-D, 2:65n301.

85. GAS, 29; Gilliam quoted in JSP-D, 4:63; "Declaration, 21 June 1834," JSP-D, 4:66.

86. "Declaration, 21 June 1834," JSP-D, 4:66, 68.

87. McBride, "Reminiscence," 6, CHL.

88. GAS, 29; "Historical Introduction," JSP-D, 4:72; T&S, Feb. 15, 1846.

89. D&C 105:23, 30–31.

90. GAS, 29.

91. Owens to Kelly and Davis, June 23, 1834, reprinted in *Painesville (OH) Telegraph*, Aug. 1, 1834; "Resolutions of Committee from Lafayette County," June 23, 1834, JSP-D, 4:79.

92. GAS, 29.

93. JS to Thornton et al., June 25, 1834, JSP-D, 4:86.

94. GAS, 31.

95. Launius, *Zion's Camp*, 152–53.

96. Elders to Dunklin, June 26, 1834, reprinted in T&S, Feb. 1, 1846.

97. McBride, "Reminiscence," 7.

98. Unsigned letter, June 28, 1834, reprinted in *Washington* (DC) *Daily National Intelligencer*, July 23, 1834.

99. Elders to Dunklin, June 26, 1834.

100. Owens to Reese, June 26, 1834, T&S Feb. 1, 1846.

101. *(Columbia) Missouri Intelligencer*, July 19, 1834.

102. Unsigned letter, June 28, 1834.

103. Majors, *Seventy Years on the Frontier*, 50.

104. *(Elyria) Ohio Atlas*, July 17, 1834. See also the *Chardon (OH) Spectator*, July 12, 1834. Numerous other papers wrote that Smith expected to "die the death of martyrdom."

105. GAS, 34–35; Launius, *Zion's Camp*, 157.

106. HC, 2:123n.

107. See, for example, Matthew Burton Bowman, *The Mormon People: The Making of an American Faith* (New York: Random House, 2012), 57; Ronald E. Romig and Michael S. Riggs, "Reevaluating Joseph Smith's 'Appointed Time for the Redemption of Zion,'" in *Missouri Mormon Experience*, 28–30, 43n6; Shepard and Marquardt, *Lost Apostles*, 79–80. For a counterpoint, see Winn, "The Missouri Context of Antebellum Mormonism," 101.

108. Minutes, July 3, 1834, JSP-D, 4:88ff.

109. FWR, 78–79, 87.

110. FWR, 89.

111. FWR, 90.

112. JS to Lyman Wight and others, Aug. 16, 1834, JSP-D, 4:104.

113. Minutes, Aug. 11, 1834, JSP-D, 4:98–101.

114. JS to Lyman Wight and others, Aug. 16, 1834, JSP-D, 4:106.

115. Whitmer, *Historian to Dissident*, 132–33.

116. *Painesville (OH) Telegraph*, Aug. 1, 1834; MoU, 163.

EPILOGUE

1. McCoy statement, Nov. 28, 1833. For discussions of finding the origins of anti-Mormonism within Mormon behavior and doctrine, see Fluhman, "*A Peculiar People*," 1–9; and LeSueur, *The 1838 Mormon War in Missouri*, 28–76.

2. MRP, 161–62, 516–17.

3. MRP, 209, 212–13; EMS, June 1833.

4. MRP, 209; EMS, Dec. 1833.

5. Majors, *Seventy Years on the Frontier*, 45.

6. Elders to President Jackson, April 10, 1834, in Whitmer, *Historian to Dissident*, 114.

7. Whitmer, *Historian to Dissident*, 115.

8. MRP, 310, 145, 371.

9. For discussions of twenty-first-century versions of this process, see Asma Uddin, *When Islam Is Not a Religion* (New York: Pegasus, 2019); and Jonathan Weisman, *(((Semitism))): Being Jewish in America in the Age of Trump* (New York: St. Martin's, 2018), 33–68.

10. Knight, "Newel Knight's Journal," 92.

11. McCoy statement, Nov. 28, 1833.

# INDEX